Dear Reader

Thank you for purchasing this book, to be honest, I need the money, and so does the mental health and arts charity who will receive a donation from the proceeds.

By getting this far you obviously have great taste, and you are clearly very intelligent, it wouldn't surprise me if you were good looking and successful too. Firstly, let me assure you this is not another boring book about boring politicians. There are no boring people in this book, although I did once spend an afternoon in Canton… and that was very boring !

Every effort has been made during the writing of this book to keep it as informative and entertaining as possible, although it is my first book, so I can't give you a 100% guarantee. So I'll tell you what I'll do, if after reading this book you feel it was a waste of your time, I'll come round and wash your car or clean your windows or something. There, you can't get fairer than that now can you ?

Personally, I think this is a really good book, in fact I'm thinking of buying a copy myself and reading it again. I would take one out at the Library but it closed down due to government cuts, and besides, I wouldn't get the royalties, and like I said, I need the money…

Tony

Reflections Art in Health Charity is dedicated to showcasing the creative talents of people who experience health problems generally and mental health problems specifically. Reflections promotes the visual and performing arts as an aid to recovery.

Donations can be made via Virgin Giving at http://bit.ly/sKmc0O

For further details please visit our website: www.reflectionsartinhealth.com and see the work of over 230 artists.

Please follow Reflections on twitter at @reflections9 and Tony at @tonyr2011

REFLECTIONS
MAKING A DIFFERENCE THROUGH ART IN HEALTH

Registered Charity Number 1141931

COMMONS PEOPLE

COMMONS PEOPLE

MPs ARE HUMAN TOO

TONY RUSSELL

Matador
9 Priory Business Park,
Wistow Road, Kibworth Beauchamp,
Leicestershire. LE8 0RX
Tel: (+44) 116 279 2299
Fax: (+44) 116 279 2277
Email: books@troubador.co.uk
Web: www.troubador.co.uk/matador

ISBN 978 1780884 752

British Library Cataloguing in Publication Data.
A catalogue record for this book is available from the British Library.

Printed and bound in the UK by TJ International, Padstow, Cornwall
Typeset in 11pt Aldine401 BT Roman by Troubador Publishing Ltd, Leicester, UK

Matador is an imprint of Troubador Publishing Ltd

CONTENTS

"For a parliamentary democracy to work, everyone has got to feel that at least one person is speaking up for them."
Philip Davies MP - Chapter 9

About Me and My Book

As I began a long journey of recovery from what, in layman's terms, I will describe as a breakdown nearly twenty years ago, I decided I wanted to do everything I could to ensure people diagnosed with a mental health problem received the best treatment possible.

It soon became obvious if I wanted to affect change I would have to sit at the same table as the decision makers, and work productively to improve the delivery of mental health services, rather than be on the outside criticising.

I have always been a campaigner, and ten years prior to my breakdown, which I would describe as my first visit to the abyss, I walked 2,355 miles to raise money for Cancer Research having had a friend who died from that terrible disease whilst I was completing the walk.

After a considerable amount of patience, persistence, luck and hard work, I was given the opportunity to have some influence, and so began my first encounters with politicians, which have continued ever since. The more contact I have with Government Ministers and MPs, the greater my fascination with their role and function within our society. And, over the past twenty years, I have had the good fortune to meet a large number of MPs and quite a few Ministers, some good, and in my humble opinion, some not so good.

In writing this book I am hoping that I can, in my own small way, create a better understanding of the people that make the decisions that affect all of our lives, and maybe even encourage the great British public to take a much greater interest in the work of our elected representatives.

We would all do well to remember that we get the politicians we deserve, and if we want to keep them on their toes and truly representative of the electorate, we probably need to be far more demanding of them, and take much more of an interest in their activities.

I truly believe apathy is one of the greatest dangers to our democracy, and we really cannot complain about the decisions our parliamentarians make if we take no interest and play no part in the democratic process.

It has been said: 'The only person to enter the Houses of Parliament with any true conviction was Guy Fawkes', which, sadly, I suspect these days many might agree with, though it is perhaps more than a little harsh. I no longer judge an MP by the party to which he/she belongs, but rather by the sincerity of their actions. It is, for example, interesting to note when an MP votes contrary to his own party whip's instructions. I have far greater respect for those Members of Parliament who have strong principles and true conviction, even if I do not agree with their political ideology.

It's probably fair to say Members of Parliament are not right up there in the popularity stakes, and the expenses scandal certainly did nothing to enhance their reputation. The esteem in which they are held in the eyes of the public has been in steady decline over the past few decades. When I ask for people's views on our politicians, responses such as, 'Well they do what they want anyway', 'They are in it for themselves', 'Most of them have never done a proper job' are fairly typical responses. Although interestingly, I often hear, 'Well my MP is good, but the rest of them are... '

At the time of writing this book, there is a debate about MPs' pay, and the public are being invited to express their views. There was a phone-in show on BBC Radio, and whilst we often accuse our parliamentarians of being out of touch, having listened to the views of many of the callers, it would appear that there is still, even after all this time, much to be done to create a better understanding of the role of an MP. I find it absolutely staggering that they have no contract of employment or even a job description, or Terms and Conditions, things most of us take for granted. How can you determine somebody's pay, or measure how effective they are, if there are no formal guidelines?

There are also plans to reduce the number of MPs from 650 to 600, and the hard of thinking say this is a good idea. Well, I would respectfully urge them to think again. MPs are our representatives, and obviously less MPs equals larger constituencies, which means more people to represent, and more constituents means less time available for each of us. The spurious reasoning for this reduction is apparently to save money. Perhaps this could be done more efficiently by reducing the House of Lords, who are, after all, unelected.

Many people, and particularly the younger generation, would probably struggle to name our leading political figures and Government Ministers, let alone the Shadow Cabinet. And perhaps it is not surprising when there is a feeling we are powerless to actually have any influence to change anything. However, it could be argued that we get the politicians, or rather the policies, we deserve, if we show so little interest in the political process, other than to turn up every four or five years to vote.

Given the impact decisions made in parliament have on our lives, perhaps it is time to re-examine and attempt to change public attitudes. In the past, society has shown it is possible to have influence. An example of this was when the nation collectively voiced its displeasure and dissatisfaction during the great expenses scandal. Perhaps we could make better use of our precious democracy if there was more of an understanding and greater engagement between the public at large and our Members of Parliament.

Having spent many years trying to engage with politicians at all levels with varying degrees of success, I have come to the conclusion that if we could achieve this, it would be much better for all concerned, and most definitely for the democratic process. It often seems that when an MP becomes a Minister they surround themselves with bureaucrats and special advisors whose sole purpose in life is to prevent them from becoming engaged directly with the public. It is almost as if they are frightened of being caught out, faced with questions they cannot answer, or worse still say something they should not as in the Gordon Brown incident during the last Election campaign. Too often they only appear for stage managed events in front of audiences who will be sympathetic to their party line. I believe it simply is not good enough to use the flimsy excuse of being too busy.

If we are to take full advantage of our democracy there has to be meaningful engagement with our political servants, for that is what they are, and they should not be seen as our masters. People would do well to remember it is tax payers money they spend – our money!

Another thing I have learnt, particularly in recent years, is that the vast majority of MPs, whatever their political ideology, do work extremely hard, and generally have the best interests of their constituents at heart. It would be wrong to think that they do not earn their keep. You only have to look at the vast amounts of committees, representing a massive variety of causes to get some idea of the work that goes on behind the scenes, and it is a mistake to think they all swan off the moment Parliament is in recess. The good MPs, of which there are many, will be working hard in their constituencies.

We should also bear in mind that there has been an election since the expenses scandal, and there is a fairly large new intake of MPs who are untarnished by that scandal.

During the course of writing *Commons People*, I have spent a great deal of time talking to Members of Parliament from across the main parties, and most of the interviews have taken place within their working environment of the House of Commons. It is a magical place, obviously steeped in history, and there is no doubt in my mind that the whole process has really changed the way I view our MPs.

Obviously, there is a degree of self selection in that I have spent time with MPs who have been happy to spend time with me, as opposed to the few that refused to see me. The whole experience has re-affirmed my belief that we need to take a far greater interest in the work of our elected representatives, and I really wish people would take the time to go and meet with their MP and get to know them. The obvious advantage of this would be the development of a far greater understanding between us, the public, and those we elect to represent us.

Commons People is very definitely not a book about political ideology, rather it is an attempt to show the more human side of our Members of Parliament, whilst dispelling some of the myths and misunderstandings. Certainly since the intake of MPs in 1997, and probably at a slower rate even before then, the demographic/make up of our MPs has changed, and whilst there is still a long way to go, they are gradually becoming more representative of the people they serve, and they must not be seen as some kind of ruling elite who inhabit an ivory tower.

Commons People takes a very clear look at the day to day lives of our MPs, examining what motivates them, who has inspired them, what they do to relax, what keeps them awake at night, and their hopes and aspirations for the future.

"I think if people felt that their voice had more of an influence it would make a difference."
Nicky Morgan MP – Chapter8

CHAPTER ONE

Entering Politics

You often hear people say of politicians, 'Well they are doing that because they can't do anything else' or 'They are in it for themselves', and, until I started talking to MPs, I may have had some sympathy with these views, so I started my series of interviews by asking: *Why did you enter politics?*

Paul Blomfield MP

"Well I never set out to be an MP, I've been involved in politics all my life since I was at school. I got involved in the anti-apartheid movement and in trying to start a school student union, and set up a school council; later on I got involved in a trade union, and after that in the Labour Party. I was an activist, involved in local issues, and for thirteen years I was Chair of the Labour Party in Sheffield, which is a voluntary role, alongside my day job co-ordinating our activities. When Richard Caborn decided to stand down after twenty-seven years of representing Sheffield Central, it was suggested I go for it, and I thought yeah, why not, as it was an extension of what I had been doing. So I went for it, as did five other people, but the members of Sheffield Central selected me."

Sir Peter Bottomley MP

"Well there are about fourteen different answers to that. One is, in December 1973, I had a job putting neon lights outside theatres and cinemas in the West End; the I.R.A. blew up Selfridges; and I had to go and clear away 30,000 lights and a hundred Christmas trees. My photograph appeared in the paper the next day being patted on the back by the Prime Minister saying 'Plucky British Workman Not Put Off By Terrorism', and I thought, he's indoors, no heavy lifting, with no need of a raincoat, I'm called out into a storm at night to deal with high voltage electricity at altitude, I'm in the wrong job, so I went into Parliament."

Ben Bradshaw MP

"I had always been interested in politics, my mum was a Labour Party supporter, she was a teacher, and my dad was a vicar. I guess I was bought up with a public service ethos, I had been a Labour Party sympathiser since my late teens. I was a journalist before, working for the BBC, and about a year before the '97 election the Labour candidacy in Exeter came up, a couple of friends from Exeter said, 'You should think about putting your name forward for that.' I had come to the stage in my journalism where I had really done everything I wanted to do basically, and I thought given the opportunity to really do something on the inside, rather than just report on it from the outside, that may be something that was worth having a go at, I didn't really expect to get selected but I was."

Kevin Brennan MP

"I think it's just in me, do you know what I mean? It's not a case of going into politics, more that politics is in me, and that's what I have been like since I was a teenager, having a passion to change the world as you do at that age. I joined the Young Communist League when I was about fifteen, but never actually did anything, just used to get the magazine and the anti-apartheid movement stuff and things like that. When I was nineteen I joined the Labour Party, and then when I settled down, it was a natural progression for me to start getting involved more in local politics. I ended up as a Councillor, and I was teaching at that time. After a while, an opportunity arose to work in politics so I went to work for Rhodri Morgan, who was my predecessor in Cardiff, then he became First Minister down in Wales, and I was selected for the seat."

Andrew Bridgen MP

"It's been an ambition of mine for a long time, and I actually won my first election at the age of sixteen when I was voted Head Boy of my comprehensive school. I went to university, have been in the armed forces, set my own business up which I ran very successfully for twenty-three years, and I thought I am now in a position where I can do something I want to do, rather than something I have to do. I have been a life long Conservative and a donor to the party and I despaired when we didn't make any traction in 2005, and I think you get to the point where, we've all done it, you go down to the pub, you moan about something, and at the end of the day you get to where it's a question of either put up or shut up. So I agreed with a few friends and acquaintances of mine, I'll stand as MP, so I did, as the candidate for the N.W. Leics. Conservatives; we had the second biggest swing in the country, 12%, and took the seat."

Andy Burnham MP

"I was born in Liverpool, my family were from Liverpool, and I grew up in the mid-eighties in the north-west, it was hard to escape the feeling that things weren't good. I think my earliest political memory was watching *Boys From the Blackstuff* with my mum and dad and asking lots of questions about it, you know the old dole office, the way in which the whole thing was presented, and then things developed. I suppose I became very politically aware very young, and joined the Labour Party in 1984."

Ann Coffey MP

"Well it goes back a very, very long way; I did a degree in sociology in 1969, it was all about looking at how society worked. I was always very interested in how communities worked: how do they deal with disagreements? How do they compromise? How do they make decisions? But following on from that, I liked helping people in the broadest sense of the word, after that, I became a trainee social worker, which you could do in those days. I think it was due to the process of being a social worker, working with families with problems, that I realised that a lot depends on the background legislation you are working with, the resources that go into communities, and the social policy on wider public attitudes. In a family you are working with the particular problems that rise out of the general circumstances in which they live. I wanted to do a little bit more so I stood for the council in Stockport in 1984 and got elected, because it was a way of influencing local policies. I was very aware about the importance of good housing, for example, it's very difficult to manage a mental health problem if you are on the sixth floor of a tower block on your own, with noisy neighbours and no support. Of course, councils are responsible by and large for housing policies, and also of course it's very nice to live in a decent environment. But then I realised that in fact councils only operate within the legislation of Parliament, that's when I became interested in becoming an MP, because I thought it's there, the place that actually makes the legislation that councils implement, that impacts on people and determines the quality of their lives. So it was that kind of process really."

Rosie Cooper MP

"I entered politics to change the world; it was almost by accident that I realised I could. Both of my parents are deaf, therefore I was their voice and ears from a very early age. I often talk about being kidnapped by the deaf community at birth. So my job was, as the oldest child, to negotiate and make life easier for my mum and dad and the family. It was not that they couldn't do it, because I can tell you now, I admire my dad and mum so much, brilliant people. My dad was awesome, born deaf, no formal education, yet the cleverest man that I have ever met. They tell me I booked my first holiday when I was four. We would go into a shop and my mum and dad were more than capable, but people didn't want to have to deal with them, they didn't want to write everything down, therefore it was easier to talk to this kid, and then I got used to making it work. This really is the bit that sorts the way I do stuff politically: I was a child dealing with all these adults, I had to find a way of making people do what I wanted them to do, cos I wasn't going to let my mum and dad down, so you develop a style which sometimes is funny, sometimes very direct, and sometimes is calculating, but you learn to quickly find a way of negotiating with adults to get what your mum and dad need."

Philip Davies MP

"Well lots of people here in Parliament have wanted to do it since they were a young age, that absolutely wasn't me. I was brought up to be interested in politics, and as a Conservative. I was born and raised in Doncaster, my dad was involved with the local Conservative Party, and there aren't many Conservatives in Doncaster. As soon as I was old enough, my dad had me out delivering leaflets and knocking on doors, I loved elections. We never used to win any, but I absolutely loved elections. I always wanted to help the Conservative Party, but had never ever wanted to be an MP, it had never even been on my radar. It was when I was working for ASDA; I was really fed up with politicians and disillusioned because nobody ever said anything that I wanted said, so rather than going down to the pub on a Friday night and complaining about it, I thought it was about time I did something. So I applied to get on to the approved list of candidates, I never thought in a million years it would end up with me in Parliament. I just thought I would go along to apply and they would probably turn me down, and that I would have given it my best shot. I applied and it just went from there really, I just took each stage as it came."

Gloria De Piero MP

"To be honest it's always been about the Labour Party for me. I tried to work for them when I was about twenty-one, I ran Labour Students and I tried to get a job as a Special Advisor or something. So I thought, what am I going to do? I really like politics, I'll have

5

to go and try to be a journalist. I started as a researcher at a programme called *Dimbleby*, and one thing led to another and I was in the media for ten years, but my heart was always with the Labour Party. So getting close to that next election in 2010, I was thinking, what am I doing here? I should be going where my heart is."

Stephen Dorrell MP

"I guess the answer is, it's lost in the mists of history. I have always been interested in politics, public affairs, call it what you like. I used to take what my contemporaries regarded as an unhealthy interest in it when I was at school, I was involved in at when I was at university, and I have always been motivated to get involved."

Michael Dugher MP

"I had always been interested in politics, even as a teenager, my mother was quite a big influence, she was not a party activist or anything but someone who was very interested in issues, debating them and talking things through. I remember a lot of conversations as a young teenager, because mum was also a mature student (she had us kids and then went back and did her degree), the house was always full of books, she did combined studies and lots of politics, she would be talking about feminism and socialism and we would be watching *BBC Question Time*. So I think it was partly that and partly that I am a product of where I came from; I grew up in a pit village in South Yorkshire, Edlington, which was the home of the Yorkshire Main Colliery. My earliest political memories are of the strike, it was a hugely traumatic event in that community and it was all about politics, I think that was what led me into it. There is a difference between being interested in politics, to then going to work in it. I think I made a decision some time ago that I wanted to be in public service, I'm not good enough at science to be a doctor, and I barely have enough patience with my own children so the idea of being a teacher was not for me, so it was trying to think of something I could do in public service where I had something to offer, this seemed to be a good thing to do."

Natascha Engel MP

"I have always been really interested in politics, and I have always been interested in the democracy side of it, the making sure that people are involved. I remember when I was sixteen, seventeen, eighteen getting really angry that people didn't care, and that they would moan about things, and I am talking when I was very young, so it was a kind of childish reaction, and I haven't changed much. But it was more the fact that I felt so strongly if we didn't take part, then the system would kind of crumble, and that people weren't really giving the system a chance by not taking part in it. People would take things for granted, as I got older (I grew up under Thatcher and the Tories), there was always that sense of growing up at a time when everything felt really pointless. Then there was the 1992 Election where I and a lot of others assumed that Labour would win, we didn't and it was another four years of Tories, it was dreadful. It just felt like it was hopeless, you couldn't influence anything. Then when I started working, I was very involved with the unions, as a Trade Union organiser, that really changed me politically. Organising is not about recruiting it's about going into a place and basically showing people how to do it for themselves, so when you leave, you leave the place independent, and people do things for themselves at a local, small level. When I saw politics like that it all seemed possible. That really changed my attitude, after that I got a lot more involved in organised politics."

Andrew George MP

"Well because I must have failed at everything else, I suppose. I didn't come from a party political background as such, mainly single issue campaigning on employment, the environment and international development, and Cornwall of course, stuff like that. I found that I kept banging my head against the brick wall of Thatcherism, so I said to my fellow single issue campaigners,

'Someone ought to do something', and they said, 'Since you've got such a big mouth, why don't you?' *[laughter]*. But it wasn't as night follows day that I became an MP. There was a bit of a road to follow. I naturally joined the Liberal Democrats. They represented the values that I felt naturally at home with, although there were inevitably some things on which I disagreed."

John Glen MP

"It was something that I wanted to do from the age of eleven, and I was elected when I was thirty-six, so it was a fascination with the process of governing really. I got involved as I went through senior school and university. It's also public service, helping people to deal with the state and all the different aspects of Government when it fails them. I suppose at one level, as I started my career in management consulting, close to business, working with and advising businesses, I wanted more to help people rather than myself to a higher standard of living. Politics for me is about public service."

Zac Goldsmith MP

"Politics colours everything, and anyone who wants change is necessarily political. As an environmental campaigner more or less since I left school in the early nineties, I have always been involved in campaigning, and stood for Parliament to try to push those same issues higher up the agenda."

Oliver Heald MP

"I came from an ordinary family and was state educated, but at school I was always someone who people turned to. If it was the question of who was going to be form captain, who's going to run the debating society or captain the rugby team, anything like that, people were kind really and asked me if I would do it. I don't really know why that was, but I think I have always liked being someone who represents people.

"Obviously I trained to be a barrister, which of course is

representing people, and have been involved in quite a lot of charitable and voluntary work over the years because I think it's good to put something back. So I have always had this desire to serve, and know that I can represent people effectively, and I have been lucky enough to be elected."

Dan Jarvis MBE MP

"Well I have always believed in the value of public service; it took me into the army fifteen years ago, and kept me in the army during some very difficult times: in Iraq, in Kosovo, in Sierra Leone, particularly in Afghanistan in 2007, but it reinforced my belief in the importance of doing something that you consider to be worthwhile, the importance of making an effective contribution to society. The reality is I had a fantastic time in the army, I was very proud of being in my regiment for fifteen years, but life moves on. After the death of my wife, I had to find something that would offer me another opportunity to make a positive contribution to society. I had been interested in politics for a very long time, and I believed before I came into politics, and I certainly believe now, that it is a very important job to be a Member of Parliament; it provides a really privileged opportunity to make a contribution to the society that you are there to serve, and I am really proud to be Barnsley's MP, and of the people who work with me. We have a really good opportunity to make a difference to the lives of the people in my constituency and that is why I want to do it."

Liz Kendall MP

"It might sound naive, but it was because I wanted to change the world. To give chances to people who have been denied them just because of where they were born, who their parents are, or what their background is. I believe that everybody should be given a fair chance to get on, and to live the life they want to lead, at the moment too many people don't get that. And that is what I came into politics to do."

Sadiq Khan MP

"It's really important to emphasise that I didn't get involved in politics to become a politician. When I was a teenager, I was angry with what was happening in my local community: my dad was a bus driver, his garage was facing closure, lots of my mates' big brothers and sisters were unemployed, my school wasn't having the investment it needed, with teachers often on industrial action, my mates' big brothers were often stopped and searched by the police, I was quite unhappy at what was happening in my community in 1985. And I thought, what can I do to get involved and make a difference? So I joined the Labour Party when I was fifteen. That was the start, I found kindred spirits, people who lived locally, who were also concerned, and I was being part of a constructive opposition to what Margaret Thatcher was doing during the eighties. I was an ordinary member of the Labour Party, going to school and on to university, still a member. When I was in Law School there was an opportunity to be a candidate for council elections when I was twenty-two. I went for the selection and was chosen to become a candidate. I was elected a Councillor when I was twenty-three, and at the same time pursued my legal career. Politics for me wasn't a full time job, I was a lawyer but also a Councillor. Later on when I was thirty-two or thirty-three, the MP for my area decided to retire, I didn't want to be an MP for the sake of being an MP, or a Councillor for the sake of being a Councillor, but it was in my own community of Tooting, so it was the only seat I have ever gone for and the only area I would have wanted to have been the Member of Parliament for."

Ivan Lewis MP

"At quite a young age I started doing voluntary work with people with a mental handicap and mental health problems. It led me to decide that I wanted to do that as a career, so I left education at the age of eighteen and set up a charity working with people with learning disabilities and mental health problems. At the same time as I was doing that I became aware of the political context I was working in. In those days it was very much the Thatcherite era, and I became quite politically aware, my parents were always interested in politics although they were never active. So I did grow up in a household where politics was talked about, but they were never involved in a political party. There was no doubt that it was always going to be the Labour Party, so I joined. I think it was a combination of being fascinated by politics from a very young age then I started doing that kind of work, and you realise there is only so much you can do because of the political climate that you work in, then I decided to join the Labour Party. Like everybody else, I had to go to terribly boring meetings, stuff envelopes, put leaflets through doors, and then after a couple of years I was asked if I would like to stand for my local council in the community that I had grown up in. I was selected to be the candidate and was fortunate enough to be elected, at a very young age, only twenty-three in 1990. Then, within a year of that, I became Chair of the Social Services Committee, which again was very unusual for someone so young, but the reason for that was what I was doing in my day job, they thought here is someone who knows a little bit about it.

"I did that for four years. Then, I had been a Labour Party Councillor for about five years when, in 1997, with a General Election on the way, I was asked to consider becoming the candidate in my area, and I was elected as MP in 1997, and came to Parliament at the age of thirty.

"So I suppose what was quite unusual was that I never went to university, I was never a Special Advisor, or a lawyer. I did two things professionally, voluntary work for an organisation called Outreach, established the charity – Contact, and ran it for about three or four years, then I went to work for a much larger charity called Manchester Jewish Federation; I worked there for eight years before being elected to Parliament."

Caroline Lucas MP

"A passionate desire to make change happen for the better. I come from a very conventional and non-political background – my father ran a heating business and an ironmonger's shop, and my mother brought up three children at home – so my first real encounter with politics came about through activism. I joined the Campaign for Nuclear Disarmament in the 1980s and protested at Greenham Common, as well as signing up to fight for environmental causes and international trade justice. In the Green Party, I found a joined up political solution to the environmental, social and economic challenges we face: how our economy is built on the unsustainable use of finite resources in other countries, for example, and how this leads to the exploitation of the people of those countries."

Nicky Morgan MP

"I really became an MP to make the best use of the skills I have got, which I think are advocacy, talking *(ha,ha)* and standing up for people; I think that is what a good MP does for their constituents, to translate what the Government is trying to do into people's everyday lives."

Greg Mulholland MP

"I decided I wanted to be an MP when I was sixteen when I started A-level politics. I saw politics as the way to be involved in shaping society, to making it and the world a better place. Politics for me is about challenge and changing things. That remains my motivation, to challenge things that are not right and to try to change them for the better."

Jason McCartney MP

"Local issues really. I had two careers before I did this, I was a Royal Air Force Officer for ten years, I wanted to be a pilot but I wear contact lenses so my eyesight wasn't good enough. I was a fighter control officer, at first, then I went to ground support, administration, finance, personnel; I did recruiting, law, court martials, then I was detachment commander. I was based in Turkey, went to Northern Iraq and Las Vegas – so lots of interesting places in the world. I came into contact with politicians while I was doing that, and sometimes I had to brief politicians who would visit where we were around the world. Then I was a journalist for ten years, and obviously I got to interview politicians, so it was always something that was in the back of my mind. Then four years ago I stood as a candidate and got selected; my mum and dad live a mile up the road, this is the area my family settled in the nineteen eighties. I am a Yorkshireman by birth, and a big Huddersfield Town fan, and I care about this part of the world, I am passionate about it. And it was probably about issues I suppose, I didn't like the way Post Offices were closing and maternity services were being cut, and I have always been someone who stands up to be counted. And here I am as the Member of Parliament."

Esther McVey MP
"To provide a 'voice' for people who don't have one and, in this ever evolving world where issues are changing on a daily basis, to promote fairness and help make things the best they can be."

Chi Onwurah MP
"Well the actual thing that made me stand was the announcement by my predecessor Jim Cousins, who was the MP for the part of Newcastle I had grown up in, that he was going to stand down. So I thought there was only one place I would want to represent in Parliament, and that was my area, so it was probably a once in a lifetime opportunity to go for it. But I had been interested in politics since I was about seven, my mother was very active in politics. I joined the party when I was sixteen, and I was elected as the MP for my school when I was seventeen. So I have only ever fought two elections and I have won both of them."

Stephen Pound MP

"I had no intention of doing so, I absolutely loathed politics, I despised it. My father, like a lot of his generation, looked east for his political inspiration, and I was bought up in a household dominated by the union of catholic mothers and the communist mafia of Great Britain, which are two of the most starlingest organisations in the world, but a lot of people of my dad's generation looked over to Soviet Russia fondly. So anyway, I breezed through the navy no trouble at all. But when I went to the *Middlesex*, I was the only person who spoke English as a first language. There were Galicians, Filipinos, North Africans, and they used to call me Mr. Steve, and just like you do I used to help them out filling in forms; they were really badly treated and after a bit I became involved with the union. And then, in 1982, in the height of the Falklands War, a mate of mine rang me up and said we were going to get hammered so would I stand for Labour in the council elections? So I said, 'Only if we don't win,' and he said, 'No chance it's the middle of the Falklands War.' So I said, 'Ok put me down then'. Unfortunately though the week before, there was a photograph published of me as a Royal Navy reservist in my uniform, so I became a Councillor in 1982, and after a year I joined the Labour Party. I think I became a politician for semi noble reasons, to help people. The truest thing is that nobody should ever become an MP if they want to become an MP; the only people who should become MPs are people who don't want to be. Anyone who wakes up reading Hansard under the duvet – take them out and shoot them."

Yasmin Qureshi MP

"I joined the Labour Party when I was fifteen years old, and that came about purely by accident I suppose. We had a fantastic lovely lady who was a County Councillor, her name was Stella Meldrum, she came to our school to talk about her work, and I was interested in what she had to say, I was asking lots of questions. She said to me that they were in the midst of local elections, and did I want to come out on the doorstep and see for myself what they did. I said yes I would like to, so she gave me her number, and I came out canvassing with her, together with another Councillor called Judy Jackson. These were the two ladies who were instrumental in introducing me to the Labour Party. I enjoyed hearing what people were saying, some people were really pleased that you came and wanted to discuss things with you, others were completely indifferent, and one or two banged the door in your face. I thought, this is quite fascinating; so I got involved in the Labour Party, and at the same time got involved in some youth community stuff, helping out, and teaching some basic numeracy and literacy in clubs and societies and things like that. I was studying of course, full time throughout all of this: I got my Law Degree, became a barrister, got my Masters, my pupillage and started working for the Crown Prosecution Service. Then I went out to Kosovo for a year, where I worked closely with the military bases there."

John Redwood MP

"I was motivated to become an MP because I wanted to help change the UK for the better. As a businessman who had many dealings with the USA and other richer countries around the world, I wanted more of the incomes, energy and success for people here that I saw elsewhere, during relatively dark days for Britain. Some advised me to emigrate, telling me the UK was finished. I decided to stay and battle for a better future."

Jacob Rees-Mogg MP

"I had always been interested in politics, I think that family conversation revolved around politics from a very early age. It's always been a great interest of my father and indeed of my mother too. So I was aware of politics. I've been very fortunate in my life, and I think there does come a time when you feel you have a greater responsibility than to yourself, to try and give something back to society which has given you a lot. That was then part of wanting to go into it. So it's interest, enjoyment, and to an extent, duty."

Jonathan Reynolds MP

"The first step to getting involved in politics, rather than being a politician, was a fairly traditional story for me. I grew up in the North-East under Thatcherism, in Houghton, heavily reliant on mining and ship-yards near to Sunderland, a family of miners, with the social economic changes in the 1980's. There was a big sense in the North-East of being miles away from any sense that the Government of the time knew about an area like ours, let alone cared about it. Looking back now I do recognise when one party has been in power for so long, and you come from an area traditionally from the other side, you tend to blame everything you don't like in the world on them. I was a teenager when they went to John Major, they didn't seem to have any answer on things like unemployment, there was all the stuff about not intervening in the Bosnian War, and selling off telecoms and things like that.

"I had a real interest at school academically; I was interested in history and I loved social history, and you get quite easily from there to politics and how things are the way they are. So when I left my comprehensive, we didn't have a sixth form, and went to the City of Sunderland College to do my A Levels, I had gone intending to do History, English and I.T. but one of the Deputy Principals convinced me to do politics as well. He was one of the most brilliant teachers you could come across, and from learning a bit more about politics, I wanted to get more involved. Through doing my A Level in politics, I did some work experience for an MP called Chris Mullin, now a famous diarist, and it was fascinating, he was a really interesting guy. So many little steps, then all these years later I am a politician myself. So it was all of that, but the fundamental thing was where I grew up."

Sir Bob Russell MP

"I don't think anything particularly made me want to be an MP, it just happened. I got involved in politics in Colchester over forty years ago; I was a Labour Councillor for ten years, and stood for

Parliament a couple of times in what were safe Tory seats. Around 1979 there was a bit of a turmoil and upheaval in politics, and I was deemed to be a right wing renegade by members of the Labour Party in Colchester, so I joined the SDP Party which was established in 1981, then I continued under my new colours and continued to get re-elected. In 1995 it was decided by the Boundary Commission that there should be an extra parliamentary seat in Essex; they created a Colchester Town seat, it was a three way marginal, all three parties fought the election believing they could win, and I stormed to victory with 34% of the vote. It was the tightest three way marginal in England, and it was the only three way marginal in England that the Lib Dems won. So I stayed there and have been re-elected four times now, with my majority going up to 48% of the vote. So here we are. I never really decided to be an MP it just happened, I had been Mayor and Leader of the Council, and would still be on the Council now being a Councillor, if I hadn't won the election in 1997."

Derek Twigg MP

"I'd always wanted to do something that helped my community or to help people who weren't able to help themselves; to make a difference and to help people who were in the more deprived section, the more poverty stricken part of the community, those who were less able to help themselves. So having become a Trade Unionist at eighteen, and then become a Councillor at twenty-one, eventually I thought I wouldn't mind giving being an MP a go. I felt I could do the job and I particularly wanted to represent my community, not just be an MP for anywhere. And the opportunity came along in 1994/1995 when my predecessor said he was going to step down. I went for the seat, and obviously here I am today. So really it was the fact I wanted to help people and make a difference coming from Trade Union and Council, it seemed like a natural progression."

Charles Walker MP

"I have always thought that being a politician was a noble vocation. It was something that had interested me since a very early age, my step-father was a Member of Parliament in the sixties and seventies and a Minister. He married my mother when I was eight, he had just left Parliament at that stage. He was only forty-four, so he needed to earn a living as politicians weren't paid a great deal of money in those days. But I grew up in a household where I had a lot of exposure to politicians, members of the Cabinet used to come round for dinner with my parents and I was allowed to meet them, I had always found it interesting, and I was encouraged to share my views round the table, so it was something I had always felt I wanted to do."

Phil Wilson MP

"If you had asked me in 1983 when Tony Blair first came to Sedgefield, if I would be taking over from him having just won a by-election, because he was leaving Parliament, having been Prime Minister for ten years and Leader of the Labour Party since 1984, as he was leaving to be a Middle East envoy, I would have said, 'What's your name, JK Rowling? As you can obviously write a good story,' but that's how it worked out. I've always been involved in politics, the first one in my family to be. I think being a politician is almost like a state of mind, you've got to be slightly obsessive, motivated and passionate about what you believe in, and there's nothing wrong in changing the way you do things as long as your values remain constant. The first time I voted was in 1979, and by the time we got back into power I was on me way to being forty; eighteen years in opposition. When I first got involved in the North East, you had the Miners' Strike, unemployment was going through the roof; you know in those days there were 5,500 people out of work in Sedgefield, today it's about 2,300 and it was just bred into you to be Labour, and because of what was going on it was very easy to be Labour."

Rosie Winterton MP

"Well my family was always very interested in politics and my dad was a local Councillor in Doncaster. My mum and dad were both members of the Labour Party, and a lot of their friends were quite political, so I was always interested in politics. I went to university and secretarial college, and got a job in Parliament, which was just perfect for me. Then I gradually began to think that maybe I could have a go at being an MP myself."

John Woodcock MP

"I was a journalist, that was my first job out of university, and I loved that, but ultimately I thought, I'm not making a difference and I could make more of a difference by changing over into politics. At every level you are struck by the genuine opportunity and privilege you get by doing jobs like this, certainly now being a Member of Parliament. Although it is deeply frustrating to be in Opposition and not able to make the changes to the country that you think are needed, and having had the opportunity to work in Government in my last job, I saw that it can still be frustrating there, but how much more you can do. Nevertheless, the platform that being a Member of Parliament gives you to hold people to account, and to be able to raise issues that are important to your constituents, is enormous."

The really striking thing about these answers is that so many of the MPs talk of having an interest from an early age, and the influence of their parents. I don't know about you, but it makes me wonder if we all as parents should encourage our children to take an interest in politics. If so, I have failed, it's too late for me as my kids have grown up now. Oh well, perhaps I should work on the grandchildren.

Certainly schools have a role to play, and I must say I am always encouraged to see so many school trips on tours in the House of Commons and Portcullis House. Forgive me, it is not for me to lecture anyone, but seriously, our democracy suffers if we, the great British public, do not take an interest. Almost every aspect of our lives are affected by the decisions our Parliamentarians make.

So it is encouraging that many of my interviewees entered politics with a strong public service ethos, with an enthusiasm to change things for the better; indeed Kevin Brennan, Rosie Cooper, Liz Kendall and Greg Mulholland wanted to change the world, now I don't know about you, but that is the kind of ambition I want from our MPs. Stephen Pound, Nicky Morgan, John Glen and Esther McVey want to stand up and provide a voice for the people – what more could we want? Dan Jarvis MBE, Derek Twigg and John Woodcock want to make a difference – what could be better? When I depart this earth, I would dearly love people to say 'Well he made a difference.'

And it is interesting that Sadiq Khan, Jason McCartney and Derek Twigg speak with so much passion about their commitment to their local communities, as do Andy Burnham and Phil Wilson elsewhere in this book. These guys don't want to be MPs just anywhere, they are totally committed to the place where they grew up.

Jacob Rees-Mogg talks of giving something back, while Caroline Lucas wants to change things for the better. Andrew Bridgen, Philip Davies and Andrew George were so fed up with what they saw happening, they said rather than just moan about it, they wanted to do something. Philip Davies also speaks of being fed up and disillusioned with politicians – does that ring any bells? – and Natascha Engel sums it all up perfectly when she says if we don't take part, the system could crumble.

We may not agree with the politics of some of these people, but they are my kind of people. They may all express themselves in different ways, but it amounts to the same thing, that strong public service ethos.

Andrew George

Politicians are people who, when they see light at the end of the tunnel, go out and buy some more tunnel.
John Quinton

CHAPTER TWO

First Day

We can all relate to what a first day can be like, so how was it for our MPs?

Dave Anderson MP

"It wasn't particularly overwhelming for me because I had been coming here for a long, long time beforehand with the unions since the mid-eighties. The only time I have ever felt that way was just before my maiden speech, one of the whips came across and said, 'Dave you will be the next but one, but one,' and I'm sitting there thinking, *this is the big one.* I had spoken all over the world, in football stadiums at big events before, but I mean the place is a thousand years old, it's big stuff.

"It was obviously good for me that I had been involved here before, but the work just kicks in straight away. We had a two day induction, then we were into business. I also had loads of friends here who I had known for years, so I wasn't overwhelmed, there were people I could talk to, people I could moan to. You come in, and you haven't been allocated an office, there were probably 150 new MPs. Now you can't say if you are going to win the election, but they knew, whatever happened that the Blaydon MP was leaving Parliament, but the offices were used like grace and favour, so it was who was considered to be a good boy etc. They give you a laptop and a locker, but it was a nonsense, some people didn't have a desk for six weeks. I was lucky because Alan Campbell, one of ours, had just been made a whip the week before, he had an office in here actually, and he said to me, 'How you getting on Dave?' I hate I.T.

and was having problems with me laptop, and so said to him 'I hate it mate'. He said I should go and use his office that he had just moved out of, and it was great; me laptop could stay there, it was online, you didn't have to wait for someone to move. So in a sense that was dead fortunate, but stuff like that is dead stupid."

Ben Bradshaw MP

"When I came in, on my first day I was awestruck, you can't help but be overwhelmed by the history of the place; all the historical events that have taken place here, you can't help but think, oh my goodness I'm part of all that now. I think it's also the humility of it, I had been sent here by the people of Exeter and had a determination to work hard on their behalf, and do what I could to improve Exeter and the country."

Kevin Brennan MP

"It wasn't totally mysterious to me because having worked for Rhodri*, although I was based in Cardiff, I would come up from time to time, and knew a lot of the Welsh MPs already, and they knew me because I used to run his campaigns and things like that. So it was great to come and feel you were representing your constituency. To be honest with you, I just felt that great feeling of privilege and that it was a real opportunity. Don't come here and waste it, try and do something positive with it."

*Rhodri Morgan, Former MP for Cardiff West

Ann Coffey MP

"I do remember the first time that I arrived, coming down to London from Stockport, when I got the notice to attend. After the 1992 election it took them a long time to reconvene Parliament, it was six weeks. I remember coming out of the Tube and getting to the barrier where there was a policeman. I said, 'I'm Ann Coffey the new Member of Parliament for Stockport. He said, 'No you're not',

I said, 'I am.' He said, 'No you are not, you are Ann Brown' which had been my maiden name, and he had known my mother. His family had been brought up in the house next door to my mother. So he had been waiting for me, and had obviously looked up who was coming, because in those days it was a matter of pride for the policemen to know all the MPs and their backgrounds."

Rosie Cooper MP

"My first day down here was weird, everyone was talking at me, really talking at me, we went into a day of what they call induction, and about two hours into it, and this is absolutely true, I could hear a song in my head: *'everybody's talking at me, I can't hear a word they say… '*. So then this person came to me, because we had to go from place to place to place, and says, ' Ms Cooper, which computer and printer do you want?' There were loads. I said, 'I've made a decision.' They said 'Oh good.' I said, 'I'm not making any more decisions today, I'm fed up.' They said, 'Pardon?' I said, 'Well if I make any more decisions today they will be the wrong ones, so rather than make one and change it, why don't I just say I'll make one when I am ready.' Then I got to the next desk who wanted to know what I would like to be called, 'Well how's about me name?.' And this person said, 'Would you like to be known as Ms Cooper, Ms R Cooper, Miss Rosie Cooper?' I said, ' I can't be doing with any of that, how about we stick with Rosie Cooper?' She said, 'Certainly madam.'

"The place that really shocked me though was the Chamber, because if you have ever been to Liverpool and seen the council chamber it's huge, so I walked in and went, this is cosy, then I nearly lost my seat before I got my seat, because you are not allowed to sit on the green benches until you have been sworn in. So we had sat on the green benches that morning because the speaker was selected, so fine, I was going to be sworn in at 2.30 pm. At 2.15 pm I said to the Sergeant of Arms, 'Where do I go?' He said, 'Go in.' So I went in and sat on the green benches and waited. Angela Eagle was sat roughly behind where Tony Blair was going to sit, she said, 'Sit with me, you'll be on the tele.' I said, 'I can't I've got to get sworn in.' Where upon the Sergeant of Arms descended on me, we got to the door of the Chamber, and he said to me, if the Speaker had been in the Chair, and I had been sitting on the green benches before I had been sworn in, I would have been deemed to be 'dead', therefore my seat would have to have been fought again, it was an old tradition. The next thing was the Sergeant of Arms, who had originally told me to go in, appeared at my side, and said, 'When I told you to go in, I meant go to the white line and wait.' I went, 'Hmm, important bits of information missing there then."

Philip Davies MP

"Daunting, very daunting, lots of people here had been before, they had been Special Advisors or researchers or whatever. I hadn't been any of that I was a complete outsider, I literally had no idea what to expect. Funny enough, because I was standing in a marginal seat in 2005, I got a letter from the chief whip about a month before the election, to say something like 'on the off chance that you win, this is what you should do.' So I was literally digging through stuff looking for that letter. I had no idea what to expect, and you actually feel quite a weight of responsibility on your shoulders. Daunting is the only word I can use to describe it."

Stephen Dorrell MP

"Well I had been around the place for some time, because Peter Walker was a friend and sponsor of mine, although I had never been, in the way things tend to happen sometimes now, an obsessive political hanger–on before I arrived here. I remember feeling awkward walking past the statue of Churchill for the first time, but it all seems like quite a long time ago now."

Michael Dugher MP

"It is different, hanging around the place compared to being a MP I think. I didn't particularly like it for the first few months, partly it was adjusting to the grim reality of Opposition; I sat there as they did their Budget and everything else, and you could kind of see what would happen as they tried to dismantle everything we had put in place, I found that quite tough actually. And I've always felt that the Government will go the distance, so I knew it was the beginning of a lot of long, hard years till 2015. In truth I was also a bit tired, I had had quite a busy job before, and had been selected quite late. I had a really nice August, I had a good rest and a good think about what I wanted to achieve, I came back in the September, and actually since September 2010 I have loved every minute of it."

Natascha Engel MP

"It was a bit different for me. I got elected on the the 5th May 2005, I then had a baby on the 29th May. I spent the first couple of weeks trying to find an office, and though it was a so called 'safe' seat, I thought it would be a bit arrogant to assume that I would win, also I thought I would have been 'cursing' it, so I didn't employ anybody. I didn't have an office in my constituency, because my predecessor didn't have an office. So I was trying to set all these things up in order so that I could go and have a baby, that was quite hard. When I came back, everyone had done their maiden speeches, I was the last one. I came in at the same time as a By-Election candidate in the October. So we had the recess, which was my maternity leave effectively, but I spent that setting up my office in the constituency and when I came back with everyone else after the summer recess, it felt to me that everyone else knew what they were doing, and I didn't have a clue, I had to start from absolute scratch. Sadiq Khan was one of the people who were really, really helpful, but the people who were really, really fantastic were the doorkeepers. They instantly recognised that I didn't have a clue what I was doing, and they were so helpful."

Andrew George MP

"You have to remember that I am an unreformable country

bumpkin really. It's like someone with a very ordinary background coming into a top public school really, with your eyes wide open, looking at a lot of famous people that you had only previously looked at from afar, and either admired or not. And then you are actually able to engage with them, it was quite a jaw dropping moment, particularly if you come from my sort of background. I am one of a very large family of eight, so I come from hand-me-downs, state education, entitlement to free school meals and that sort of stuff. And this wasn't something that I had always worked for, it wasn't something that I had had big ambitions to do, it was purely that in order to be able to help secure the political change I wanted, I had to come to this place. Yes it was daunting, but also inspiring and enthralling."

John Glen MP

"It was a lot how I expected, I'd had the privilege of working here for three and half years before, so I knew what it was like in an MP's office. I still feel in awe of the place, it's a special place where I have been put by my constituents, so I have never really lost that sense of *wow*. It is a real privilege. But in the early days it was very much getting to know processes and procedures, and getting to understand the slowness with which things worked."

Zac Goldsmith MP

"Bewildering. There is no job description, and no real steer. You find yourself falling in line with customs that initially mean nothing, and it takes a few months to learn all the mechanisms, levers and tricks available to a backbencher."

Liz Kendall MP

"Honestly, it was a shock in a way because the Chamber, and what happens within it, can be a very aggressive environment. People can do and say things, that I don't think they would do or say in any other place of work. It was interesting because some of the behaviour that goes on in there, I would never behave like that at work. And it was very interesting because Dennis Skinner was brilliant, really supportive of the new intake of 2010, and he said, 'This is a place of work, go in there and do your job. And that has always really guided me, *you are here to work, to do a job*, and I want to do that job in the same way I would in any other environment.

"That has been the biggest difference, being first and foremost a constituency MP, with all of that, it can be difficult, challenging but I love it. The Chamber is a very different environment, and I think it takes everyone a bit of time to get used to it."

Sadiq Khan MP

"I describe it to my daughters by saying, imagine watching Harry Potter where he goes off to Hogwarts – a totally different world! The induction's not great, you're a small fish in a big pond, I didn't have any mates here before I became an MP so I had to start building friendships, there are cliques around. You make mistakes, you are learning all the time under the glare of publicity. It's a scary place, there are people from backgrounds which are far more privileged than yours, and they have friends or family who are, or who have been, MPs. So it is tough. I don't want you to feel sorry for me, but I always knew, coming from my background of primary and secondary school, that had given me the skills to achieve what I needed to do, so I didn't lack confidence. That's one of the things I keep saying when I meet the kids in my local schools, you can be an MP, don't allow people to give you the impression that it's too tough a gig, because the reason they do that is to make you think you can't do it, so I always try and encourage them. Of course you have to work hard, there is no substitute for hard work, but don't let others let you think it's so hard that you can't do it."

Caroline Lucas MP

"Strange, wonderful and slightly overwhelming. The House of Commons is a beautiful place, a site of great history and culture.

But it's also stuck in the past. The first thing I was shown was not my office – that took at least a month to be allocated – but the pink ribbon where I was to hang up my sword! From the start, the antiquated language which parliamentarians are still expected to use in the Chamber, the late night voting and the unpredictability of the daily agenda all felt pretty anachronistic. I've also been shocked by the lack of efficiency. Half a dozen votes with electronic voting, used in a number of countries and in the European Parliament, would take you a couple of minutes, but thanks to our antiquated voting system, the same votes can take you an hour and half in Westminster. That is not a good use of anybody's time. The style of the Chamber itself is hugely problematic. Everything revolves around adversarial, bully-boy exchanges where MPs shout across the room at each other. Not to mention the fact that there are 650 MPs in this place, yet there's only room for 450 people to sit down. It's madness. I think we need to find a far more effective way of doing business, and of making Parliament a more accessible and inclusive place for people outside of the Westminster bubble."

Nicky Morgan MP

"I think for about three or four weeks I was in a state of complete shock. I was fighting a marginal seat, I had no idea if I was going to win or not, and I had been trying for such a long time to win in Loughborough. When it finally happened, I arrived here on the Monday afternoon, having been to my old workplace, who gave me a very nice send off with a big bunch of flowers. Then I arrived here with my husband and there was a doorkeeper saying, 'Hello Mrs Morgan, Welcome!' And it was just all very surreal. Of course, we didn't know if we were going to be in Government or not, because the coalition negotiations were carrying on, so it took a while to settle down. For a while I was thinking, what on earth have I done, to my life and my son's life and my husband's life? So it does take a while to get used to it all."

Greg Mulholland MP

"The only thing that I could compare it to is the first day at a new school. All the new boys and girls are looking around wide eyed. Going in and sitting in the Chamber for the first time is surreal, but you soon get used to it. The whole place soon becomes 'the office', though sometimes you are reminded where you are and what it means."

Jason McCartney MP

"Well when I first entered the House of Commons on the Monday morning after the General Election, I basically didn't know where I was going. I had been twice before in my life, for a combined total of forty minutes, and I turned up not knowing what entrance to go to, not knowing that as well as the historical Palace of Westminster, there was a whole new building called Portcullis House, I didn't even know that existed, so I was like a wide eyed little boy on Christmas Day. I had never worked in politics before as a researcher or as an MP, I had two previous careers: ten years in the R.A.F. and ten years as a journalist, so it was all new to me, it was a massive learning curve.

"And because so many new MPs were elected at the same time, 242 I think it was of all parties, they had a proper induction day, they gave you a pass, they gave you a laptop computer, a locker key for where you could keep all your things, and we actually 'hot desked' it for about seven weeks. They turned one of the committee rooms into a shared office, where we would just have desks back to back until you got allocated an office. But by doing that, we communicated, we made friends and shared ideas. So I got there on the Monday, by the Wednesday, I was looking at my neighbour saying, 'You've got a lot of post there, where do you get your post from?' I hadn't collected any post, he said, 'Well there is a Post Office.' So I followed him down to the Parliamentary Post Office, and already there were three sacks of mail, about a foot high in those green Royal Mail sacks, I think about 100 constituents and about 400 charities and businesses must have written to each of the candidates just on the off chance of who would win with their issues and problems. And I remember I started opening the mail at one o'clock, and I was still opening it at six o'clock. Just opening it and sorting it out into piles – one a hand-written pile, one a constituency pile, one with invites, one with briefing notes. It took me so long just to open, take out the paper, glance at it and put it in the right pile, and that was just opening it, let alone dealing with it. Then the next day we were given an email address, so I started getting lots of those coming through too. It was a massive learning curve but it was very exciting!"

Esther McVey MP
"Exciting, exhilarating, but also overwhelming."

Chi Onwurah MP
"Well the House of Commons is a very weird place, I wouldn't exactly say it was daunting because I was quite determined not to be scared, but it was a lot to go through in the first few days. Because you become a Member of Parliament, the moment the returning officer says that, then you are one, without getting any training or support in it. The first day I came into Parliament they had all the doorkeepers, with their white ties and strange clothes, and they didn't make it seem any more twenty first century, but since then I have learnt that they are very twenty first century, it's just they dress strangely."

Stephen Pound MP
"Absolutely chaotic! Sorry, can we just rephrase that, it was rather confusing. The point is there was no induction, when I came in in 1997 I had no office, no equipment, no staff and no secretary, but I was given a sack of post, so I went off to St. James' Park, sat on a park bench, opened it, and hand-wrote the replies, because there was no other way to do it. Then I met this guy called Jimmy, who was from Glasgow, and was sitting there shot-gunning Special Brew,

and he helped me sort the post out. So I just sat there and went through the whole lot, went back in, sat down for a pint, which I did a lot in those days, only to find that I had another sack to get through. This really came to a head when one of the new MPs who came in the 1997 intake, went on the *Today* programme and was asked the self same question, and although she came from the north-east she was Welsh, and John Humphreys said to her it must be very difficult: 'Oh you don't know what it's like to wake up each morning with nine inches of mail'. To which someone else said, 'Chance would be a fine thing!'

"So you don't know where you are, you have no idea the whole place is constructed to confuse, it's a nineteenth Century Boys Club crossed with a Magistrates Court, and it's only after about three months that you get an office. I had never opened a computer before in my life, and I had to go and buy one, but fortunately I had an Olivetti typewriter, which I used till the ribbon broke and there were no replacements available. It was all very confusing, and the first thing you have to do is to respond to your constituents mail which is pouring in, and you don't have any space or mechanism to do that.

"In those days you had to get your own computer and claim back for it. The other problem was, like a lot of us in 1997, I was still working. So I rang my boss up on the Friday morning after the election, and said, 'I won't be in today I'm an MP now'. So he said, 'Well you'll be in on Monday then' and I said, 'Well actually no.' And he said 'Yes you will, sorry mate but you've got six weeks notice to serve, so come in on Monday.' So for the first six weeks I was here, I used to work 6 am till noon at my job and then get down here for one pm and be here. In those days frankly I often just used to sleep in a chair here, cos there was no point in going home. You understand from your firm's point of view, you can't just walk out of the door."

Yasmin Qureshi MP
"Oh it was brilliant. My chambers as a barrister were just down the

road in the temple, so of course it's by the edge of the river, and when you come out you could look into Parliament from my chambers. I have to say that many years ago when I decided that I wanted to become a Member of Parliament, every time I would drive past, I would say, 'I want to be in that place.' Oh and it was exciting and challenging, but it was a bit like being at school as well. It's awesome, when you walk up the steps and you see the hall."

Jacob Rees Mogg MP

"Amazing! I had been here before occasionally, but never very much, and I didn't know my way around. It's a wonderful feeling to suddenly be able to come in by right, rather than as a guest. You are now here representing, in my case, 69,000 people. It's a huge responsibility, but very exciting."

Jonathan Reynolds MP

"It was just crazy for me because I was selected just over a month, thirty six days I think, before the General Election. So I had gone from a really intense, happy experience as a trainee solicitor in a big Manchester firm which was all encompassing, and I was a local Councillor in Hyde as well at the same time, and then really within two months, life had turned completely upside down. So it was a really strange experience, but very exciting as well. It wasn't until I was walking down Victoria Street on my way to Parliament for the first time, that it really sort of hit me as I turned up at the gates. Obviously no-one really knows what happens when you get elected as an MP. I was given an envelope by the Returning Officer, saying I might want to report to the House of Commons at some time, obviously no-one had won the election, so there was all this confusion. I had no idea when to go down, no-one told me when to report for duty. I had a call from Jack Straw saying, 'Hi I'm Jack Straw, and this is the picture at the moment.'

"On our first day, all the new MPs gathered in the Chamber for a talk from a figure from each of the parties. Everyone filed in, and the Liberals and the Tories immediately went to the Government benches. And it was only then, sitting on the benches for the first time that I thought, '*Here I am in the House of Commons*', it was incredible."

Derek Twigg MP
"A bit bewildering I think is the best way to describe it. I remember having to bring my election leaflet with me to prove who I was. What you have to remember was in 1997 there was I think a record number of new MPs so it was somewhat overwhelming. They said to bring some identification with me, and it was suggested that I bring that to show to security. So I met one of the doorkeepers who showed me around a bit, then the key factor for me was to find somewhere to put my stuff, I got this locker, just off the Chamber and that was such a relief, for the tons of paperwork I had already. Then you had to pick your constituency post up in a big bag, with no office, no staff or anything like that. It was bewildering, exasperating and of course exhilarating. Here you are, elected to the Mother of Parliaments, to represent a community you were born in. It was a completely new Government, a new beginning, so it was totally exhilarating as well."

Charles Walker MP
"Overwhelming, when I was selected for Broxbourne, it was very exciting, I had a fair idea that whoever was selected to be the Conservative candidate for Broxbourne was probably going to win because it had been a Conservative seat for a long time, I won't be silly enough to suggest that I thought otherwise, but absolutely wonderful up until the very moment it was announced by the returning officer that I was now the elected Member of Parliament for Broxbourne, and I was handed a letter with my instructions with what I needed to do, and at the moment I felt total and utter fear. It was fight or flight, I wanted to run away. I drove home with my wife after the celebratory drinks, I don't drink, but after a celebratory

Diet Coke, it was overwhelming, exciting but actually extremely worrying because if you take this role seriously as most of us do, I was suddenly responsible for the hopes, aspirations and dreams of potentially 72,000 people. That was quite a responsibility to bear."

Phil Wilson MP

"Well I'd been involved in politics for a long time, so it wasn't an unusual place for me, but it was still awesome really. What I will never forget is when you are sworn in; you have two sponsors, and they stand each side of the doors and you look into the Chamber, it was like walking on to the stage for the first time. You could see through this little bit of net curtain, and you could see them debating, you were just waiting for your time, and that's what I will always remember, that was special, walking in that first time."

John Woodcock MP

"Slightly daunting actually, I had been around this place for a number of years. I had been an advisor to Cabinet Minister John Hutton, I'd had a year working as Gordon Brown's Political Spokesman, going into the most famous front door in the political world every day, but I always remember coming out of the Tube station for the first time, the week after I was elected, and that sense of responsibility hits you, that you are there to stand up for the people who have just elected you, and sent you down here, it's a big responsibility on your shoulders."

Call me sentimental, I actually found the answers to this question heart-warming, maybe even reassuring. These do not sound like people who are in it for themselves. There is a real sense of awareness of the responsibility bestowed upon them, by we the electorate, as they became our Members of Parliament.

Considering it is the very seat of our democracy, the

Mother of Parliaments, it would be reasonable to expect it to be very slick, well organised and professional; it has after all, had hundreds of years to perfect its' function.

So when Dave Anderson talks about not having a desk for six weeks, and Jason McCartney remembers having to 'hot desk' (share) for seven weeks, you may be a little surprised, but perhaps they were lucky? If you listen to the accounts of some of their colleagues who entered the House years earlier such as Derek Twigg and Stephen Pound, neither of whom had an office, equipment, staff or a secretary, and yet sack loads of mail already waiting for them, you have to wonder if this is a sensible way to treat our elected representatives. Many of them speak of chaos and bewilderment. It is all a bit strange to say the least, and it appears some of the old customs are too when we hear the thoughts of Rosie Cooper and Caroline Lucas.

Rosie Cooper describes her first day as 'weird' and with her story of almost being deemed 'dead', which would have resulted in her seat having to be fought again, you can certainly see why. Perhaps one of the most interesting observations is that of Caroline Lucas, one of the very few independent MPs who does not have the luxury of support from a huge party behind her (incidentally it was Sadiq Khan who urged me to interview her); whereas Rosie used the word 'weird', Caroline chooses 'strange' as she refers to another old custom when she was shown the pink ribbon, the place where she should hang her sword. Isn't it amazing that we are in the twenty-first Century but the House of Commons still has these customs. Personally I think it's a good thing to give a nod to history.

However, Caroline makes you think with her observations regarding the antiquated voting system in Westminster, as opposed to a much more efficient electronic voting system, and we all know what she means when she talks about the adversarial bully-boy exchanges where MPs shout across the floor of the House at each other. But if one thing sums up how crazy the House of Commons is, it is the fact that there is only room for 450 people to sit down in the Chamber, and yet there are 650 MPs! You can see why Rosie and Caroline use words like 'weird' and 'strange'.

But perhaps it is another of Caroline's thoughts that is worthy of repeating: 'We need to find a more effective way of doing business, and of making Parliament a more accessible and inclusive place for people outside of the Westminster bubble.' AMEN to that.

Liz Kendall is another of our MPs concerned by what can sometimes be, as she describes, 'an aggressive environment', when she talks about behaviour and people in the Chamber who can do and say things that she thinks would not happen in any other place of work, and of course she is right.

And perhaps Nicky Morgan gives an indication of the enormity of the task of becoming an MP when she tell us of that thought, 'What on earth have I done to my life, my son's life, and my husband's life?' As with Sadiq Khan, I have met Nicky on a number of occasions, the first being during my charity walk. She is another really nice person who we could all relate to, so much so that I wanted one of my daughters to spend some time with Nicky in the hope of getting her interested in politics, and to demonstrate that even as a young mum it is possible.

Natascha Engel, one of the most endearing and engaging MPs I met, is another wonderful lady who performs the difficult tasks of being both a mum and an MP.

And don't you just love the way that Sadiq describes his first day to his daughters by a comparison with Harry Potter setting off for Hogwarts. You can also feel for him when he talks about not having any mates when he arrived there. I have met Sadiq on a number of occasions, including the first time when he turned up to support my charity walk. I know what a good guy he is, so I feel sure he will have plenty of mates by now. But Sadiq makes a very serious point when he tells the schoolchildren he meets (and it actually applies to everyone, and is a point worth repeating), 'Don't allow people to give you the impression that becoming an MP is too tough a gig.' Like anything else that is worthwhile it may take a lot of hard work, but it can be done.

Kevin Brennan, another nice guy, who it's easy to relate to, speaks of the privileges and the great opportunity to do something positive, as does John Glen. I only visit the place for occasional meetings, and of course to conduct these interviews, but I totally relate to that feeling of awe, and he is so right, it is a special place. Then there is Ben Bradshaw. This is a man who had been an experienced journalist, and witnessed the destruction of the Berlin Wall, yet even he was awestruck upon entering the Palace of Westminster. This gives you a flavour of just how magical the House of Commons is. Interesting to note also the humility Ben felt having been elected by the people of Exeter.

Andrew George describes himself as a 'country bumpkin', so you can imagine how he felt on his first day, and you can understand why it was a jaw dropping moment, describing his first day experience as 'daunting, inspiring and enthralling.'

However, it is that word RESPONSIBILITY that keeps cropping up. Both Philip Davies and John Woodcock talk about the huge weight of responsibility on their shoulders. Charles Walker and Jacob Rees-Mogg speak of the responsibility of representing 72,000 and 69,000 constituents respectively, and Charles expresses that real human emotion of fear at the prospect.

Undoubtedly, one of the most important points of all is

made by Chi Onwurah when she says, 'You become a Member of Parliament without getting any training or support'. I ask again, is this any way to treat our elected representatives?

The last words on the first day experience must go to Greg Mulholland: 'The only thing I can compare it to is the first day at a new school, all the new boys and girls are looking around wide-eyed'. Don't we just know exactly what he means.

Andy Burnham

The hardest thing about any political campaign is how to win without proving that you are unworthy of winning.
Adlai E Stevenson

CHAPTER THREE

Inspirations

For my third question, I thought it might be interesting to know who has been the inspiration for our MPs.

Dave Anderson MP

"Margaret Thatcher, I wanted to do everything I could in my life to destroy that woman. Every day I come into this place, it's revenge for what she did to me and my community, the people I love."

Paul Blomfield MP

"I got involved through the Anti-Apartheid movement, when I was a teenager at school. I know a lot of people say it but Nelson Mandela was an extraordinary influence. I was very involved in anti-apartheid, and spent some time in South Africa with the African National Congress. Mandela's vision and courage through all those years he was in jail, and then to come out and build a country around the principles of reconciliation was totally inspiring."

Sir Peter Bottomley MP

"My wife. I am the founder member of a group called the Dennis Thatcher Society; it's for men married to women more important than we are. The reason we have never met is our wives won't let us. Dennis said it should be called the Prince Albert Club after Queen Victoria's husband."

Kevin Brennan MP

"Yes I think probably my predecessor Rhodri Morgan. One thing I think I learnt from him as a politician, was to actually always be interested in people and what they have to say, whoever they are, and to always try to help somehow or other. There is always something you can do, and some people don't expect you to be able to solve their problem, but they would like somebody who is going to listen to what they have to say about it, and who will at least try and do something. I always say to people, I can try, I'm not saying it's going to work, in fact it probably won't, but let's give it a go, and ninety-nine times out of a hundred people are perfectly happy with that. You had a go, you didn't flannel me, you told me it might not work, but you gave it a go on my behalf. So Rhodri was an inspiration to me in a personal sense.

"There are also various people from history who inspired me when I was younger, like Nye Bevan and so on, but I do think in a personal sense it would be Rhodri."

Andrew Bridgen MP

"I think it's a great privilege to be an MP and think about the people you are in Parliament with on both sides of the House. Obviously you have images of people, you see their media image, and some people have not lived up to that in my expectations, but some have exceeded it. I would say if I was to pick one person who absolutely exudes decency and it is a privilege to know him, it would be Iain Duncan Smith. When he was Conservative Party Leader he was a bit of a failure, I didn't know him personally and I thought goodness me, but when you actually meet the guy and see the work he has done around social justice, and his work on welfare reform, he's just an absolutely decent human being, who it's an absolute privilege to be in the company of. So he has really impressed me."

Andy Burnham MP

"The person who I always thought was closest to where I was on the political scale would have been John Smith, kind of like having old fashioned values around the working class culture. In terms of political inspiration now though, I would definitely say Nye Bevan. The more I have learnt, the jobs I have done, I constantly refer back to him and what he did."

Rosie Cooper MP

"Well internationally JFK is my hero from when I was a kid. People talk about the flawed man, but I am not really interested, it was at the time of the race riots in America, and all that went with it, and the beginnings of Vietnam. So, Kennedy, internationally. In Britain, Shirley Williams was somebody I admired greatly, and the other person was Barbara Castle. I saw her on her ninetieth birthday tell the Prime Minister off, and she had everyone just dancing to her tune because she was not having pensioners defeated. Apart from the people I have already mentioned, the person I admire most in this world, who started off with all the disadvantages, is my dad. He is a brilliant man, with no formal education, and he is the cleverest person I have ever met."

Philip Davies MP

"My political heroes when I was younger were Margaret Thatcher and Norman Tebbitt. They were my two absolute heroes, without a shadow of a doubt. They were my early inspirations. My inspiration since I came into Parliament was Eric Forth. He was my mentor when I first got into Parliament, and he died a year later, and I still miss him now. He was a great man. If you were to ask me to pick one political hero, mine would be Eric Forth."

Gloria De Piero MP

"Oh gosh, I mean there are people I admire like Tony Blair, Mo Mowlam, Clare Short – I mean she left the Labour Party but flippin' eck what a woman, so I admire lots of people in politics. But schoolchildren often ask me, who has inspired me, and you know, as I get older, I think the most amazing people are – my mum and dad. They are the ones that kind of instill this stuff in you and make you what you are, so they are the real inspirations. But you don't realise that till you are 'knocking on' do you?"

Stephen Dorrell MP

"Inspiration is an interesting word, I guess when you have been around the political world for as long as I have, you get to know people warts and all. What I now do is read history, and I enjoy trying to understand people as human beings, warts and all, so there are a number of people who I admire in history and in current life. Inspiration is a funny word though.

"Going back into history which is always safer territory, I admire Churchill, as everyone does. And if you look back at some of the nineteenth century figures, there is a biography of William Pitt, which brought him to life as a human being, which I would recommend to anyone, I think he was an interesting character, at an interesting time."

Michael Dugher MP

"I don't have one figure who is my 'hero' in politics. I have been fortunate enough to work for and with a lot of big figures, I have tried to learn from all of them, I think a lot of those people had tremendous strengths. I never looked at anyone and thought that they were perfect, but I have tried to learn from all of them, which hopefully makes me a better Member of Parliament because of it. I am a product of where I come from, my mother was a big influence, and her father as well was very interested in politics, and would read *The Guardian* cover to cover, talking politics all the time. He was another influence, but there isn't just one person. I have lots of people who I think have done amazing things in politics that I admire, and I have been fortunate to work with some of them."

Natascha Engel MP

"Lots of people have in lots of different ways, not necessarily in organised party politics. I think in the unions people have inspired me politically. I think people in smaller leadership roles have inspired me. Sometimes it's quite overwhelming when you are an MP where the pressure is on you to do something massive, to change the world. You speak to a lot of MPs and you say, 'Why did you go into politics?' They say, 'To change the world', and I think if that's the attitude you go in with, you are going to be quite disappointed. And actually those people who have a smaller scale idea of doing things, I think tend to have happier outcomes. So my inspirations mainly have been a lot of women in the unions who have had a massive impact on the way that other women can work, and they have been amazing."

Andrew George MP

"Inspired me? The unsung heroes, not the great orators and front bench people. They always get all the attention and accolades they deserve. So it's people like David Drew who lost his seat last time, a Labour MP, he was a really hard working, campaigning MP and there are many others like him, who I find very inspiring. They are kind of role models for me: independent minded, passionate about what they do and committed. I am not claiming to have any of those virtues, but those are the kind of people who inspire me. The others are my constituents, decent, hard-working people I feel inspired to represent. Many have to endure things which they don't deserve, and I feel motivated to help. They and their plight motivate me if I ever feel I'm flagging, when I start thinking, *'what the hell am I doing this for?'* Some will come to an MP with naive faith, perhaps thinking they can wave a magic wand and solve their problems for them. But I am often re-invigorated by the decision to use the privilege of the position I hold, to do my best for those many deserving folk who have often been ill treated by the system."

John Glen MP

"I think it's a combination of personal experiences and characters in politics. I remember my father talking to me about politics from the age of eight, when the Falklands War happened, he explained about that, and with the election campaign the next year, I kind of had a sense of what was going on. He was a key influence on me. At school I was head boy, and was always someone who tried to take responsibility for things, and my old headmaster, who is in his seventies now, was a big figure for me. But I think William Hague was a key influence, I admired his ability with words, his ability generally as a speaker, so they were really my three influences. But it's evolved, it's been a passion, it's been a vocation for me for a long time."

Zac Goldsmith MP

"Many people. My father and my Uncle Teddy, who devoted his life to green causes."

Oliver Heald MP

"Well I had the inspiration of a great teacher. My school had a history teacher, Mr Terry, who was very interested in politics, he used to encourage us. There are four of us in the House who have all been his students, he is now ninety-one I think, and in terms of a personal influence Frank Terry is an influence on me. In terms of politicians, I always admired the one nation style of politicians like Willie Whitelaw, and some others, so I wouldn't say that I am a right wing Tory. But on the other hand, when it comes down to it, in 1979 the country was in a terrible mess, and Mrs Thatcher and the Conservatives that she led did change the country for ever. I would say they rescued the nation. So I would say a combination of one nation conservatism, but also a good deal of respect for Mrs Thatcher and her team, that's where I am."

Dan Jarvis MBE MP

"My family set an example to me at an early stage. The values of my family have stayed with me so that has been very important to me. They are the same values I try to make sure my kids grow up with.

It's quite fashionable for MPs to quote Churchill or Gandhi, but I think what really inspires me is being out in my constituency of Barnsley Central, talking to some really decent people, who inspire me to go and do the best job that I can for the town. So my inspiration isn't Gandhi or anyone like that, it's old ladies in Athersley, who are such brilliant people they just make me want to do the best job I can."

Sadiq Khan MP

"Before I became a politician the person who inspired me to get involved in politics was Neil Kinnock, some of his speeches were amazing. He made the hair stand up on the back of my neck. He was inspirational, trying to bring the Labour Party back into the centre ground, to make it sensible, and to take on those who were causing problems in the party, so I really admire Neil Kinnock. As far as other more recent politicians, I thought Tony Blair, Gordon Brown and Peter Mandelson did an amazing job getting Labour elected again. Some of the things they did in those thirteen years, the minimum wage, investment in the NHS, investment in schools, equality laws, improving the plight of those who are poor in the developing world, so I really admire their achievements too."

Ivan Lewis MP

"Well there was a guy, and the interesting story is that I would never have gone back to a second Labour Party meeting if it hadn't been for this particular older guy; in those days he would have been in his fifties, he was a real character and had a pony tail, he used to sit in the pub all day and he used to paint. I don't think he had ever worked a day in his life properly, but this guy really encouraged me. He said I must come back, he introduced me to other people, and did that with quite a few younger people who came. What usually happens is you would come along, be made to feel unwelcome and walk away, but this guy really made an effort to support me and others. He was very, very important to me. It wasn't just me, there were four or five of us that got involved in that locality, and he was really encouraging. Often what you would get when younger people would turn up, you'd be told to told to wait your turn, and it could be twenty years before you get your chance, you were not really taken seriously, he was just really good. He died unfortunately a few years ago, but he will always be a special guy for me. He was a brilliant organiser politically, and we started to win well, some of that was due to his very astute organisational skills. So right from day one he was an important person. Then, when I was elected, I will never forget that famous night in 1997, they didn't finish the count in Bury till about 4 am, we went back to the sort of headquarters, it was still packed cos people were so excited, we hadn't won in that constituency for thirteen years, and obviously we hadn't won nationally. I remember, it was just me and him left watching the telly in the community centre when Tony Blair made that famous speech 'a new dawn has broken'. It was really special, so he was someone who was quite important in that respect."

Caroline Lucas MP
"Petra Kelly, one of the founders of the German Green Party, one of the most passionate advocates of Green politics."

Nicky Morgan MP
"I joined the Conservative Party because of Margaret Thatcher; I mean as a woman, and as a strong Prime Minister, like her or loathe her you knew where you stood, she was an inspiration to female politicians. I suppose there is an amalgamation of people from all parties, people who stick by their guns, people who have the courage of their convictions."

Greg Mulholland MP
"My father who stood for Parliament four times in the darkest days for the Liberals; Paddy Ashdown who led the Liberal Democrats to a notable presence in Parliament; Jane Tomlinson from Leeds who

was the first terminally ill woman to run the London marathon and went on to achieve extraordinary feats of endurance; campaigners the world over who have fought for justice and the ordinary people I meet who are quietly doing amazing things such as coping with difficult situations, caring for loved ones or campaigning to help others."

Jason McCartney MP

"I think fellow local MPs, I got to know Phillip Davies, who is the MP for Shipley, really well. He had actually stood here for election in 2001 and was unsuccessful, but then stood in Shipley in 2005 and was elected with a small majority, and then was re-elected there in 2010 with a 10,000 majority. Why? Because he is a good local MP. His mantra is, community and country before career. I have a clear conscience when I go to bed at night, why? Because I genuinely believe that I have voted in the best interests of my constituents. So on Monday, against the whips, I voted for a referendum on the EU, not because I necessarily believe it's right to come out or go in, but because I believe it's important to show that we keep our promises, and show that we trust people to have a say in the future. But I sleep better, and I think that is what people want. I also rebelled on tuition fees, I was one of only five Conservatives who did so. Not because of the policy, but because I was concerned at the message it sent out. You don't start paying them back till you earn £21,000, but because a lot of people do not understand the policy, young people have been put off, it has stopped them applying to go to university, and that's what I feared, and why I voted against it."

Esther McVey MP

"I've always been inspired by the great philanthropic industrialists from William Hesketh Lever to Bill Gates. Oh yeah, and my dad for being a great dad!

"But if you are talking of a modern day politician, it really does have to be Iain Duncan Smith, who after walking away from being leader of the party, established the Centre for Social Justice and produced a wealth of work on societal failings and now, on becoming the Secretary of State for the Department of Work and Pensions, has put that knowledge into action ensuring welfare works, so helping those most in need and ensuring it always pays to work."

Chi Onwurah MP

"Well no, there wasn't one person in particular, although my mum inspired my interest in politics and she was a very committed activist. Then I think George Orwell inspired my belief in the importance of politics, and the need for honest politicians."

Stephen Pound MP

"For people of my generation Nye Bevan was the man. Of course I never met him, but he was a Welsh miner, left school at fourteen with no qualifications, went to evening classes (I left school at fifteen with no qualifications and went to evening classes but that's neither here nor there), but he created the National Health Service, I mean he *created* the National Health Service. So he was a true inspiration. And again the other person, it's a generational thing, but people of your age cannot imagine what it was like when JFK got elected in 1959/1960; Kennedy was the first modern politician. Suddenly politics was different." [Steve shows us a picture of Kennedy and his wife smiling] "I mean it's a bit of a false picture because they weren't happy, but he was the other person for me."

Yasmin Qureshi MP

"The Councillors I talked of earlier, Judy Jackson and Stella Meldrum, although Stella has died now."

Jacob Rees-Mogg MP

"I know a lot of Tory MPs will say this, but Margaret Thatcher was the Prime Minister when I was nine, and she first won the election.

Her conviction and her strength of character have always inspired me. I think she inspired a generation. And looking back, I am interested in history, and there are historic figures whom I have had an interest in and have had a great appeal to me; for instance Palmerston, as a rather romantic figure of Britain at her best. And then Robert Peel, who was not a romantic figure at all, but a fantastically good administrator, and he knew the business of what Government ought to be doing. So I would say those two as historical figures, other than the Pitts of course, father and son, who were on a different scale from anybody else. They all seem to be MPs for some reason."

Jonathan Reynolds MP

"Definitely a guy called Andrew Patience, who was my politics teacher. I did write to him after I got elected, but I think he had moved on to be the principal of an F.E. College somewhere else. My mum and dad were pretty inspirational, my dad's a fireman, so my ideas of public service come a bit from there. They are the main people, although there are various politicians I admire too."

Sir Bob Russell MP

"Lots of people really, obviously my parents, my scout leaders, my church and church youth club, there are not many church youth clubs run by a QC, who actually helped me to get my first job as a trainee reporter. My meagre academic achievements didn't help but the fact that I was a touch typist did. My biggest regret though was that I didn't do shorthand, but I was typing at fifty words a minute and had just become a Queen's Scout and it was those things that got me the job. I would go out and find stories because I just loved the job."

Derek Twigg MP

"Probably Clem Attlee, I think he achieved most as a Labour Prime Minister, and was very understated and not seen as a great orator, but just got on with the job and delivered, probably some of the biggest changes we have ever seen in society, in a very difficult time after the war, and also he was a decorated war hero himself, so had been through it. He wasn't from my background, but he achieved so much I think in such a short period, five or six years I think."

Charles Walker MP

"Well my step-father Christopher Chataway inspired me – he was a Member of Parliament and prior to that a well known runner – because he is such a decent and honourable man, and if I can be a fraction of the person he has been, and it will only be a fraction, I think it will be a life well lived. If you have a life model who is decent, kind and generous, you see the good side of politics and its ability to affect meaningful change."

Phil Wilson MP

"One of my big heroes is Abraham Lincoln, who I think was a pragmatic politician whose objective during the Civil War was to keep the union together, and he succeeded in doing that. Someone described him as a man who was brave because he was brave enough to be inconsistent, and he did what he thought he had to do to keep the union together, therefore he ended up contradicting himself. Like he did on slavery, the only slaves he released were the ones in the slave states, and the ones who weren't, weren't released. Everybody thinks they were all released. So it's that kind of pragmatic approach to it, but also a principled approach. Other people have inspired me too. I always talk a lot about me dad, cos I know what he went through. His mum was a single mother through the 1930's, his dad died of cancer when he was about eighteen months old. He knew what it was like to struggle, and he never really complained. I think also all that happened in the 1990's, with the crew that Tony Blair had around him, like Peter Mandelson, Gordon Brown, Alistair Campbell, Angie Hunter, Sally Morgan, and John Burton – it was like your England 1966 World Cup Squad.

It all came together, and it all produced something that saw us into power for thirteen years, something that we should never forget."

Rosie Winterton MP

"Well lots of people have. I suppose starting personally, my dad was a great inspiration because he was a local councillor in Doncaster, and has always been very interested in politics, and that was inspiring to start with. And so many people here, they contribute in different ways."

John Woodcock MP

"Yes, there are people all around this place and outside, who are so focused on getting things done and on changing things. I have an enormous amount of respect for my predecessor, John Hutton. I don't know if you agree with this assessment but I was giving an introduction to John when he came up to speak at my dinner in Barrow last week, because it's twenty years since he was elected in 1992 to the month. I was saying that there are different types of people in politics, there are people who look at a situation, decide what is going to be popular, and then convince others that is what they believe in; there are other people, of which John is one, who decide first of all what they think is right, and then try to make that popular, that is the only way to do politics. It is the only way that will change things, and the only way that I think people will gain respect for politicians, which is wavering.

"There are others outside of here who are really determined to get things done too. Yesterday I was up in my constituency launching a charity called Alice's Escapes, which gives holidays and respite for seriously ill children and their families. It's been pioneered by a young woman Alice Pyne, who has had a lot of national attention for her bucket list – things she wants to do before she dies which went global on Twitter. She's an amazing woman, with an amazing family around her. She is one example of many, many people who don't have the levers of power, but decide what they want to do, and use whatever means they can to make things happen."

Well that was fascinating don't you think? I believe you can learn a lot about someone by knowing who they are influenced by.

Interestingly Dave Anderson chooses a negative influence in Margaret Thatcher. Well I guess she is like Marmite, you either love her or hate her. Personally I think hatred is a very unhealthy emotion. And what a great answer from Sir Peter Bottomley, of course many of us will remember Virginia, and some of us may even say our husband or wife inspire us too.

Kevin Brennan's predecessor and inspiration offers some excellent advice: 'always be interested in people and what they have to say, whoever they are, and always try to help.' If only all of our politicians, particularly our Government Ministers, followed that guidance. And having worked with the NHS for the past twenty years, I wholeheartedly agree with Kevin's other choice (shared with Andy Burnham) Nye Bevan. And to think at the time of writing we have Andrew Lansley as our Health Secretary, oh dear… ah well…

Within the introduction to this book I talk about having learnt to judge an MP by the sincerity of their action, rather than along party lines. Andrew George, a Lib-Dem, is a perfect example for me, not unknown to vote against his own party, and it says a lot about the man, that he chose a former Labour MP as his inspiration. It may be a bit naughty and out of place, but it is my book so I am going to say it: given Andrew's political persuasion, I want to publicly thank him for his support of our NHS, as I do Greg Mulholland, another Lib-Dem supporter of the NHS.

While I am handing out plaudits, I'll come clean and say

Dan Jarvis MBE is my MP, and as a resident of Barnsley, I am proud that he is. It tells you all you need to know about the man, that he is inspired by the old ladies in his constituency.

As a campaigner myself I appreciate the words of Greg Mulholland, and I defy anyone not to have the upmost respect for Jason McCartney and Philip Davies with their philosophy of community and country before career; again it's about the sincerity of actions, rather than party lines. If more MPs shared their mantra, we would have something approaching a real democracy.

All dads will appreciate the sentiments of Esther McVey, and interestingly there is another mention for Ian Duncan Smith. And every single one of us will agree with Chi Onwurah and her expression of the need for honest politicians, even if it's not related to my question – naughty Chi, oh, and naughty Jason too.

Nye Bevan gets another mention this time from Stephen Pound, who is not only incredibly smart, but in the opinion of many of his peers, the funniest MP in the House! Having had the pleasure of his company on a couple of occasions during the writing of this book, I would have to wholeheartedly agree.

As a big supporter of the NHS, I am delighted Nye Bevan got a few mentions, and I guess it's not surprising that Margaret Thatcher did too. And really nice to see so many mention their parents don't you think?

In case anyone is interested, my inspirations are Winston Churchill, Nye Bevan and all the people who have served in our armed forces and the people who are having to defend our NHS.

Stephen Pound

Ann Coffey

I have come to the conclusion that politics is too serious a matter to be left to the politicians.
Charles de Gaulle

CHAPTER FOUR

Day to Day Life

I had intended to ask all my interviewees to tell us about the day to day life of an MP, but it soon became obvious I would get the same answers from all of them, so here are some accounts to give you an idea of how our MPs spend their days.

Sir Peter Bottomley MP

"It varies, and it may mean getting up at half past three to get to an airport, by five to fly at six thirty. It might be taking one morning off in three months and you're in the bath, reading a book or eating an apple, and the *Today* programme ring up at twenty to nine to ask you to be in the studio at five to nine to talk about MP Expenses. It has some of the happiest things in life and some of the most miserable. To me there is no pattern. The difference between my father who, was a civil servant, and me, is he would look at his watch and say, am I hungry? I look at my watch and think when did I last eat?"

Ben Bradshaw MP

"Well it varies very much from day to day, I mean a lot of the work is responding to events, taking up issues as they arise, there is a certain amount of work that you do regardless, like your case work, helping constituents with problems they might have with the local authority or with the benefits system, or with neighbours or something like that. A lot of it is obviously about if you are a back bencher spending time in Parliament, if you are in opposition holding the Government to account, but then I think it makes sense for MPs to focus on some issues that they will spend more time and get some expertise on, some MPs will sit on committees on specialist issues. I was a Minister for nine years, and that is again a very different role as you have an extra three jobs, obviously there is the tooing and froing from Westminster to your constituency, and that's some kind of summary of what the job involves.

"The difference is dramatic when you are a Minister, I was one for nine years, and basically when you are a Minister you work all the hours that God sends, seven days a week, and probably 80 – 90 % of your time is spent on your Ministerial job, and obviously when you are not a Minister that time is freed up. I have a lot more time now to focus on issues I like to get involved with, and a bit more time to catch up with friends and family, who sadly I had to neglect really over the last few years. In day to day terms of course as a Minister, you are part of, or run a department, and you have a lot of support in terms of civil servants and officials around you. If you are an ordinary back bencher your budget only really stretches to having one or two people working with you, so you are much more restricted in terms of the research or admin support you have, you have to do a lot more on your own."

Andrew Bridgen MP
"Well it's two jobs really, it's the job down here in Parliament, and there's the job in the constituency. The constituency work probably didn't exist thirty or forty years ago, because MPs would normally live in London, and maybe only go to the constituency a couple of times a year. I live in my constituency, and I quite honestly believe that it's best to be of your people, to represent your people. In the constituency you obviously get a lot of correspondence, now we get a lot of emails mostly, as that's the new medium of communication, far quicker and far more efficient. We still get letters, and phone calls, and people who want to meet face to face. We run surgeries every other week on a Friday and we see eight to twelve people somewhere in the constituency for fifteen minutes each. Most

things can be dealt with over the phone or by email or letter and don't really need a face to face meeting, but some people just want that contact. So you've got all that stuff going on in the constituency, and then in Westminster you are a legislator. I support the Government on the bits I agree with, I think I have voted against the Government six times so far. *[I interject] – Top Man!* Well I am not necessarily a favourite of the whips office.

"Today we had a meeting with the Countryside Alliance, then I had a group of constituents and other people from the National Trust who were in Committee Room 10, so I gave a speech to them for half an hour, then we had lunch with a Lobby Group about some work I am doing, then I had a Select Committee meeting which I thought was going to last for about two hours, but actually lasted for about ten minutes on the Regulatory Reform. That then meant I could go into the Chamber for questions, and managed to get a question in, then I listened to Philip Hammond's statement on Afghanistan, then I've come straight here to meet you. I have another meeting at six, a dinner meeting at seven, and then another meeting to go to between nine and half-past, and that's the day gone isn't it. *It's a long day isn't it?* Well we've got votes at ten o'clock too. I don't think most people in the country realise that we will still be here voting at gone ten o'clock tonight, but that's quite normal on a Monday and Tuesday. Most people who come to Parliament will go away with a more positive feeling about MPs and what they and their staff do. Harpreet and Woody work really hard for me here."

Rosie Cooper MP

"Nuts, the days are crazy, you can see my timetable here for this week. I like to be busy, and I don't like to waste my time, so I won't just do stuff for the hell of it, I do it because I believe either I will get something from it or the people will. My background in P.R. means often I will go and help groups that have come in here, and they haven't quite got their thinking right, so I will help them do their P.R. a bit better."

Glora De Piero MP

"It's completely different when you are in Westminster, to when you are in your constituency. To be honest I like it more in my constituency with 'normal people', you can get wins for your community and see things happening. Here it's really weird and even though I was a political journalist coming here, as an MP it's just so odd, because of the hours, not that I am complaining about them. But basically you arrive on Monday and you go back on Thursday. You are kind of stuck in this place, you don't get any air and you don't see any normal human beings, so it's quite nice to see you two here today! I am going up early tonight, and it's like ooh I am going to see some real people tomorrow, and that lifts me a lot. It's relating the two that I still struggle with sometimes."

Michael Dugher MP

"Well the House sits about thirty weeks a year, generally now around the school term, which is good for me as I have young kids. You tend to be in the House Monday to Thursday, you come in on Monday and tend to be here late on Monday and Tuesday night. When you arrive on Monday mid-morning, it's kind of like getting on a conveyor belt really, in that the House is pretty structured; you have questions at half past two on a Monday and Tuesday, and on a Wednesday you have PMQ's. There are various parliamentary set pieces that shape your day, but also you have back to back meetings. I am also a Shadow Minister, so we have team meetings, and I have work involved in my portfolio. Thursday comes around pretty quick, and by the time it does you are already thinking about Friday and being in your constituency, and Saturday, and because they have not had you all week there are pretty strong demands on your diary there too. We joke at home that Sunday night has become the new Saturday night. I try and keep as much of Sunday as possible free for family time, I often do work on a Sunday night, and often we have constituency engagements and things, but I try to keep them free, because as you say with a job like this, I have little kids and they do tend to grow up pretty quick."

John Glen MP

"There are really two halves: the Westminster half and the constituency half. I come up on a Monday morning usually, sometimes on a Sunday night, and my days here are spent having meetings, doing interviews, also preparing for speeches and questions in the House of Commons, meeting pressure groups about possible changes in legislation. There are a lot of seminars, dinners, policy briefings, the list goes on. It's a pretty intense life, it starts at 7.30/8.00 every morning and finishes at 10 pm with a vote on a Monday and Tuesday. There are lots of engagements with different groups and I am on a Select Committee as well which involves scrutiny of defence issues, and involves a lot of hours each week. For constituency work it is usually a twelve hour day: visits to schools, businesses, opening a village hall, having a two to three hour surgery, speaking at an Association dinner, opening shops, one to one visits to constituents, a whole variety of things. That's it really. And you are a figurehead; here at Westminster you are a sort of 'F' list celebrity because there are so many of you, and it's difficult to distinguish yourself, but you are perhaps a 'B' or a 'C' list celebrity in your constituency where there is only one of you. You are also there as a leader in your community, facilitating outcomes for people by encouraging other groups to do things. So you are not actually in possession of much power, but if you use the office you are given wisely you can influence things. So I have a weekly column in the local paper, I have good relationships with different people in the local Council, and can make things happen. I would say 70% of the things that people come to my surgery about aren't things to do with national Government, but are to do with local Government."

Zac Goldsmith MP

"Surgeries in the morning on Mondays and Tuesdays; Parliament in the afternoons and late into the evenings. Wednesdays and Thursdays are dominated by Parliament until evening, and Fridays and Saturdays are constituency days almost entirely."

Oliver Heald MP

"It can be as demanding as you want it to be, some people do more in Parliament, or some people specialise in Foreign Affairs or whatever. I personally like the constituency role, so I put a lot of time and effort into that; I have a lot of surgeries and I was the first MP who had an email that was open to the public to use. I take a lot of steps to give good access which means that I get a lot of correspondence, a lot of emails and letters, and we take up a lot of cases, so that is my main focus. I also get involved in debates here to stick up for my area, and get involved in the big national debates about issues that interest me, which tend to be work and pensions. And in the past I have spoken quite a lot about mental health issues."

Dan Jarvis MBE MP

"The day to day life is incredibly busy, there are two aspects to it; there is life in Westminster and life in the constituency. There probably isn't such a thing as a typical day, but in Westminster I have meetings programmed from first thing in the morning (about eight o'clock) quite often through until midnight. So it is very busy, the nature of life in Westminster means that no day ends in the way that you thought it would. My diary is constantly chopping and changing, as urgent Ministerial questions or statements take place in the Chamber which mean I have to re-jig my diary, but I am very well supported by a good group of people which makes it work. It's always great to be back in Barnsley on a Friday and at a weekend, it's my opportunity to get out and meet people locally and listen to the issues that matter to them and be involved in our community. So I really enjoy the different aspects of the job, being in Parliament representing Barnsley people's views, and being back in Barnsley talking to people about the issues that matter to them."

Nicky Morgan MP

"That's the fascinating thing about the job, because every single day is completely different. You end up doing things that at the beginning of the day you would not have realised you would be doing: interviews, meeting different people, speaking in debates, you get pulled in all sorts of different directions. There is no standard day. The toughest challenge about the job is trying to stay on course so that you get to do the things you really want to do."

Greg Mulholland MP

"A typical week for me involves travelling down on Monday late morning, to arrive in London for the start of the week's business at 2:30 pm, which is departmental questions. The rest of the week involves spending some time in the Chamber, depending on the business and whether or not you wish to make a speech, or just ask questions in question times and statements, plus meetings with organisations and some desk time trying to get through the in-tray. I usually travel back on Thursday afternoon, hopefully just in time to put the children to bed. Friday is the constituency day, with surgeries, visits and constituent meetings then the weekend is also often busy with events and surgeries, with Sundays spent mainly with the family, wherever possible."

Jason McCartney MP

"Every day is completely different, I have just been on Radio Leeds doing a phone-in about the role of MPs, and that's the variety. You can do big international things; I could be in the Pentagon in Washington DC, as I was in January having a briefing on Libya, Morocco and Tunisia, and then I come back here and could be helping somebody with a wobbly paving stone outside their house, with both issues being important to members of the local community. So the variety of issues is amazing, no day is exactly the same. In terms of a basic structure, I generally go down to Parliament first thing on a Monday morning from my home in Honley, which is in the heart of my constituency, do parliamentary things, and come back on Thursday night. I then work in my constituency on a Friday and Saturday; Saturday is either holding a surgery, visiting businesses, or at a community event. I try to keep Sunday free, but every now and again something crops up, like Remembrance Sunday, or a community event which is quite nice as I can take my children along and get them involved. So there is a rough structure there, but every day is completely different which is what I like about it."

John Redwood MP

"There is no greater privilege than representing people in Parliament. The highlights of my Parliamentary life have been the election victories, following intensive conversations with voters. I have drawn most inspiration from the electors themselves. They bring me their problems and their solutions. I work away to try to resolve difficulties and improve the malfunctioning of public service as a result of those continuous discussions. I keep in touch by knocking on doors, by listening in the market place, and by reading all the incoming emails and contributions to my interactive website."

Derek Twigg MP

"It depends how you work. I tend to get in very early in the morning around seven, and will be here till around ten o'clock at night. It's a mixture of dealing with your correspondence, having meetings about a variety of issues, constituency issues, meeting organisations like yourselves: charitable, social, business, medical, educational organisations, listening to their concerns; then go back of a weekend and do all your surgeries, meeting lots of community groups, going to schools and businesses, doing speeches, speaking to people, being in Parliament, asking questions. Every day something different tends to happen. A week last Monday I was talking about Hillsborough, and that was very important because I was at Hillsborough; you wouldn't have thought all those years ago that here I would be talking about it in Parliament. Talking about other issues emerging through Parliament, education and health, and issues affecting business, all those things you talk about."

Charles Walker MP

"It's extremely busy, there are a lot of demands. I suppose the one thing I find most frustrating, and I say this tongue in cheek and with a smile (for when it appears in your book), is when constituents say, 'so you are going back to work on Monday?' when the House is sitting, as though when you are in your constituency you are not working. Politicians have two places of work, there is the House of Commons where we are to hold the Government to account, peruse legislation, amend legislation and there is our constituencies, who we are responsible for representing and most Members of Parliament work very hard in their constituencies, to ensure that their constituents have access to them and that they see them around. There are very few countries in the world where the public have access to politicians in such an open way and such a regular way, as in this country, and I include Europe in that, so all this nonsense that politicians are out of touch is total rubbish."

As Ben Bradshaw describes, clearly the day to day life of an MP is different dependent upon if they are a Minister, a Shadow Minister, or just a back bench MP, in which case I suspect that the workload is pretty similar whether you are in Government or Opposition. We should all bear in mind that MPs are representatives of we the public, so just like us, some will be extremely hard-working and ambitious, and some may not be.

It is interesting when Ben talks about the dramatic difference being a Minister, and it taking 80% to 90% of his time. I often wonder if constituents get a raw deal if their elected representative becomes a Minister, as she or he has less time to focus on local issues, and whilst they probably receive more administrative assistance, I am not sure that is adequate compensation for the people they represent.

Interesting how Gloria De Piero uses words like 'weird' to describe her day to day life in Westminster, and that she doesn't see 'normal human beings', and it's only when she goes back to her constituency that she sees normal people. I expect a lot of people will understand where she is coming from, although I am not too sure I would agree with her. Most of the MPs I have met have seemed normal to me, and, as I keep saying, we elect them and they represent us.

Michael Dugher's account of a typical day provides a very good insight into the day to day life of a Shadow Minister, and we should all bear in mind, they are entitled to at least a degree of normal family life, like the rest of us. Indeed, I would argue they cannot function properly if they do not have any quality time with their families.

John Glen also provides a great insight into his day to day life, and isn't it fascinating when he says 70% of the things people come to see him about are local issues. Perhaps we should consider this when we vote, do we want an MP because of an often spurious party manifesto, which is not adhered to anyway, or do we want an MP who will represent our best interests locally.

Oliver Heald demonstrates the flexibility MPs have, we all have to hope we have a hard-working MP, and if we do not, it is up to us to call them to account. Dan Jarvis MBE, Andrew Bridgen and John Glen, like many of their colleagues, draw a distinction between their work in Westminster and in their constituencies.

I would like to give the final words in this chapter to Charles Walker, I have met him on a number of occasions, and he is a thoroughly decent man, and what he says is worth remembering: "There are very few countries in the world where the public have access to politicians in such an open and regular way, as in this country, and I include Europe in that, so all this nonsense that politicians are out of touch is total rubbish."

Caroline Lucas

A politician should have three hats. One for throwing into the ring, one for talking through, and one for pulling rabbits out of if elected.
Carl Sandburg

CHAPTER FIVE

What is the Biggest Issue Raised by Your Constituents?

Now we have an idea of the day to day life of an MP, I thought it might be interesting to find out what the most common problems brought to our MPs are.

Dave Anderson MP

"In terms of their day to day life it's housing. It's a question of supply and demand; there's not enough to go around. We had the huge Right to Buy issue that people got into, the Council weren't allowed to build any replacements, and we didn't build any, we were crap. Then you have the break-up of personal family structures, so you have lots and lots of people living on their own, divorces etc. Whereas before it would have been a man and woman getting married, and living in a house, that's broken down in many cases. Housing stock is getting more and more worn out and hasn't been replaced."

That's really interesting, because the southern MPs we talk to, all say that CSA is the biggest issue, whereas with the North East MPs it's always housing.

"CSA is an issue, but not as big a one. In terms of volume, we feel it more because we have probably always provided housing for people in the North-East, we had a huge stock of ex Coal Board housing that has been pulled down, and not replaced. I guess in the south housing has always been an issue, and what's the point of complaining to your MP if there's nothing they can do? The trouble is there is very little we can do, apart from making sure that the Council treat them decently, and that they know about other agencies and the decent private landlords, which I guess some people don't. Down there it's just a struggle to find a house. Some people just take it for granted, it can still be the attitude in the north, people think they need a house so they will just go and get a council one, well actually they won't, cos there aren't any, even for people in desperate need. Sometimes you have to tell people the only thing they can do is to make themselves homeless. You've got to tell your mother, just kick me out, cos if you go to the council and say, 'Me mother's threatened to throw me out,' they will just say, ' Come back when she has.' So I think in terms of volume that's without doubt the biggest one we get, in terms of day to day casework, I mean campaigning wise we get other stuff, but on an individual basis that's it."

Roughly how many people contact you a day – how many emails do you receive?

"I wasn't on the email over the weekend because I was away for my thirty-ninth wedding anniversary, and when I got in here there were 219 emails, and my office deal with a lot of stuff directly too. Every day my people locally are doing great stuff for people in the constituency. The best thing about being an MP is that the office carries weight, we can get special access to hotline numbers, and it tends to generate more urgent responses."

Paul Blomfield MP

"Well people come either because they want to make their voices heard on an issue, or they have an individual problem, where the intervention of an MP can make a difference in their lives. It really is too diverse, I get around 200/250 emails, letters and phone calls a day, which my office processes and talk to me about. For example when the Government were planning to sell off the forests, I had a good few hundred people contact me, and that was just from Sheffield Central, and we don't have many forests in Sheffield Central [laughter]. The next biggest issue people contact me about is the NHS, concerns about Government reforms on the NHS, and certainly that is something that I have taken up, but I couldn't really identify just one issue, and that's what is so good about the job. There are a fantastic range of things that people want you to get involved in."

Andrew Bridgen MP

"I think the CSA probably. They seem to me to be an organisation completely in crisis. We had one today where the case officer sent the wrong thing three times. Fortunately for our constituents, MPs have a hotline to the very best people the CSA have got, but it's rapidly becoming the case that the only way anyone can get any movement in the CSA is to go through their MP. I think that whole organisation always has been in crisis and it hasn't got any better. So almost the only way to cut through the red tape and bureaucracy is to use your MP, it's not serving the public well or those it is supposed to serve, or even the absentee fathers."

Philip Davies MP

"I do surveys of my constituents, and ask them what issues they are most concerned about. The top issue, always, always, always, is crime. Whatever else is in the news, that is always what people are most concerned about. In terms of what people come to me with issues about, it tends to be very local; politics is becoming more and more local. I can't remember the last time anyone contacted me about the war in Afghanistan, I'm not even sure if anyone has ever contacted me about the war in Afghanistan. People come to you with very local issues, or very personal issues. So it tends to be around things like not getting their kids into the schools they want to, I spend lots of my time contacting the local authority on behalf of my constituents, or it's things like the Child Support Agency, or the Tax Credits Office. It tends to be either local authority issues, or Benefits Agency related issues, and housing."

John Glen MP

"I would say the most common are probably housing issues. People come to me with a concern that their housing is inadequate, that they need better housing. That is the one that comes up every week, usually twice or three times, or something relating to the quality of suitable, available housing."

Oliver Heald MP

"Well my area is, in its own way, unique; it's in a large part of Hertfordshire, probably 20% of the county, it's a big semi-rural area, I think there are some key issues – environmental issues, issues about sustainability, I have seven streams in my area which are all threatened in one way or another, and I am part of a big campaign that WWF are running about that. I am very much against some of the big planning proposals that have been put in for my constituency, because it's the lungs of Hertfordshire, it's the green area and people want to see that respected. Obviously we need housing as well but there has to be a balance. So I think issues to do with my own area, and the environment, keeping it special, are probably the things that people have taken up most. And then you get all the other issues, when I was a barrister I was on the committee for the free representation unit, I used to do the employment cases for people who couldn't get a lawyer and my wife used to do the benefits cases. Over the years we have done literally thousands and thousands of these."

Nicky Morgan MP

"Well the big one has been the Child Support Agency, that has been a huge issue. I knew I would get casework about people not getting their pension, or their benefits, that sort of thing, but dealing with the Child Support Agency and HMRC have been absolutely huge. It seems to me in particular that the CSA is an organisation that is failing everyone: mothers, fathers and children."

Jason McCartney MP

"It's probably things like benefits, the Child Support Agency, and because I have a substantial Kashmiri/Pakistani community, there are also visa issues, immigration, indefinite leave to remain appeals, because of the nature of my population. I didn't really know much about the Kashmir/Pakistani community, so have tried to make a real effort, and in November I visited the region in a private capacity with friends I had made locally in Huddersfield, and met the Prime Minister there, so I now understand the issues a lot more, and realise how close they are to Britain. I have learnt so much, and that is another really wonderful thing about being an MP, I didn't know much about that part of the world, so I flew to Islamabad and travelled across the region from there, but now I feel really confident about speaking about the issues in Parliament, as I understand so much more, which areas are ruled by India, which by Pakistan, and which are independent."

Chi Onwurah MP

"I would say it's probably housing, either not having a council house, or having a council house which is wrong for whatever reason: too small, or because of social abuse they are experiencing, or damp or no heating or whatever. So that's probably the most common problem I get."

Sir Bob Russell MP

"Two weeks ago I held my 700th advice bureau since becoming an

MP – that's over 8000 appointments in fourteen years. The Child Support Agency still remains the single biggest issue, and in my view the organisation is not fit for purpose. Most of the time they do get it right but there are too many occasions where they don't; this ranges for absentee parents, the majority of the time it's the male of the species, there are some right bastards out there, generally men, but occasionally the women can be the bastards too, and both sides use the children as bargaining tools. Some of the scenarios that are portrayed to me are absolutely awful. There are too many dads who refuse to pay for their children, they expect others to pay, they think it's funny that the tax payer should. If I allocated all the cases I see under a single heading the CSA would definitely be by far the biggest issue."

It's interesting that is the biggest single issue that you deal with, is that anything to do with where you are an MP?

"We have some soldiers, breakdowns, but I would say it's less of a proportion than the general population. The two rapidly growing issues are housing issues and anti-social neighbours. Some people seem to take perverse pleasure in making other people's lives a misery. I just don't understand what sort of lives they have cos it's so much nicer to be pleasant to people."

Derek Twigg MP
"Most common issues are housing, either getting a house, or trying to get a more appropriate one; benefits problems, particularly in the current climate where the Government have changed the rules, there are a lot of people now losing out, and there are a lot of appeals going in, and probably things like anti-social behaviour and policing issues. They tend to be the big ones, although you name it, any issue can be brought to an MP. In the surgeries at the weekend, it can be

anything from housing to Child Support, to debt issues, environmental issues, to some pretty unusual anti-social behaviour, so it's a variety."

Phil Wilson MP

"Well there's more than one I think. At the moment we have got this big wind farm development in the area which is getting a lot of interest. If it's as big as they say it's going to be it will be the biggest in England. And I think that County Durham has got enough of the things. County Durham produces 22% of its energy from those sources, which is well above the national average, so I think we have done our bit. Other things I find it's obviously jobs, the other big issue I've been involved with is private landlords, because we've got a big waiting list in the area. We've got social housing providers, obviously a lot of people own their own homes and have bought their council houses. What happened though is they bought their council houses, but the money never went back into building more, I think that's a tragedy really. What happens is, if somebody buys a council house, the money raised goes towards helping to build more council houses, and those people who live in those council houses, further down the line have the right to buy it; what it does is, it locks in aspiration, and also wealth distribution, but we never did that. So what we've got is, not just in Sedgefield, but around the country, there's a big problem, and it's also because of the credit crunch, we've got a big housing problem. People can't afford mortgages, you've got to get a big deposit, which is putting out a lot of young people, people aren't building the houses they used to for social housing, and then what you've got, especially in places like Ferryhill, Chilton, Trimdon Station etc., is a lot of terraced housing, very cheap housing, private landlords have moved in, and I have more anti-social behaviour issues in areas where there is a predominance of private landlords than I do anywhere else. I think it's a whole area that needs to be regulated and looked at, especially by 2020, as over 20% of the housing stock will be private lets.

"It's something that really frightens me, I sometimes think that all the fundamentals are out of kilter now. An economy where kids can't get jobs, but the bankers get away with murder. You take a long time to get up the housing waiting list and get a decent home. You talk about the National Health Service, which is turning into just a Health Service, and all those issues are coming round again. And in a way I know we've had thirteen years of a Labour Government, and I don't think you can say it's the fault of the Labour Government, or indeed the Tories before, I think it's just trends, and it's unintended consequences of policies that have been pursued over the years in good faith. But I think there's a disconnect now of people and politics because we are not addressing the fundamental things."

Rosie Winterton MP

"People come quite a lot with housing problems, and all sorts of things, people may come because they have problems with their neighbours, in terms of anti-social behaviour. CSA can be an issue. It can be almost anything literally, particularly problems associated with the coal mining industry, whether it's COPD or Vibration White Finger, a whole series of issues really."

So there you have it, a flavour of the issues that we raise with our parliamentary representatives. On average our MPs receive over 200 emails/letters per day which must be pretty time consuming, and the most common problems are housing and CSA. This is why, when we vote, we need to consider who will represent our best interests most effectively rather than simply voting on party lines.

I'll leave the last word to Sir Bob Russell: "It's so much nicer to be pleasant to people, if everyone took that advice the world would be a far better place."

Derek Twigg

Bad officials are elected by good citizens who do not vote.
George Jean Nathan

CHAPTER SIX

Expectations

We all have hopes and aspirations, so I asked if being an MP had lived up to expectations.

Dave Anderson MP

"Yes because I didn't have very many expectations. I had done a lot of work previously with the unions so I wasn't particularly 'enamoured' by it, not overawed, I wasn't carried away. I treat it as a job of representing people in Parliament. I'd like to think I did the same when I was a union rep."

Paul Blomfield MP

"Yes it's been extraordinary really. It has its frustrations, but nevertheless the opportunity to represent the city that I have lived in for most of my life – it's a fantastic privilege to be able to voice the concerns of the people you represent, and to help tackle the problems they face, and help them in resolving them. It's tremendous, and I hope for more."

Sir Peter Bottomley MP

"I don't think I ever had any expectations, and bluntly, some of the horrors, whether it was being an MP or a Minister, I was present at the funeral of Arch-Bishop Oscar Ramirez in Central America in 1980, when fourteen people died around me. I was at the King's Cross fire, and the Kegworth Air Crash, partly from duty, partly because I had to be there. On the other hand, if someone can't get out of a hole they have dug themselves into, or someone else has dug them into, and suddenly with one bound they are free, that's great. And there are other times when you start asking questions, and you never quite know when the answer is going to come. So for instance, in this country if I had said in 1975, when will the colour of my skin be as important as the colour of my eyes… when would people no longer be stopped by the police on the grounds that they were black. How do you change that? I have just been to a Memorial service in Westminster Abbey for Sir Simon Milton who was Jewish, a glorious service in a Christian church. It's the oneness that matters."

Ben Bradshaw MP

"It has more than fulfilled my expectations. I didn't really know what to expect when I started because I am not one of those people who had always wanted to become a politician. There are a lot of people in politics who I think you could describe as career politicians, politics is all they have really done, I mean I had another career beforehand. I came into politics by accident really, but I think the privilege and wonder for me of representing a community, is a truly wonderful feeling. I feel that I belong, I am the property of my constituents really, and you build up a real relationship with your constituency over the years; you can make things happen for them and deliver things. Realising you have the ability to do that is great, obviously I had no expectation when I was elected that I would become a Minister, that was a great privilege and amazing to see how Government works from the inside, having been a journalist and seeing it from the outside, and ultimately serving in the Cabinet in the last year of the Labour Government was an amazing experience. So for me, it has more than fulfilled my expectations."

Kevin Brennan MP

"Yeah I would say it has, I mean I would like to be Prime Minister by now, obviously [*laughter*] but there we are, there's still plenty of time. I think in some ways it has probably exceeded my expectations because what is great about being an MP is that you can genuinely unlock the bureaucracy on behalf of ordinary people, when they are batting their head against a brick wall and don't know where to go, they haven't got a voice or any real influence, you can actually make a difference for them. The great thing about being an MP, especially in the UK, is the constituency link; the fact that our constituencies are relatively small by international standards, so you are looking after about 70,000 voters and their families, and generally things come to you from that contact that you can do something about.

"To give you an example, when I first started off as an MP, this guy came to see me and he said, 'My son has this terrible condition, it's going to kill him: Duchenne Muscular Dystrophy what you going to do about it? You're my MP.' I said, 'Well I don't know, but I will join the All Party Group and take an interest in it, and see if I can bring any influence to bear in Parliament about research and so on.' Well it turns out there wasn't an All Party Group, so I set it up, I ended up chairing the group, and we worked with his little charity, as well as others, and as it happens a fund came along for genetic research at that time, so we got a big chunk of that fund for research into Duchenne Muscular Dystrophy; now several years down the line, it's undergoing human trials. So that came about from a constituent coming along to see me in a surgery. It doesn't always work like that, but that is the kind of thing you can do. Some people come along thinking nothing will change if you see your MP, but it can."

Andy Burnham MP

"Yes and no I would say, it's a hard life at times, and I know people won't give any sympathy when I say that, but it's mentally tough; it's hard emotionally as well, with all the time away from your family and the pressure it adds. In some ways it has been harder than I thought, but the moments of exhilaration have been better than I would have thought too. When you do things that genuinely matter, you feel you have done something. The biggest issue for me, that I got more personal satisfaction from than anything else, was the Hillsborough story. It may not have changed as many lives as some of the other things I have done, but it matters massively on a personal level. When you can do things that alter the course of issues, it's hard to describe the sense of reward you get from that."

Ann Coffey MP

"It's so long ago I can't remember what my expectations were. I think they have probably changed over time; I have had different expectations at different elections, I think the more I have got to learn about the job, the more I have been able to 'peg' my expectations to the reality of it. Whereas, I think when you are first elected you think you are going to come and change the world. I think in time you come to understand that you are part of a very big team, you can still make a difference, but maybe you look for smaller things, different ways of making a difference."

Rosie Cooper MP

"No. It's a strange life, running up and down to the constituency, remembering where to leave all your stuff, I have clothes everywhere, so that is difficult, but that's logistics really. But I think the idea that you have power as an MP, I realised that wasn't the case very quickly. The power struggles and the house authorities, I call them the invisible men; they are the people who make all the decisions, then they get passed down to us, and we are supposed to think that we have made the decisions and we haven't really. If you look at the House magazine, about four or five weeks ago, I said I wouldn't let the House authorities run a cattery, they are all very upset. What they do is they take these decisions, then send them to the administration committee for example, and I think they just think that we are going to agree, but I think we have been quite difficult about it. They make decisions, then we are just supposed to go 'oh yes that's fine.' Well people like me are dead awkward and tend to go, 'why should we?' They want to spend £50,000 on two cameras that will look directly at the Prime Minister and the front bench, well if BBC or ITV want that they should pay for it. They have all walked away and left the taxpayers of this country paying over a million pounds to televise Parliament, so I asked the question, when you first started out, what happened. Well they said, Mrs Thatcher was the Prime Minister and she said, if you want to televise Parliament, you pay for it, and they paid for it, but now they won't pay at all. So the thing is, the deal has been struck by the invisible men, but I don't think that the taxpayers of this country should be paying for Americans to watch *Prime Minister's Questions* and all the rest of it, it's outrageous, but there is nothing we can do to stop it, the invisible men win again."

Philip Davies MP

"To be perfectly honest I didn't know what to expect. Again, I'm an outsider, a lot of people who get into politics have been researchers, or special advisors, and have spent a lot of time here, so they know what the form is. I knew absolutely nothing about it, I think I had only been to visit Parliament twice, and that was my knowledge of Parliament. So I didn't know what to expect. To be perfectly honest, when I was selected as the candidate for Shipley, I had no idea if I was going to win or not. It was a marginal seat, and I mean if you are selected as the Conservative candidate for Kensington and Chelsea, a few weeks before the election you can allow yourself the luxury of thinking about what it might be like in Parliament. You could knock on every door in Kensington and Chelsea and hurl abuse at anyone who opens it and still get elected. Where as in Shipley, it was less clear cut, so all of my focus was on trying to win the seat, I didn't think about what it would be like. In the end I only won by a majority of 422, after two re-counts, it was a close run thing. I didn't really have any idea of what to expect. The only thing I would say is that it is far harder work than anyone could ever imagine, and I would support people in some of their criticisms of MPs, but not in terms of how hard they work. When I was the candidate for Shipley I still had my full time job at ASDA. And as the election approached, I didn't know if I was going to win or not, but I used to think to myself that at least after the election I would only have one job, I might be back working for ASDA or I would be an MP, at least I wouldn't be in the situation of having two full time jobs. But I can say in all honesty, I work harder now than when I was doing those two jobs. And I would probably have never imagined that could have been possible, but it's absolutely true. You never sit back and think, oh I am up to date now, you are always chasing your tail."

Glora De Piero MP

"You know what, I took the decision so quickly, I was selected as a candidate five weeks before the election. So I was just like, oh my god, I'm a candidate, gosh knock on doors quick and try and win this election; so I don't know, that was such a whirlwind. I always thought I would be an MP, but I always thought I would have longer to think about it, everything was so quick. The constituency stuff is more fulfilling, I thought it would be, but it is incredibly fulfilling, I have a total love affair with my constituency."

Stephen Dorrell MP

"I don't think I arrived with lots of illusions. Peter, my friend and sponsor, had always discouraged me from the idea that you could arrive at Westminster and change the world. If you have the opportunity in life to make a difference, you take it, and I have had the opportunity on a few occasions, both on a small scale for individuals, and on a bigger scale, and I have sought to take it."

Michael Dugher MP

"I don't know really. I really enjoy the constituency, if I'm being honest, I have been in and around Westminster for a lot of years. The bit that I really, really enjoy, and this is also a bit about being in Opposition, I vote a lot here, although we don't win many of the votes, and that's reasonably predictable before you go into the Lobby. But actually in the constituency, you can still do an awful lot. You can support good causes, like your own. You can genuinely make a difference to people's lives. It might be in quite small ways, but the people who come to my surgery are a lot of desperate people, many of whom have fallen through the cracks of the system, and I can actually help them; whether they have a problem with the CSA, or if it's a tax issue, or whether they are not getting a benefit they are entitled to, or they have a problem with the Council, I can actually help people. I think most people from all parties go into politics for the right reasons, or at least I would hope so, and the most rewarding thing is that if you work hard, you can make a real difference in your constituency, and that is incredibly rewarding."

Natascha Engel MP

"I didn't have any false expectations about being an MP, I knew a lot of MPs and I knew what the lifestyle was, I knew what the hours were, and it is different in some ways; I didn't realise – I don't think you can realise – how it will take over your whole life. Your whole life is just that one thing. I find it quite different being in the public eye, I mean I'm not famous or anything, but even in your own constituency, you go shopping in a supermarket and you get people look at you, and you think *what have I got on my face* [*laughter*] and then you remember what you are, and that's quite odd. Somehow your self image and what other people see of you are a bit different. The hours are unbelievable, the amount of work that you have is not physically possible to do, but the nice part of that is that actually it is down to you to decide what you do and what you don't do, given that it is impossible, you manage that yourself. And you don't have a boss. Apart from your constituents who you represent and who elect you (or don't elect you), you don't have a boss and I really like that. I like making decisions for myself."

Andrew George MP

"Yes it has, I think possibly one side of it that I hadn't fully anticipated was just the extent that you do become a kind of lightning conductor for some of the most vexatious and unpleasant people. You just have to bite your lip and carry on. I know we are all supposed to have thick skins, and I am sure that many do, but the fact is that you do put yourself in a position where you can be 'shot at' at all times. You just want to get on and do your job, but the fact is, you often become distracted by nonsense."

John Glen MP

"Well it was pretty similar to what I anticipated. I had worked for two MPs between 1996/1997, and then in 2000/2001 and also in 2006, so I had three periods before I came into the House where I had quite a lot of intimacy with the role of an MP, and the day to day challenges. I think probably the bit that hasn't lived up to my expectations is the frustration one feels when you are apparently not making much of a difference. You can sit for four or five hours in the house, make a six minute speech and think great, it's on your website, someone might have read it, but then you think, *have I really changed anything*? And there's a gap between your own hope to change the country, culture, whatever, and the reality that it's plugging away week in week out. And actually the amount of effort it takes to become a specialist in an area you are interested in, it is quite challenging and if you do that in two or three areas, whilst you have a high volume of emails, and day to day postbox like stuff, i.e. posting stuff out to get some answers. You need to reassure yourself that you are not being inadequate."

Zac Goldsmith MP

"I suspected before becoming an MP that our democracy is dysfunctional. I now know it is. I hope the new intake, as well as a few long-time reformers, will succeed in bringing in a few changes. I hope we'll see, for instance, a mechanism that genuinely allows people to recall representatives that no longer inspire confidence. I have introduced a Bill to that effect."

Oliver Heald MP

"Very much so. It's one of those professions which is not for the faint hearted. You can get a lot of criticism. Sometimes, you can have done absolutely nothing wrong, but people still think you have because you are an MP. So you can get on the doorsteps, well they are all the same, which can be quite upsetting, but at the same time, to have the opportunity to represent someone to take up a case and get it solved for someone who wouldn't have been able to do it themselves, to be able to take up an issue for your area and get it done. You know I can drive round my constituency and see campaign after campaign, most of them hopefully successful, the odd one not. And then all the big national issues, you know; to be able to make a difference on a campaign or an issue is fabulous, and it's very rewarding, you feel you are doing a bit of good for your country."

Dan Jarvis MBE MP

"It's not a job, it's a way of life. It consumes every breathing moment of your working existence, and I knew that it would. I believe very strongly in public service, I believe that if MPs do their job well they can make an enormous difference to their communities. I believed that before I came into politics and I know it to be true now. The standing of MPs is quite low at the moment, and I think those of us who have the privileged position of serving our constituents have to do all that we can to rebuild those bridges. Yes it's an incredibly important job, and I feel incredibly privileged to be able to do it. If I won the Lottery tomorrow, I can absolutely guarantee I would continue to do it."

Liz Kendall MP

"Oh it's has exceeded them, again it might sound like a bit of a cliché but I love people. Life is about people, and you get to meet and talk to people from all sorts of backgrounds, and although there are huge problems and difficulties that we face at the moment, every single day I am in the constituency I meet people who I am absolutely inspired by. There is bad in the world that you hear a lot about, but there is also a lot of good too, there are people who do phenomenal things, and that really inspires you."

Sadiq Khan MP

"And more, it is an amazing job. I have been very privileged; in my previous life I was a lawyer, and had a number of big cases, test cases, which set precedents, where I changed the life of a number of my clients, but I realised even as a good lawyer where you win cases and change the law you only impact on your direct clients, and maybe if it is a test case a few thousand people are affected by the law. But if you are a parliamentarian and a legislator, you can pass laws that impact on millions of people, so your ability to influence things is much greater. Sometimes you realise that you are a small cog in a machine, you need to dampen your expectations a little and work as a team player. At other times, you can give issues a public airing and bring about change, and give people access to decision makers. Once you realise the tools you have in your toolbox, you start to cope more effectively, but I still love being an MP for my own community. There is no more humbling experience than being the MP of the manor you were born and raised in, cos there is a pride they have in you. One of their own has done good. I get old ladies, black, white, Asian, whatever, coming up to me and telling me they are proud of me, which is important to me, and there are things that I can point out that I have improved, and where I have made a difference."

Ivan Lewis MP

"I don't think I had even begun to think about what becoming an MP would mean to my life. I was elected on the Thursday, with that massive euphoria in 1997, over that weekend I was mobbed going down the shops. I then had to come to London, with nowhere to live, no office, and I didn't know anybody; I had two young children, two babies really, and a wife, life changed overnight. It was obviously a mistake not to employ a temporary secretary, I used to sit in my office and it used to take me five or six hours to open my post, not to sort it, not to deal with it, just to open it, in those first few weeks. I used to sit till four or five in the morning hand writing responses to people because I didn't want to let them down. The policemen used to laugh at me when I used to walk out of here at four or five in the morning. Those early days were really tough, nobody really prepares you, and there wasn't much of an induction, or a mentoring system, so I found it really difficult. Then I was given the opportunity to serve as an assistant to a Minister, I was asked to second a Queen's speech, and then I had nine years as a Minister. I would say that the experiences I have had have been unbelievable, remarkable, and I have no regrets, but it can be tough."

Caroline Lucas MP

"Yes and no. There's no doubt that by simply being here in Parliament, you have an incredible opportunity to contribute to the political conversation – and to take the concerns of your constituents right to the heart of politics. Even as one MP from a smaller party, I think it's possible to make a significant impact, partly by asking the questions that no one else will – on withdrawing our troops from Afghanistan for example, or on the urgent action needed to tackle climate change. I've also found that most people here are very friendly and accommodating, and often willing to work together on specific issues, regardless of political persuasion. On the downside, I find the glacial pace of change and the archaic Parliamentary processes deeply frustrating. The traditionalists who cling onto their old-fashioned procedures claim they're defending our heritage – but the fact is, things need to change. The disconnection between Westminster politics and what is actually happening in local communities is deeply troubling. Most people see Parliament as remote, unaccountable and incomprehensible. There's definitely an appetite for change – a Westminster Hall debate I hosted on the need for Parliamentary reform was one of the best attended in years. But there are also those people who say, as Margaret Beckett did, 'Don't worry, don't try and change things too fast, you'll get used to it.' The fact that people get used to it – become institutionalised – is precisely the problem."

Nicky Morgan MP

"I didn't expect to win a seat like Loughborough. I think the honest truth is I didn't have a pre-conception of what is was going to be like, as I had never worked at Westminster before. One of the things that strikes me most is I have been involved in politics for a long time, and have always had great respect for Members of Parliament. And I think that has changed, the relationship between the outside public and MPs has changed a huge amount and that is perhaps different. I expected to build up to making difficult decisions, but I expected to be able to work with other people. I think people are very quick to judge outside, and to question the motives of Members of Parliament, and that's probably the hardest thing and the thing I least expected."

Greg Mulholland MP

"I am not sure how much time I spent wondering what it would be like, once I was seriously engaged in trying to get elected. I did always believe that it would be a position where you could speak up, challenge things and help encourage change. I have not been disappointed and although clearly as one MP, you can only really effectively be involved with a few issues, you do have the opportunity to be heard and to encourage change. Locally, the role includes the more formal one and it is a pleasure and a privilege to see how much it means to people when you attend their events as the local MP and that is something in our system we should cherish."

Jason McCartney MP

"In some ways I was sort of prepared for it after being a candidate for three and a half years, as I had begun to help people with issues and concerns, I had been visiting businesses and schools. It's just stepped up a whole notch really. It's a whole range of issues. Here in my constituency office I have two members of staff, Sally and John, and we are currently helping over 800 people with different issues; it's anything from benefits, housing problems, a leaky shower, planning issues, the Child Support Agency, right up to weird and wonderful things like people having lost their passports and being stranded overseas. And then there's the parliamentary things, legislation down in Parliament and voting on issues on behalf of my constituents."

Esther McVey MP

"In many ways, I believe it has. If there are people you want to help and things you want to pursue, you have every opportunity to do so. The downside has been the negative perceptions the public hold of MPs, which is inaccurate because I have to say, MPs of all parties are very good people who work very hard."

Chi Onwurah MP

"Didn't have any expectations. I thought it would have been unwise to have had expectations, and would have been a little bit arrogant as well, being newly elected."

Stephen Pound MP

"No cos you could never imagine it; every single person knows a little about an MP, nobody knows everything about an MP, it's a bit like everyone thinks they own a bit of the police or a bit of nursing or medicine cos they have experience of a bit of it. Everyone knows a bit about politics cos they know a little bit about it. One of my brothers is a priest and I think he is the only one who isn't an MP who understands what it is like to be one 24/7; you can't walk down to get the papers without being treated like you are public property. It's like last night, twenty past eleven, I was on the bus, coming home and I put my Oyster Card up and some guy said, 'Bet you'll be claiming that on expenses won't you' I mean f**k off... but you get that all the time. But what has lived up to it is sometimes you can do something that nobody can, even if it means pulling things together, sometimes it's nice to be able to do something that others can't. I am thinking of a particular nightmare case, with some people in supported housing, who are falling through the gaps, with everyone saying is it the PCT's responsibility, or is it the mental health trust's, is it the local authority, is it the GP, and you can actually pull the whole thing together and for me that's brilliant. I never realised how powerless we can be, but the power is there if you take it but you actually have to go out and get it."

Yasmin Qureshi MP

"Yes it has in many respects. In the context of where it is not quite as I thought it would be is that sometimes you are not in a position to be able to achieve as much as you would like to. It's hard to know how to put it, but I thought I may be able to do more, but in reality there is only so much you can achieve. Maybe I had unrealistic expectations. And I think more to do with the whole party systems, with the party structures."

Jacob Rees-Mogg MP

"Yes I would say more than. It's twofold; one is when constituents come to see me and I write to people on their behalf, MP's letters do get treated reasonably well, you don't always get what you want, but you always get a serious reply for your constituents' concerns; and the other things is, when Parliament is sitting, the Ministers are all here, and the Ministers are intelligent people so if a good argument is made, they listen and a policy develops. I think that is very important. I thought Ministers were very remote figures in an ivory tower somewhere special before I was elected, and suddenly I realised when I got in that they are normal people too, and therefore they want to do their best; and if an argument, sometimes put by an Opposition Member, persuades them of something, and there is a policy that is going wrong, they are willing to change it. That's very impressive, it's not just automatic as it may appear from the outside."

Jonathan Reynolds MP

"It has I think, yeah, that's an interesting question. Because I was a local councillor, I sort of knew what it was like to be an elected person, and that's good training, but nowhere near enough training for the all encompassing experience of being an MP. At first it is very hard to get your head around the fact that you are an MP. If for instance you happened to say that a local institution wasn't good enough and needed to improve the paper would immediately print it; you also have the power to intervene in things. I think it takes about year to get your head round, but once you have, and you have your staff set up right, and know what local campaigns you are interested in taking forward, then it really does live up to your expectations. This is where I lived anyway, so there were lots of things I was aware of, whether it be a motorway junction that needs to be changed, or a hedge that needs to be cut back, you start being able to see things you can change and that is quite nice. Because we are in Opposition, the satisfaction is through local campaigns. Once you get a sense of being able to use the levers of power in your local area it really is good. Last month we brokered a deal for the canal that runs through Stalybridge to be cleaned more regularly, and Tesco are going to pay for it because they are next to the canal – things like that, practical things. And because of the Expenses Scandal you are conscious that the profile, the general image of MPs, is pretty low, so it's nice to prove that an MP can do some useful things."

Derek Twigg MP

"I wasn't sure what to expect to be honest, I think I was surprised by the variety of issues that people come to you about and want your help with, there's such a vast range. And here of course, it's a matter of getting yourself confident enough to speak in the House, to be able to take part in debates and to be able to hold a Minister to account. So that took a bit of getting used to. In terms of influence though, that's quite surprising, because no-one says no, well almost no-one says no to meeting you, including the Prime Minister, well I don't know about this one. But previous Prime Ministers, to heads of multi-national firms, all sorts of businesses, to organisations such as councils and other public bodies. So that's why as an MP you can use your influence to get in there and get your point across. Someone once refused me a meeting, and I pointed out that the Prime Minister never refuses to meet me nor do any of the Secretaries of State I ask, yet you refuse to. Anyway, it didn't last long and we did get to meet them. So that sort of influence that you have as an MP did surprise me, which is great as you can represent the interests of your constituents much more effectively."

Phil Wilson MP

"I love it! I love being an MP! Especially when you are representing the area where you grew up and you can go back; I think it was Thursday or Friday night last week when I went to The Black Bull in the village and just sat down with people I had gone to school with. That's special. So when these big constituency issues come up, whatever they may be, I just feel when I'm dealing with them, I'm not dealing with them in the abstract cos I know the people personally that are affected by them, which makes it easier."

John Woodcock MP

"I was so focused on winning, on being able to convince the people of Barrow-in-Furness that I was the right person for the job, and passionately believing in the things I was standing for, that I don't think I actually thought about how it was going to be. It's very different from being an advisor in Government, but it's something where you are learning and finding out new ways to be effective all the time, and I am sure that will go on for however long the people of Barrow-in-Furness want me."

Once again, I find some of the answers to this question really rather heart-warming and reassuring; Paul Blomfield and Ben Bradshaw speak of the privilege of representing their constituents.

Kevin Brennan, Ann Coffey, Stephen Dorrell, Michael Dugher, John Glen and Dan Jarvis MBE all speak of the opportunity to make a difference.

Then there is Rosie Cooper's intriguing reference to the House Authorities and invisible men, all very mysterious, and Philip Davies sums day to day life up very succinctly when he says: "You are always chasing your tail."

I will admit to being a little biased when it comes to Michael Dugher and Dan Jarvis MBE, both Barnsley MPs, which is where I live, but they are both so committed to their constituents, and we are very lucky to have them.

It is MPs like them that make me want to defend the role of MPs, although it is interesting how Caroline Lucas makes reference to the need for change and disconnection between Westminster politics and what is happening in local communities. Sadly I suspect she is right when she says most people see Parliament as remote, but she is wrong about it being unaccountable. It is accountable as long as we take an interest.

Kevin Brennan's account, for me, is perhaps the most important one, as he provides a perfect example of just what an MP can do for us, if we can be bothered to engage with them.

The final word in this chapter must go to Zac Goldsmith, who is another example of what, for me, is all that an MP should be. Zac says: "I hope we'll see, for instance, a mechanism that genuinely allows people to recall representatives that no longer inspire confidence. I have introduced a Bill to that effect." I suspect we would all wish him the very best of luck with that.

Gloria De Piero

A politician thinks of the next election; a statesman thinks of the next generation.
James Freeman Clarke, *Sermon*

CHAPTER SEVEN

High and Low Points

All of us have high and low points throughout our working life. You may be surprised by what some of the MPs consider to be their high points, but there are no prizes for guessing what many refer to as their low points.

Dave Anderson MP

"I don't really know, I was very, very satisfied with my election result in 2010, because five years previously we were the number one targets for the Lib Dems almost in the country, and we held the seat with a bigger majority than we thought we would, and then we almost doubled the majority. We had a swing of effectively 13% better than average for the rest of the north east for Labour, which was pretty good.

"Low points, well getting beat wasn't very good, although it was probably on the cards. I haven't had what you would call a low point, other than coming here everyday and knowing that you are going to get beat, so I feel bad for the people I represent. I have always tried to be optimistic, and have been a trade unionist all my life, but now we are rehashing arguments that we had twenty or twenty-five years ago, the arguments are the same and the outcome will be the same, which is bad news for ordinary people. So it's not like I lost this, that or the other, it's just general."

Paul Blomfield MP

"The high point was winning! Particularly as mine was a constituency that Labour was predicted to lose, it was very marginal.

So out of 41,500 votes cast, I won by 165. It was tight because primarily the two universities are in the constituency, with around 20-25,000 registered students, and my opponent was a Liberal Democrat promising to abolish tuition fees. I do think it will be different next time. So that was a high point. It was clearly a low point that Labour didn't win the election. I actually looked back over the previous thirteen years with an immense amount of pride, in terms of what Labour achieved, of course we got some things wrong, but overall the country in 2010 was a great deal better than when we inherited it in 1997. In the year that I have been here, high points are getting stuck into the work, I am on the Business Select Committee, and working as a PPS to Hilary Benn, who is Shadow Secretary of State for Local Government and Communities. I'm secretary of the All Party Group on Universities. Low point is I think disappointment that we haven't seen the support to match the rhetoric sometimes from the Liberal Democrats in terms of the potential that there is on crucial issues for them to play a role, for example on saving the NHS. They talked about it a lot, but when push came to shove both in the House of Commons and the House of Lords they stuck with the Government."

Sir Peter Bottomley MP

"Yes, if I can't cure an injustice, I think there must have been something more I could have done. For example, there is an acquaintance of mine, who I got to know after he went to jail, sentenced to death in America for murdering two people he hadn't murdered. It took five years to get him off death row, and he's still in prison twenty-five years on, so that was a half success, but not a full success. If I have someone who needs a hospital procedure, and either it's a new procedure so there's a big queue, or something may have gone wrong that's not so good. And then if I read the hospital board meeting papers and see that things are now better than they were a year before, and how dramatically better it is than twenty years ago, you think three cheers for the administrators, the nurses, the doctors, everyone who is working together. So the low points are unfinished business, and the real fun is just seeing happiness on someone's face."

Ben Bradshaw MP

"I think one of the things that motivated me to switch careers was the fact I had covered the Berlin Wall coming down very early, in fact I was only twenty-nine/thirty when that happened; it was an amazing experience, I remember thinking afterwards, *oh heck what am I going to do now, how am I going to beat that, is it all going to be downhill from now on?* So actually I think moving into politics was the right thing for me, it was something different, a new experience, and I have to say the thrill of getting elected on May 1st 1997, particularly after a very nasty election campaign against someone who was quite nasty personally towards me, was a huge thrill. I think if anything that was as big a thrill as covering the Berlin Wall, if not more, and of course becoming a Minister and becoming a Cabinet Minister was also a big thrill, and holding my seat, because I won a seat that had always been Tory before, except for a brief period in the 1960's. Although I was quite confident of being elected for one term, I didn't have any expectations that I would be in Parliament for any longer than that. So it's been amazing.

"I think the MPs expenses saga was not so much a low point for me personally because although the *Telegraph* tried to have a go, my expenses have always been very low. For me personally, I think the expenses saga helped me locally because whenever my local newspaper printed a league table of expenses I was always at the bottom. But I think in terms of the 'hit' it had on all politicians, all of us were in some way tarred with the same brush at that time in terms of public anger. Normally the reception I get in the streets of Exeter is very friendly, people come up and talk to me. At the height of that you did get people shouting and making snide comments. But you do have to have a bit of a thick skin if you are going into politics, you get those sort of 'brickbats' from the media all the time, but I take great comfort in the feedback and support I get from my constituents, that makes it a lot easier to bear the 'brickbats' that our feral media, as Tony Blair calls it, throw at us at regular intervals."

Kevin Brennan MP

"I suppose one of the most difficult times was around the vote on the Iraq War in March 2003. There were 139 of us, Labour backbenchers who voted against the war, it was a very, very intense pressurised time. I'll be perfectly honest with you, it was equally tough and difficult, but equally exhilarating to be part of history, part of making that decision. I remember one of my colleagues who was sat on the back benches with me when all the debates were going on and we had to decide, cos I am not normally a rebel. I genuinely believe by working together it's how you get things done really, you have to try to stick together, as hard as that can be sometimes. And one of my colleagues was saying to me, it's a really difficult decision, but I said this is why we are here, if we are not prepared to do this we shouldn't be here, you have to be able to look at yourself in the mirror tomorrow morning and say I did what I thought was right, especially about this, because it's life and death. So that was probably both a low and a high point."

Andrew Bridgen MP

"I really enjoy speaking in the Chamber. Last year there were only two MPs out of the 650 that spoke more often than I did. I wasn't counting it was just at the end of the year that's how it came out. I really enjoy being in the Chamber as much as I can, and taking part in debates. To give a speech you have to put a card into the Speaker, that works on the basis of who's spoken the most often gets pushed to the back, and you speak in order of priority, so obviously if you are a new 2010 intake MP you are pretty much at the back of the queue. But you put in everyday for your questions and it's a lottery, if you are on the order paper you get a question. But we have worked out how to get supplementary questions, because obviously when the Labour Party have got so many, the Speaker will generally come back to our side for a supplementary one. I think the Speaker does reward people who attend, at the end of the day the Speaker wants people in the Chamber, there's nothing worse when there is a debate and the camera looks round and there's one person on one side and three on the other, one of which is the Minister, it doesn't reflect very well, so I genuinely do think that he rewards people who attend a lot."

I think Joe Public would appreciate an MP more who they see in the Chamber.

"Yeah but also the public want you to respond to their emails in ten minutes.

"I had a pretty bad summer, with the media attention you can get for the wrong reasons and also the effect it can have on your family, that was pretty low. The journalists are just desperate to fill the papers with anything, they are not generally bothered whether it's true or not, they don' think of the consequences. As a politician, you need media attention to get your message across, and then when you get burnt by it, I guess it comes with the territory, you are fair game, because none of us are pressed to become MPs. You come into this knowing the media are not always your friend."

Andy Burnham MP
"The low point, I think the hardest point I have had in politics, was when I was deciding whether or not to stand for the leadership, and my wife was going through a pretty difficult health situation, it was like everything came together at once, with the personal and the political, that was a particularly hard moment. I think every politician would say to you sometimes when a problem at home coincides with a challenge professionally, it can become intolerable at that point.

And I remember what happened was, because of me being in the spotlight, it brought the spotlight on to her and her situation, I hated that, I absolutely hated that. So that was a low point.

"High point, the best individual moment I have had as an MP, was when Steve Rotherham sat down after his speech in the House. If I could pinpoint one single moment in time, because it just felt like a moment of triumph. All he did was read out the ninety-six names of the people who died at Hillsborough, but it was a moment of triumph against the odds, I will never forget that moment."

Ann Coffey MP

"Well I think obviously it makes a difference if you are in the party of Government, rather than the Opposition because you have more access to Ministers, having said that, it is possible as a backbench MP, if you can get support from other MPs across the parties, to actually get Governments to listen even though it may not be 'your Government'. The high spots for me have been the tiny advances that I have helped to make, for example, the last Government agreed to the registration of small childrens' homes, the implementation of a care plan for children leaving care, and when you see that being implemented – that is a real high spot. Obviously the low spots are when things don't work out, when you can't get Ministers to do what you want, or when a particular piece of legislation is passed that you don't feel is very helpful."

Rosie Cooper MP

"High points are when we manage to pull something off for the constituency. A high point for me was with the debacle of F.E. colleges, only twelve were approved, I fought like a tiger, and Skem College is the only college in the country that went back on that list and it opened in September; I know that if I had not done the things that I did, it wouldn't be there today. We might have got the money eventually, but we wouldn't have it now, it has started the regeneration of Skem, so that's a real high point.

"A low point. I am not good at being beaten by the system, sometimes I just want to keep on going and going at it, when good sense says cut your losses and stop. In terms of patience and frustration, that is when I am at my lowest. I just can't accept that we have a great country like we have, and we do some of the things that we do. Sometimes our values get skewed dreadfully."

Philip Davies MP

"I think the high points in Parliament tend to be when you are bringing something to the attention of the world which otherwise would not have been brought. Or when you have a constituent who brings you an issue and you sort it out for them, and you can see that you made a difference. I think everybody in life, in whatever job they are in, want to make a difference. I think the things that are high points are when you can look back, and think, in my own little way, I made a difference there.

"I don't think there have been any low points to be perfectly honest. I've absolutely loved every minute of it. I've been lucky that throughout life I have always enjoyed every job I have done. I guess there are low points in a way when the Government does things you don't want them to do, but if you took those as low points you would slit your throat in no time at all, you've just got to take those on the chin."

Gloria De Piero MP

"My high point was when someone came into a surgery with his mum and said, 'The PCT have just changed their policy on free incontinence pads, so now my mum has been told that I have got to take them in 'soiled' so they can weigh them and then they will decide if they are soiled enough.' I was in the surgery, open mouthed. You think of your own mum and dad. Getting that changed – that was my blooming high point. You know what, the *Daily Mail* is good for some things. So I rang the *Daily Mail* and said you will never guess what… that's disgusting… I was just horrified, how the hell did some pen pusher think that that was a good idea?!"

Stephen Dorrell MP

"Well I would have to say the high point is when I became the Health Secretary, that was a big job, and I got a lot of satisfaction out of doing it.

"Low points, well I guess the result of the 1997 General Election certainly was a low point, because it was at least as bad, if not worse than most of us had expected.

"Pre '97 I had spent ten years, first as a whip, then as a Minister, I had been engaged in making decisions which I felt moved things forward, and in the immediate aftermath of '97, I used to characterise my job; I was Education Spokesman briefly in the Shadow Cabinet, my job was to get up each morning, read David Blunkett's press releases and invent reasons for disagreeing with them *[laughter]*."

Michael Dugher MP

"I remember the 1997 victory being pretty good, having been out of power for so long, if I remember my earliest political memories of the miner's strike in the mid-eighties in my pit village as I was growing up. It was basically a decade and a half before we got back into office again. That was a really big moment. I am also really proud of my election in Barnsley, it was a great moment for me; I felt so proud becoming a Member of Parliament, in the Metrodome on the night I was elected, I thought about being sworn in as an MP. Also when I did my maiden speech, it was quite a nice moment. I mentioned before about my mother being an influence in terms of me going into politics, and also about where I come from. Well when I did my maiden speech, which inevitably is about yourself, your journey and what you want to do, as I was doing it I was talking about the area I grew up and how similar it is to the area I was representing, and I looked up at the gallery at the side, and both my mum and my dad had come down to watch my maiden speech. And

I was talking about the house that I grew up in, so that was quite a nice moment.

"I think the election defeat was really a low point. Although I expected us to lose, I found that quite difficult really, particularly having worked in Government for so long, I had been able to do things and deliver things. We have been beating ourselves up a lot since the election, but we did do a lot of things that I am really proud of and we helped a lot of people, particularly the sort of people that I represent. And my biggest frustration is seeing things happen to those people, and me being powerless really to prevent what I see as some really disastrous decisions. I think we have delayed certain things and forced U-turns on a whole bunch of things, we are an effective Opposition. I do my best to represent my constituents, but in politics, Government is where you need to be to really deliver for those people you represent, and the limitations of Opposition can be quite frustrating."

Natascha Engel MP

"The high point, oddly, was the General Election campaign because of the other candidates who stood against me; we spent so much time together, we did so many hustings together, that we all got to know each other very well, and obviously politically we agreed on nothing, but as people they were all really decent, and getting to know them was great *[laughter]* it was really odd.

"And I guess the other high point was after the General Election, I went for this chairmanship of this committee, it was a brand new committee, and I won. I probably shouldn't have done *[laughter]* no-one else was paying any attention I think *[laughter]*. But it was absolutely amazing. I was campaigning very hard in order not to be humiliated, because I was standing against somebody who was very famous and very well liked and respected, who everyone knew was going to be a shoe in. So I campaigned my heart out, so that I wasn't completely annihilated and humiliated, but I ended up winning by a tiny margin. I stood against Alan Hazlehurst, who had been

Deputy Speaker, and he is an absolutely lovely man. He sent me a note, and I nearly cried it was so lovely. He's a Tory but he is known to be incredibly fair, kind and generous, just a very, very nice man, and very senior.

"I think the low point was also the last General Election, just because things really changed. We had the Leaders' debates on the TV, and I think that all of us found that knocking on doors became pointless. People were making up their minds according to what they saw on the television, and suddenly everything we had done over the last five years if you were an incumbent MP didn't matter. Also the after effects of the expenses scandal, it really undermined people's faith in politics, that was terrible to see. And being part of that was terrible, because that's not what anyone goes into politics for, to turn people off like that."

Andrew George MP

"High points – yesterday, the supermarket adjudicator, I am privileged to chair the Grocery Market Action Group, and have been campaigning for ten years to get the supermarkets to stop beating up their suppliers. We led that campaign nationally to secure this important Watchdog. You don't have to be a Minister to get a policy through. We secured all party support for the policy.

"I'm proud to be involved in the campaign to remove the council tax discount on second homes. Something which affected my area, again that was a campaign on which I originally ploughed a lone furrow. But support grew and we got it through. So I hope I am living proof that you don't need to be in the front line of politics to achieve positive outcomes.

"I could point to various amendments to various bills, but in terms of a whole Act of Parliament the Supermarket Watchdog (Grocery Adjudicator) will be the first. But like so much else it was team work.

"Lots of lows. You try to set the highest possible standards, but you're always aware that you are spinning thousands of highly brittle ceramic plates, and you can't keep them all up, so you risk letting yourself, and others, down. It can be very hard.

"Also, during my time as an MP I have tragically lost two of my older brothers. I remember the day my eldest brother Mark died in 2001. I was trying to get back to Cornwall to see him but I couldn't get back quite in time. Instead of going by train I switched to a flight, and just as I was getting on the plane, I phoned the hospital again and a nurse told me, 'sorry love he's dead'. I then bumped into Charles Kennedy, he was flying to Scotland. He kindly delayed his flight somehow and said, 'listen here have a fag.' He must have seen that I was so distraught at the time. Eventually, I got on my plane, and a couple of days later a woman came up to me and said, ' I think you are disgusting, my son was on a plane with you the other day and you totally ignored him'. Of course, I realised it must have been shortly after hearing that my brother had died. She didn't want to know and just stormed off. And, you know, even in those sorts of moments you are still on show, you are not even entitled to grieve. I felt quite shattered and even angry about it. And I didn't even get the chance to say to her 'well, I had just heard that my brother had died, how would you feel?.'

"So, there are those types of things. The reporting of the expenses 'scandal' and the way that the papers ripped in to my family. I mean, I don't mind them having a go at me. I am the worst accountant in the world, an absolute mess, I hold my hands up to that. They created a story that I bought a flat for my daughter. It was on the front of the *Telegraph*. So there is my daughter, totally innocent and living in student halls of residence but because she had been a model and they had some nice pictures they seemed to cleverly conflate information to create a story. So that too was also very much a low point."

John Glen MP

"I think the high point was getting selected itself, that was on the 31st January 2010, which was really good, a culmination of a lifetime's ambition. Not that I could take anything for granted, but being selected in a seat that had been a Conservative seat for ninety years gave me some confidence that I would win three months later. That has to be the high point. I think just those early days, entering Parliament, seeing David Cameron form a Government, acclimatising to a world that hopefully I would be part of for some years ahead was a very exciting time. With trying to see it in a rational way, I am not sure I was blown away by it because it is my vocation, my mission, it's where I want to be, but it's not the be all and end all. My family is more important to me. I enjoy politics very much, it's rare really for someone to find a career where they are truly at least 95% satisfied, and feel they are making a contribution that adds up to something.

"It was a long and sometimes difficult path to get to Parliament, the tribulations of the selection process are well attested to by many people. It took me ten and half years, not that long really. I was first selected on the candidates list in August 1999, and then ten and a half years later I was selected in a safe seat. The party had different priorities and changed the way the selection process worked. But in the end, I have always had a strong Christian faith and purpose, and a sense of if it was going to happen it was going to happen. And it came together in my home county three months before the last election, at a time when I was going to take a redundancy package from my former employer, so it couldn't have worked out better. But it's only looking back that I can say that, there were moments when I didn't get interviews for other seats along the way, where I thought my moment had gone, and probably Salisbury was my last chance, before the last election, so it was just as well I got it.

"You tend to fight a seat you can't win first, most MPs do that, so there are four or five years up to that, and there is another four or five years where you are in the hunt for a marginal or a safe seat. Mine was a bit different in that I was only selected a few months after I was on the list to start off with. I didn't get one in 2005 because I was in a reserved occupation working for the party, running the 'war room' for Michael Howard's campaign. So I was denied the right to apply for seats in the twelve months up to it, quite legitimately as it wouldn't be good to have someone working for the party centrally and then clearing off to fight for a seat when you are doing a job for the party, so that extended it, but it's not unusual for someone to be on the list for ten years."

Oliver Heald MP

"Well the highs have been where you feel you have made a difference, made a positive change, either for an individual or via a policy. I was lucky enough to be on the front bench for thirteen years, there are all sorts of policies now being put in that I was the originator of. I see a lot of things happening, and think, well I had a hand in that, so that's a high. As for lows, I think not seeing your children grow up, because you are spending so much time here, and I think the expenses scandal was very depressing for all politicians. Clearly a significant number had let the public down, and even those of us who had a clean bill of health, felt we should have done a bit better as a group."

Dan Jarvis MBE MP

"I think securing a debate in Parliament on regenerating the economy in Barnsley was a high point, in the sense it gave me an opportunity I think potentially for the first time to have a specific debate on Barnsley, and on what practical measures the Government could be using to stimulate the Barnsley economy and to create jobs. And that was my debate that I applied for, I was quite proud of the speech I delivered in that debate so that was one of the high points. I think speaking in the Chamber is a really important part of the job – Prime Minister's Questions is quite an intimidating environment, for the first time, as a brand new MP to ask the Prime Minister a question – I was pleased that went pretty well, and I managed to get the question out. There are very senior experienced politicians who have been there for decades who still sometimes make a mess of it, so I was pleased to be able to do that. But you know the most important thing is to just be able to get on with the job with a good bunch of people, working out where we can make a difference.

"I don't think that there have been any obvious low moments. I came into Parliament just after the by-election in March, and straight away I was confronted by a very difficult decision about Libya, whether it was right for our country to deploy military assets to Libya, that was something I took very seriously and thought long and hard about. But based on the evidence that was placed in front of Parliament, it was a relatively straight forward decision to make in the end. I have been able to recruit a fantastic team of people to work with me, I have a very good office in Westminster and Barnsley, and we have set ourselves a number of objectives, and we work incredibly hard. I have always known this is what I wanted to do, and that it is a privileged position. People often ask me if I miss the army, I always say I think it would be quite self indulgent to say that I miss the army, as this is such a privileged life, this is what I wanted to do. You know there are moments where I think about thing I had done in the army and acknowledge that my life is different now. I think I am very lucky to be an MP and I really can't think of any low points so far."

Liz Kendall MP

"High point was a constituency issue, I have been really involved with Leicester College which has brilliant courses for Adult Learners, often women who want to get back to work, or people who didn't do so well at school, but are now determined to try again. They had a brilliant 'hustings' event where they had different teams trying to win for the best speeches and points that they made. I went along, it was really interesting because it combined both issues that they cared about, but it was also about democracy, it was showing people that democracy matters: have your voice, make an argument, tell the politicians. So it was a really exciting event, and it was very difficult to choose who the winner should be.

"My lowest point was recently, when a guy in my constituency came to see me because his wife had diabetes and ended up having her foot amputated, and they needed some adaptations in their house; handrails, stair lift that sort of thing so she could get upstairs and have a wash. They had been told that she needed them and they waited ten months to get them, her health deteriorated, the council came back and saw that, and realised she now needed a total bathroom refit to have a wet room. When they finally came round with the stuff needed to do it it was four days after she had died. He was really upset because the woman he loved had ended her life feeling that she had lost her dignity because her children were having to wash her. He was really upset because she hadn't had the help she needed, and he felt that when they finally came round he had lost his rag a bit with them. When I went to the council to look at what had happened, they said it was because of the pressures on their budgets, and the cuts they have to concentrate on the terminally ill who only have six weeks to live. For me to see somebody so upset that the woman he had been married to and loved for so long had ended her life like that, was a real low point for me. People probably don't think that is what politics is about, but it is for me, that was a real low point."

Sadiq Khan MP

"There have been lots and lots of high points. Being elected was a dream. Making my maiden speech, I mentioned my father and my children, it was a great high for me. Getting involved in committees and making legislation is obviously important to me. Whenever I name check Tooting, whether it's Springfield or St. George's or things locally in Parliament it makes me proud. I do lots of assemblies in Tooting, because I went to a local primary school in Tooting and a local comprehensive there, and I want young people in Tooting to see someone like them in Parliament, walking the corridors of power is important. Getting involved in Ed Miliband's leadership campaign and winning was a high point. Being in the

Shadow Cabinet, helping to develop our policy to get re-elected is a high point. So there are lots of high points. Raising issues about mental health is also a high point. In my previous life, one of the cases I did was Rocky Bennett. Rocky Bennett was someone who had mental health problems who died as a result of control and restraint in a clinic in Norfolk. I did the inquest and there was also a public inquiry into lessons to be learnt, and one of the things that the public inquiry concluded was that there was institutional racism in the mental health world, and that it was a Cinderella service, so I was able to make changes as a lawyer. But as a parliamentarian I can argue for more resources, and make sure that mental health issues are raised. I am lucky because I have got Springfield Hospital in my patch, so I can point to something that makes a positive difference to people's lives, without institutionalising them. Having twenty-first century facilities is very, very important.

"Yes of course there have been some low points. Voting against your party is not nice, people send you to Coventry and don't talk to you cos they see you as disloyal. Obviously, well publicised, having my meetings with my constituents bugged wasn't nice. Obviously the press intrusion, there are some odious people who will write nasty stuff that isn't true, you just have to deal with it, get on with it. What people don't realise is I have not yet met a politician who has got a thick skin, and who it doesn't upset. It does upset you, and anyone who claims it doesn't is either someone I haven't met yet, or someone not being completely straight. It really does affect you because your children, your wife, or your family could read it. It affects your mood, it's not nice people being personal. I have no problem with people assessing my performance, but when it gets personal, unjustified sniping, it is just awful."

Caroline Lucas MP

"Being elected as the first ever Green in Parliament was obviously the major high point, representing the hopes of so many people who've worked incredibly hard over the years to get the party a seat in Westminster. Since then, I've felt proud to be able to stand up for my constituents on a huge range of issues – from challenging the Government's plans to privatise the NHS and sell off our forests, to defending the most vulnerable from disproportionate cuts to welfare.

"Among the many highlights has been gaining the support of the city's Chief Superintendent for a new debate on drug and alcohol addiction in the city – calling for a rethink on the failed 'war on drugs' and moving towards a more effective, evidence based approach, which reduces harm and treats addiction as a health issue, not a criminal one. I was also glad to be able to play a key role on parliament's Energy Bill committee, proposing measures to increase the affordability of energy efficiency measures, tackle fuel poverty and create jobs. Alongside this, I launched a national campaign, End the Big Six Energy Fix, calling on the Government to introduce a levy on the huge profits of the energy companies to help make our ever-increasing energy bills more affordable. I'm also pleased to have secured an opportunity for cities like Brighton and Hove to bid for funding for ultrafast broadband, which would make a big difference to the growing digital business sector here.

"Another high point was securing agreement from Brighton and Hove City Council that it will develop a domestic violence strategy as part of pioneering work to end violence against women and girls. And after I lobbied the Government over the lack of funding for local rape crisis services, the local survivors' network was promised an additional three years' funding for their work.

"In terms of a low point, there certainly have been frustrating moments – you have to accept that one MP out of 650 is very rarely going to be in a position of swinging majorities, and some days it feels like you're pushing water uphill. But perhaps the worst times are those Prime Minister's Questions when all the braying and name-calling in the Chamber makes you wonder whether Parliament is really fit for purpose at all."

Nicky Morgan MP

"I think high points are being at the centre of national events, I mean Prime Minister's Questions every week is fantastic, because you know that the eyes of everyone interested in politics is on the Chamber, so to be there and sitting in a front row seat is a real privilege. Helping people, and getting thank you letters. I had a letter /email from someone yesterday saying 'thank you for sorting out my problem with the CSA, if you hadn't intervened… ' It wasn't because it was me, it was because as their MP I could intervene. Well that's lovely to make a positive change to someone's life – that's what it's all about.

"I think sometimes the frustration of not being able to get things done, things taking a lot of time, you can't just snap your fingers. In a business environment if you want something done you just go ahead and do it, there are not layers and layers of bureaucracy as there are here. And there are also daft ways in which the House of Commons is run which make me angry, so it's probably not the job itself, it's all the stuff that goes around with it. The majority of my constituents are absolutely lovely, but there are always a few who can't see a different point, or they get frustrated if they think you can't help them, although you have probably done as much as you possibly can; it may be a situation that it literally insoluble, then you hear that they have been dealing with the last three MPs about it too, and if they haven't sorted it out, I am probably not going to either."

Greg Mulholland MP

"High points, there have been many; winning the seat from third place, the sense of actually changing things for the better. There have been a number of things I have achieved, both locally and nationally. Locally, I led the successful campaign to secure funding for the long awaited multi-million Holt Park Wellbeing Centre, which is currently under construction. I also worked with the Friends of Spring Gardens to earn a reprieve for Spring Gardens

Care Home in Otley, which faced closure as part of a raft of council care home closures. Nationally, following my involvement in the campaign for High Speed Rail to Yorkshire, I was delighted when the Government announced this would be happening. I was also proud, as chair of the Rugby League Group, to ensure the funding for the 2013 Rugby League Cup was guaranteed and also managed to force a rethink over cuts to BBC local radio sports coverage. I was also delighted to be voted by the 100,000 members of CAMRA as one of their top forty campaigners of all time for my work to protect and preserve the Great British pub. Away from politics, I am very proud to have successfully completed the Jane Tomlinson Anniversary Challenge, completing the Paris and London marathons and cycling in between via Yorkshire, and delighted I raised over £6000 to assist this fantastic cause, inspired of course by the inspirational Jane Tomlinson, and also the excellent Leeds Rugby Foundation and Kidz in Kampz, both based in my constituency. Above all, however, my greatest moment was welcoming constituent Mirza Tahir Hussain back to the UK after we managed to free him from death row in Pakistan, a moment I will never forget.

"Low points of course are not succeeding in campaigns – I was very disappointed at the Government's decision to place the headquarters for their flagship Green Investment Bank in Scotland, despite the strong and well presented case put forward by the Leeds City Region bid team. It was also a real blow when, despite a city wide campaign, we failed to stop Carlsberg closing the famous Tetley's Leeds brewery in June 2011. I was also bitterly disappointed that the Government failed to legislate to stop the abuse by the giant pueblos but continue to campaign to get them to do so. You have to accept as an MP you can't win every battle but the key is to ensure that such disappointments make you even more determined to succeed next time. For all MPs the expenses scandal was a low point. As well as the MPs who abused the system, all MPs were tarnished and some very unfair things were said to the point that for a while, spouses and partners didn't feel like going out of the house. Also during the last general election campaign I have the new experience of facing religious hatred by being abused in the street for being a Catholic, thanks to attacks on me from my Conservative opponent, but such things make you stronger."

Jason McCartney MP

"I haven't had a real low point as such, but it is the cynicism and mistrust of MPs. I genuinely believe I am working really, really hard, trying to do my best, but there is still this mistrust that we are all in it for what we can get, and that we are all millionaires. A lot of things have changed, expenses have all been sorted out and rightly so. I publish all my expenses on my website, I don't claim lots of things I am entitled to. I do not claim parking, I could have a free permit from the council, but I want to pay my parking charges like everyone else; I could claim petrol and I don't, so I have to pay the extortionate costs like everyone else, which keeps me in touch with reality. There are also lots of myths that go around, like when we are on summer recess, it's reported as MPs going off on their seven week holiday. I am here as I am today, seeing eight different lots of people in my constituency, that's what I did in the summer. I had a one week holiday when I took my girls to Spain. I was elected to represent people, and that's what I enjoy. I live and breathe this. The thing is when you get elected, there is no job specification, no terms of reference and I haven't signed a contract; I could, I suppose, if I wanted to, just stay at home all day but I don't. There is no holiday entitlement, you make the job what you want to, nobody tells you to have an office in Holmfirth, or what issues to get involved with. So you sort of form it in your own mind what you want to do, and I want to be a very Yorkshire based MP.

"There are loads of high points: helping people with local issues, helping people with benefits issues, getting the council to come and sort out someone's leaky roof, helping out with school issues, sorting out lost passports, doing things in the best interests of your constituents. It's also nice to vote with your heart, and quite frankly to get a thank you email. Positive feedback means the world to me. I want to be Jason McCartney, your MP, rather than Tory… I am in a party because I believe in about 80% of what my party does, and I feel you can get things done working together as a group. However when I disagree with the 20% I will say so, but I will do so in a constructive way. Just about everyone who is an MP, has gone into it for the right reasons."

You are a perfect example of what Joe Public would like an MP to be.

"I hope so. I think having a positive attitude is really important. I have just produced my newsletter which goes out a couple of times a year, it's all positive about what I do: visiting local companies, care homes, schools, the Huddersfield to Brighton bike ride I took part in. I don't care what anyone else does, I don't slag them off. That went down really well during my campaign, a number of candidates said negative things, but I just concentrated on who I was, what I had done, and what I wanted to do."

Esther McVey MP
"Highs – collectively working with: the Department of BIS, education, school children and some of the country's most successful women, to promote careers advice and role models to youngsters and then having the career book I wrote turned into a play by the National Youth Theatre, which is now going on tour around the country to help those kids most in need of support, and having David Cameron at No. 10 launch this initiative.

"Lows – never having a weekend and a permanent home!"

Stephen Pound MP

"One of the best was the election in 1997, the election was on the Thursday, and then by the Friday morning there was that picture of Cherie Blair opening the door at Downing Street in her nightdress, and the attack had begun. My present job in Northern Ireland also means a lot to me as it's something I have worked on for a number of years.

"I think one of the greatest lows was the 1992 General Election, I just couldn't believe we could have lost it. The idea of John Major becoming Prime Minister again, I found it impossible to believe, although I know Edwina Currie was quite relieved. It's unfortunate the bloodstream of politics is elections, and the heartbeat is the vote."

John Redwood MP

"In the 1980s I campaigned for policies that would give the UK the chance of faster growth and higher living standards. I had the chance to see some of these put into effect when I acted as Margaret Thatcher's Chief Policy Adviser. In the 1990s I successfully campaigned to keep the UK out of the Euro, and was delighted with the victory of the minority of us who always argued it would end in tears and would do damage to jobs and economic prospects. Today I am campaigning to see through the public service reforms and budget changes needed to sort out the UK's precarious financial position."

Jacob Rees-Mogg MP

"Oh gosh that's difficult. I think my maiden speech was a high point, because I have always enjoyed public speaking, and have done quite a lot of it, but it's a very, very different environment to speak in. I wondered if I would be able to do it, whether the way I speak would go down well in the Chamber. Once I had finished, I felt much more comfortable that I could speak in the Chamber confidently and not make a fool of myself, which was of concern. One of one's great aims in life is not to make too much of a fool of oneself, and as long as you can get past that, then it's alright. I felt that my maiden speech didn't make a fool of me, that was very reassuring.

"Low points, if I have had any, I have forgotten them, I never really dwell on these things."

Jonathan Reynolds MP

"There are obviously some, getting promoted in re-shuffles is quite nice because you are getting some recognition. The highest points for me come from the constituency work. When you are a councillor there are all these things that you want to push, but you are one of about fifty and you don't have the resources; once you are an MP you have much more of a platform to do things, like some of the campaigns we have run in Stalybridge town centre, stuff like that, when you get local wins, they are quite modest, but actually are the more tangible things.

"Low points? If I looked through my diary I would probably find bits, a lot of the experience that makes it feel as though you've got this job as an MP and it's brilliant, but at the same time, this is an area that is suffering quite badly under the Government's decisions. So personally you are happy to be an MP, but you wouldn't wish to see your area suffering so much with unemployment, there are a thousand kids in this constituency alone on Job Seekers' Allowance. Sometimes I think people make a mistake of thinking that Opposition parties don't want to see good news on the economy and things like that, well actually it is heartbreaking to see what poor economy figures do to your local area. You know people locally and you see what it is doing to them, it's pretty grim when you see that."

Sir Bob Russell MP

"I was disappointed when I was convinced that the last Government were going to drop the drink/drive levels and they didn't; that was a campaign that I ran with a local newspaper and the parents of a fourteen year old girl, killed by a driver, below the legal limit here, but only just, but above the limit in other countries. I was absolutely convinced that we were going to get a lower level with Ministerial support at that point but we didn't, when it was passed over to the incoming Government.

"One of the phone calls I shall be making after you have gone is to start another campaign after three questions I tabled last night. A few months ago, Colchester police were called to Tesco's car park, where an elderly gentleman had parked his car by the filling station, it had been concluded quite rightly that he was unfit to drive. They drove the car home for him, this was on the Friday, and told him they were going to contact the DVLA at Swansea to revoke his license. Despite that, he went out in his car again on the Monday into the town centre, mounted the pavement and killed a sixteen year old girl on her way home from college. Because of my own family bereavement way back with my daughter, something I do in situations like that is very privately write to the family explaining that I have empathy and that they should get in touch if they would like to. This lady contacted me about a month back and said as time had now elapsed she felt she had the strength to move on, so I put her in touch with the local paper, and they made it the lead story. They are now going to take it forward. So I am working with these two mums in my constituency, and one other, whose son was stabbed to death at a cashpoint, who is now running a national knives campaign. The police have the power at the moment to stop you driving if you are under the influence of drink or drugs, or if the car is unroadworthy. They don't have the power it would appear to stop someone driving if they are unfit to drive.

"We have also had some sad moments with three military funerals, with Colchester being a garrison town, two of which I was able to attend, where the soldiers were actually living in the area. One of the army wives, was Victoria Bateman; Vicky came to see me before her husband was posted, and of course I tried to reassure that he would be fine. Of course, he was very sadly one of those who didn't make it. On the anniversary of his death I was volunteered by the Minister for Defence at the time, Kevin Jones, to do a parachute jump in his memory. Anyway, in about the February or March, my office said to me that the Minister for Defence had just been on the phone, and that I would be doing my parachute jump on 12th June. In the end I psyched myself up to do it. I went down in the Minister's car at about five o'clock in the morning. So the first jump was Victoria and the Commanding Officer from 2nd Battalion Parachute Regiment, and at a 1000 feet there was this little black cloud, where she scattered her husband's ashes. It was like being at a funeral. So the next thing is the Defence Minister and I go up, and I need to say we were piggy backing, we did it 13000 feet. It was exhilarating but I was glad when I got to the ground.

"As for high points, I have been very fortunate, we had a Royal Visit to Colchester, the Queen came and that was very nice. I have met Prince Charles a couple of times, I have met Princess Anne. I have actually met the Queen four times as an MP."

Derek Twigg MP

"That's a really good question that I haven't really thought about before. I think probably two particularly big constituency things were the Mersey Gateway, the new bridge, that we've got the almost final go ahead to start the building of a few weeks ago, which we had campaigned for for ages. High points are helping individuals too; I remember a lady with a terrible pension problem, she couldn't get a settlement, and we ended up getting her a three figure sum eventually. The old lady who has been trying to get a repair sorted out on her house for ages, and we can make it happen, or the poor family who have had benefits problems and no-one to advocate for them, those sort of constituency issues mean a lot, they are really important. In terms of low points, clearly losing the election, was an obvious low point, and I think for me, losing my job at The Ministry of Defence, when the re-shuffle came in 2000 was a real disappointment, because I loved the job and worked hard at it."

Charles Walker MP

"I'll tell you what the high point is, often you will look at your diary, and you have had a busy week, and you will see that there is some appointment in it for the weekend in your constituency, and you may say to yourself, '*why on earth did I say to my staff to put that in the diary?*' And actually you get there and people are so happy to see you, they are so welcoming, it's a total affirmation of their event because their MP has come along – and I really do find those events totally heart warming. Because it's very easy to think when you are a politician that everybody is against you, all your decisions are second guessed, nobody likes you, everybody loves you, but often when you are in your constituency you meet remarkable people, warm-hearted people, not all of whom support you, but you meet people who are genuinely for democracy and your place in democracy, and I just think it's a very affirming experience.

"Far too many low points to mention, what do they say about life: life is a slow progression towards death punctuated by many low points and a few high points. I have to say there have been low points in politics, sometimes I am very disappointed with the decisions that are taken. I have to recognise that we live in a democracy, but I am not always sure they are taken for the best or most honourable of reasons. I keep being told that politics is a dirty business and I am sure it is, but I like to see the best in things, and sometimes politics does disappoint me when it seems to be worst of things, or the motivations for a decision don't seem to be the best. One of the low points was the whole issue around MP's expenses, where it seemed almost regardless of who you were, you were positioned as a criminal or a crook, that was a very distressing time for Members of Parliament, constituents and the nation at large, so I would say that was the absolute low point."

Phil Wilson MP

"A high point locally for me would be getting the Hitachi deal, which means they are going to build a factory where they will build the new generation of trains for the East Coast Line. It will bring about 500 jobs, and cost £90 million, the biggest investment in the North East since Nissan, so being involved in that has been the high point.

"The low point would be losing the 2010 election cos no-one likes being in Opposition."

Rosie Winterton MP

"Obviously first coming here in 1997, and all the elections since. Every election, I am so grateful to the electorate for electing me, and putting their faith in me, so those are always high points. And I have been very pleased to become Chief Whip too.

"I think the whole issue of expenses was a low point for everybody. That was probably the time when MPs felt very demoralised, and obviously there have been various other political ups and downs. I suppose if you are talking about Parliament though, that is when it fell to an all time low."

John Woodcock MP

"Well I am two years in and I am just hoping it continues. It's amazing to be able to stand up in Parliament and speak out for your constituents. I wish we could have had more successes and you feel you're swimming against the tide when you are in Opposition. There have been individual things where we have forced changes. I was delighted just this week that we got a change regarding Mesothelioma compensation. A lot of sufferers were due to have a lot of their compensation taken away, and it's an awful illness. My constituency has the second highest rate of sufferers in the whole country, and the Government were set to make changes which would have seen a lot of money taken away from people when they only have months to live once they are diagnosed. So I was delighted that we were able to get a change on that.

"I was also recognised nationally for my campaign on bowling greens which is on-going, and that's fantastic.

"As for low points there haven't been that many, but the relative impotence of Opposition hits home when you stay in Parliament till 2 or 3 am, and you think you are doing your bit and holding the Government to account, and you are making a nuisance of yourself. Spirits can get buoyed up when you are in the Chamber, everyone is supporting and shouting at the Government, and then the vote happens; you lose, your constituents are no better off, and may be much worse off because of the changes, and you haven't been able to do anything. That is why we have got to get back into Government as soon as we can, because we can't stand up and ultimately do the right thing for the people we represent until we are."

I have tried not to be political whilst producing this book, but sometimes it is difficult when Paul Blomfield makes the point that there are 25,000 registered students within his constituency, and his Liberal Democrat opponent promising to abolish tuition fees during the election campaign, and ok, he failed to win, but actually his party subsequently did no such thing. You can't help but think about Zac Goldsmith's idea to recall representatives that no longer inspire confidence, and he is absolutely right. How can we say we live in a democracy when a party can be elected on a manifesto which they then renege on the moment they gain power? That is a perfect example of what causes people to disengage with politics, although of course they should do precisely the opposite, and call their politicians to account.

We can all relate to Philip Davies when he says many of us, whatever our job, want to make a difference, and Michael Dugher illustrates how much easier it is to make a difference when he says Government is where you need to be to really deliver for the people you represent. Although wait a minute, Andrew George says, "so I hope I am living proof that you don't need to be in the front line of politics to achieve positive outcomes" – so there you go, politics is all about opinions.

Like me, you may have been moved by Andrew George's account of the death of his brother, and how sad it is that we can all be so quick to make judgements about people without knowing all the facts, that old saying 'a mile in my shoes' springs to mind.

Another moving account is recorded by Liz Kendall, it is another perfect example of why we should all take an interest in politics and what decisions are being made that can have such a devastating effect upon us. What happened to her constituent should be a salutatory lesson for us all.

Liz Kendall, like Gloria De Piero, Natascha Engel, Yasmin Qureshi and Nicky Morgan are people I just wanted to give a big hug to, they show such compassion for their constituents, just what you want from an MP. Is it because they are women? I don't think so, the same could be said for most of the male MPs I interviewed too.

Sadiq Khan, now he is an example of a guy you could give a big hug to, but he raises interesting questions about the way we and our media treat our MPs. Greg Mulholland illustrates precisely the same point, as does Jason McCartney. Three politicians all from different parties, and all thoroughly decent people, any right thinking person would be happy to have them as their parliamentary representatives.

You will realise by now that I like to give somebody the final word on each chapter, but I am spoilt for choice here, so here are a few contributions.

Sir Peter Bottomley – High Point: "It's just seeing happiness on someone's face."

Kevin Brennan – "You have to be able to look yourself in the mirror tomorrow morning and say, I did what I thought was right."

Natascha Engel – Low Point: "The after effects of the expenses scandal. It really undermined people's faith in politics, and that was terrible to see. And being part of that was terrible, because that's not what anyone goes into politics for, to turn people off like that."

Caroline Lucas – "Perhaps the worst times are those Prime Minister's Questions when all the braying and name calling in the Chamber makes you wonder whether Parliament is really fit for purpose at all."

So the expenses scandal has left a deep scar running through our political system, and maybe it should, but is it time to move on?

Greg Mulholland

*One of the penalties for refusing to participate in politics, is
that you end up being governed by your inferiors.*
Plato

CHAPTER EIGHT

Five Years Time

Where do you see yourself in five years?

Dave Anderson MP

"On a beach in the Bahamas *[laughter]*. I genuinely don't know. One of the big issues for all of us is we have the Boundary Commission changes, and that will have a big impact on my constituency, it virtually disappears. We have put in alternative proposals that have got support from surrounding constituencies, but whether that will get anywhere I don't know. I genuinely don't know where we will be, I could probably win a selection process if I needed to go through one, given the likely nature of the seats, but it's a matter of personally if I want to do it, at sixty one/sixty two years old and my wife's three years older than me, and a lot of the other MPs are younger than me."

Paul Blomfield MP

"Having just been re-elected for the new constituency of Sheffield Central, because boundaries are changing, I think the Government know exactly what they are doing with the boundary changes and they are trying to do us over. The lack of flexibility that they have provided for in the way that the boundaries will be changing, the lack of accommodating local communities, the strict numerical formula essentially means that it builds in an advantage for the Tories over Labour. If you look at my seat, there are 17% of households where nobody is registered to vote, and often the people in those households are the people I spend a lot of time working for, the disengaged, disempowered people, they don't count in the new equation. Numbers are based on the amount of registered voters, that means is that a seat like mine is artificially depressed, it gives a political advantage. Most people assume when the Government say they are trying to make every constituency the same size, that it's based on the number of people who live there, it's not, it is based on the number of registered voters, which works against inner city constituencies like mine, where there is quite a high turnover, with many people staying off the electoral roll for one reason or the other, and they are often the people who need your time most, but they are not counted. There are real worries about the next step which the Government is looking to put through, which will force a boundary review every Parliament, but they are also changing the way that people register. At the moment the head of the household registers everyone that lives there, but they are going to ask every individual person to register themselves. My guess is there are a lot of 16/17 year olds who are approaching eighteen who probably won't get round to doing it. The Electoral Commission say it will take around 30% of people off the Electoral Register, and it will probably be the sort of people who need their voice to be heard, young people, often people with mental health problems, older people, people who are in community living, or who live a lifestyle where they move around. In practice it's a lot of people who vote Labour, so they know what they are doing."

Sir Peter Bottomley MP

"I hope to be in Westminster or Worthing – holding the same role, as MP for Worthing West. Fortunately they are not proposing any changes to my boundary, I want to continue to show that being a Member of Parliament is a worthwhile thing. When they restarted some kind of recognition of the honours service in the political system, they chose me because they didn't want to spend an extra ten minutes finding someone who was duller and safer. The reason they gave it to me was for public, rather than political service. If you are in a position where you can help people, you can do that by being a Minister a friend, or a neighbour, but MPs do it for everyone – which sounds like a bit of a bumper sticker, but I would like to carry on doing so, if the good Lord, the doctor and wife allow me *(laughter)*."

Ben Bradshaw MP

"Well politics is one of those careers where it is not possible to look that far ahead, if you are someone like me who doesn't have a safe seat. I tried very hard to win my seat, and to keep my seat. I have a small majority now, and depending on the outcome of the next election, I would hope to still be here. Obviously if I am still here I hope to be here under a Labour Government, and who knows, maybe back in Government myself, that's what I would like to happen. But I am afraid that gift is not in my hands, it's in the hands of the great British Public."

Kevin Brennan MP

"I'd see myself still in the House of Commons, if re-elected after the next election, hopefully with us back in Government, and hopefully working for that Government. I'm in my fifties now, and you do think how long will you stay in this place for, but I think I have two or three elections left in me yet.

"I am still hoping to be rock star too, but it hasn't happened yet, although there is still time.

(absolutely)

It's an interesting question, because I used to teach, there is nothing so ex as an ex MP. It's actually very difficult for some colleagues, because when you go into politics, you step off whatever career ladder you may have been on, if you are not one of these people who have just worked in politics all your life, you step off that ladder, and into a world where when you finish, it's probably going to be because you have lost your seat. So you come out of your job as a loser, you've been sacked if you like, from a job where you can't apply for another one just like it, you've probably lost many years of your career path, what would I have been, a head teacher by now probably if I had stayed in education, a much better paid job than I do in practice. But I couldn't go back into that, if I went back into teaching, although I loved it, I couldn't realistically go back into the classroom and pick up my career as before.

"I met a guy who used to be an MP after the 2005 election who had lost his seat, and he was walking up Whitehall, I said where you going, and he said to meet the Chief Whip (who at that time was Hilary Armstrong), to have a chat about things. I said what you doing now, this guy had been a university lecturer before, and he said well I am trying to find a job, I've applied for all sorts of things, and now I've applied for a job as a bus driver. So I think it's a real issue for people, if you come into this world, what do you do when you come out of the other end. Now if you are lucky enough to keep your hand in like some lawyers do, but that's frowned upon more these days about having an outside interest. Although my personal view is that it can be quite a healthy thing to have some other interest that you could pursue if you came out."

Andrew Bridgen MP

"As Napoleon said in every soldier's back pack there is a Field Master's baton. I would like to be the Business Secretary. Having grown a business from one member of staff to two hundred and seventy, I think I would have a good appreciation. It's the Private Sector that generates all the taxes that keep everything else going. As I have said in the Chamber the business of business is business and the business of Government is creating a situation where business can thrive. We need to nurture business as it pays for everything else, and in this current economic climate things are pretty grim. If we can get the business through this, that is honestly the goose that lays the golden egg. If we kill it, there won't be any more golden eggs, so I think that is a crucial job."

Philip Davies MP

"I would like to still be the MP for Shipley in five year's time, but that seems to be not an option, as the Shipley constituency will not exist if the Boundary Commission get their way."

Gloria De Piero MP

"Some people think that I am really ambitious, I am not. Being an 'important' person doesn't fulfill me, so I really just want to keep feeling like I do every time I go to Nottinghamshire. Apart from that, I don't have any grand plans, I just want to keep sticking up for my community."

Stephen Dorrell MP

"My father always taught me that a career is something that you look back over, you do your job because you want to, you feel that you can contribute, and don't worry about where you will end up in five years time, because you will end up just wishing your life away. It's advice that I have always tried to follow."

Michael Dugher MP

"I would like to see us, Labour, in Government that's the most important thing, it's the only thing that matters. I can continue doing the best job I can in the constituency, where I can make a real difference, but to be able to make a really big difference you have got to be in Government. So we need to work really hard over the next three years to persuade people who had lost faith with us, lost trust in us, and new people as well to put their trust in us because we have got to get back into Government. I think that should be what motivates all of us."

Natascha Engel MP

"I don't know, I think it all really depends on what happens with the coalition politics. I love doing the job I am doing, the Backbench

Business Committee, it's about giving backbenchers of all political persuasions a voice. It's been really interesting getting to know the other parties, and the committee has given backbenchers a real boost. Certainly from the people that I speak to, and from my own perspective, I love being a backbencher now, whereas before you kind of felt like you were waiting for someone to pluck you out from obscurity *(laughter)* now it has much more become a job in itself, it's brilliant, it's really brilliant. I get re-elected at the beginning of every session, so in a way I hope I am still there in five years, cos I really love it!"

Andrew George MP

"Probably as a curmudgeonly, awkward, rebellious, trouble making back bencher, as I am now."

John Glen MP

"I hope I will be really established as an excellent constituency MP, and in time that I would be able to make a contribution in national politics, whether it be on an issue, or as a Minister or an assistant to a Minister. I am quite realistic about that, I mean I started in active politics in the 1997 election where a good friend of mine lost his seat up in the North East, and frankly there have been lots of disappointments along the way. I have seen so many disappointments, I am in this for the long haul, and I don't have any fixed expectations of advancement or whatever, because I want to make a meaningful contribution. That may be on a single issue that might emerge, or it might be that I am given an opportunity to serve in the Government, either one would be attractive. What's important is that I continue to feel that I am making a worthwhile contribution, both to my constituency primarily, but I also feel I have something to give more broadly."

Zac Goldsmith MP

"It is impossible to know where politics will take me. I am a committed and active backbencher, doing my best to push issues I believe in, to hold Government to account and to represent my constituents. If I stand for election again, and if I am elected, I suspect I will do the same, but better."

Oliver Heald MP

"Well I would like to still be here, representing North East Hertfordshire in whatever form it is then, after any boundary changes. They are saying that 80% of it will be under a new name, but it will be basically the same area, and I am hopeful that I will get the nomination for there. It is disruptive. I have parts of my constituency that I have represented for fifteen years, being put elsewhere, and all those friendships and campaigning, and occasions where you have done something in a civic capacity, all that builds a relationship, you get to know them and they get to know you, and to break that is damaging."

Dan Jarvis MBE MP

"Well it's 2012 now, I'm going to be doing everything I can to represent my constituents and to hold this Government to account until we have a General Election which I hope my party will win. Therefore Labour will be in Government in 2015, and I really hope that I will be given the opportunity to serve in that Government. So in five years time, I hope to be still here as the MP for Barnsley, but also doing a job to support a Labour Government, with my kids having moved on five years to be in Secondary School, thinking about their longer term futures. One of the frustrating things about Opposition is you haven't got the ability to change things, you can hold the Government to account, but it's being in Government that gives you the opportunity to make an even greater contribution. So I hope in five years time I will be able to do that."

Liz Kendall MP

"I honestly don't think about that, I just want to do a good job for my constituency and in my national role, at the same time as staying as normal as I can, getting the right balance, as well as doing the job as well as I can, seeing my mum, my dad and my friends."

Sadiq Khan MP

"Hopefully less grey than I have turned recently, with less wrinkles, and less black bags under my eyes! In five years time I would want there to be a Labour Government, making the quality of life of the people of Tooting better. It's not about what job I've got, it's about what I am able to do. If you are able to influence lawmakers, to make laws that you think are good that's the great thing. So in five years time, I would like to see a Labour Government in the second year of our term trying to help young people get jobs, get a good start in life, go to university, get an apprenticeship. Try to make sure that doctors and nurses have the right tools and skills to be good ones, and just generally making sure that there is hope rather than despair."

Ivan Lewis MP

"With Man. City having won at least three Champions Leagues *(laughter)*. That's a really good question and I don't know. I hope my party will be back in power. Whether I am or not is a different matter. I hope that is the case, but the opportunity to serve your party or country in whatever way is an honour. Being a Minister, a Shadow Minister or in the Shadow Cabinet are all really important, but backbench MPs can also make a contribution."

Caroline Lucas MP

"In Parliament surrounded by more elected Greens, I hope! And still fighting hard for constituents in Brighton Pavilion, making real progress on improving everyday life for people in the city."

Nicky Morgan MP

"I don't know, in five years time we will have had the General

Election, and I very much hope that I will still be Member of Parliament for Loughborough, that we are still in Government, and I would love to be doing something in Government. Alternatively, if that's not an option and it's not my choice, I would like to be doing something really worthwhile on the backbenches. I always said that I wanted to be Loughborough's voice at Westminster, and I would like to continue to be that loud and clear voice."

Greg Mulholland MP

"In politics it doesn't make sense to be looking ahead 5 years. We have an election between now and then and it is complacent and foolish to look beyond it. All I know is how old I should be and my children, where they will be up to at school etc and that is what matters. What I am focused on now is achieving all I can as an MP and a campaigner in the next few years, so that I am challenging and changing things for the better."

Jason McCartney MP

"Hopefully at Westminster, having just been re-elected as the Member of Parliament for Colne Valley. Look anyone can work it out, I have been voting, I wouldn't say against the Government, but instead for my constituents, so I don't expect to get the call from the Prime Minister at any time. I get my satisfaction, my thrill from looking after my constituents. If I can go on and be a good hard working local MP for the next couple of decades, I would look back at my time with a lot of pride after all, I am not some London barrister who has been floated in by the party."

Chi Onwurah MP

"I would hope to still be the MP for Newcastle Central, hopefully in Government, but the most important thing for me is to be still representing the people of Newcastle."

Yasmin Qureshi MP

"Well, how honest should I be now *(laughter)*. I would like to see myself in a Ministerial position because you can change things at that level, and therefore, yes, I would like to see that. But if it doesn't happen, I'm not one of those people who will sit in the corner and cry. I actually think that the job of an MP is a pretty good one anyway with how you can serve your constituents. I am not sure that anything else I ever do will be able to beat that."

Stephen Pound MP

"In an allotment, outside a shed, smoking a pipe and being a really miserable, grumpy old sod *(laughter)*. And I'm going to sit there saying 'don't ya talk to me like that', 'in my day we had real music – *Smack My Bitch Up* by Prodigy, it had real lyrics, none of this modern stuff' *(laughter)*. 'Now get orf my allotment!' No, no I'll be gone in five years time, I'm too old now mate. You know I don't know, I said to two of my girlfriends the other night *(laughter)* I said this will never stand up in court *(laughter)*. My powers are not what they once were."

John Redwood MP

"One of the pleasures of my job is I have no idea what I will be doing in five years time. I would like still to be the MP for Wokingham, as much remains to be done."

Jacob Rees-Mogg MP

"I want to carry on being returned for North East Somerset, that's what I love. My family live in the area that I represent, have done for hundreds of years, and one of my favourite stories, and I tell everyone this, so I will tell you about it as well. One of my first events was a coffee morning, and a lady who must have been ninety came up to me, Mr Rees-Mogg, I used to know your father, and he was a very serious little boy. Now there aren't many people who refer to my father as a serious little boy in recent years *(laughter)*, and when I told him about this, he knew exactly who I meant. She had been a great friend of his sister's when they were school-children, and you feel so much part of a continuing community. So as long as I can represent North East Somerset, I am happy."

Jonathan Reynolds

"Most of all I would like to be re-elected, the last Election was really hard, and I would like to be returned with a certain degree of enthusiasm, to have made an impact. So the top of my list is very definitely to be recognised as a good constituency MP, not just in the results but for people to speak highly of me, like they do of my predecessor James Parnell. Getting that positive word of mouth would be nice. I think if you are really serious about some of the issues locally, you do also want to put those further up the national agenda. As much as I love being the local MP with all those local campaigns, you are not just a super councillor, the whole system works by you taking on things beyond your parish.

"I have been a Whip for the Labour Party which was great, and I am now Ed Milliband's PPS. To be PPS to the Leader is quite prestigious, you get a seat at the table at the Shadow Cabinet, you see a side of it in Westminster, how the Leader's Office works that few others see, unless they work in it. So it's really good. I would like to do this job for Ed, gain more experience and try to support him, and then maybe take on more of a Spokesperson role. I didn't know Ed at all previously to this, I had worked for David, and it says a lot of the man, Leaders have two PPSs – John Denham is his other, a really close ally of Ed and one of the first people to support him, but he has me as well, and I have enjoyed getting to know him. Whenever I go to places to do speeches not so much now, as he is ahead in the polls, but at the start when people didn't know so much about him, I would say don't under-estimate this guy."

Derek Twigg MP

"That's a really good question again, you think of some really hard ones. *(laughter)* To be quite frank I haven't given it any thought. I would still like to be doing a job that is helping people and making a difference to them, and working to represent my community, because my job is really important, because it's not just any seat, it's my constituency."

Charles Walker MP

"Sitting hopefully in this office, and if I am still here I would love to be the Member of Parliament still for Broxbourne, it's a job I love very much. I hope that we will have got rid of many of the discriminations against people with mental illness, the discriminations such as a very high bar to serving on a jury, being a school governor, sitting on company boards, and of course being a Member of Parliament. And the more we do on this, because as you know there is a Bill being brought forward by Lord Stevenson in the Lords, which hopefully when he's done that a Private Member's Bill will be brought in the House of Commons to end these discriminations. But the more we look at it, the more of these discriminations we find in the areas of business and education, we started off with four, it looked like then at one stage we were going to get three, and now I think we are up to seven. That sends out a very negative message. Not that a lot of people know about these discriminations, they tend to know about jury service and being an MP, but actually in turning over these discriminations we will send out a very positive message to people, that being mentally ill isn't something to be ashamed of."

Phil Wilson MP

"Hopefully here. In five years time which will be 2017, we will be halfway through a Labour Government, that's where I want to be."

Rosie Winterton MP

"Well I would hope to still be the Member of Parliament for Doncaster Central, because that will obviously be post election, and to be a member of the Parliamentary Labour Party which would be the governing party. It would obviously then be up to the Labour Prime Minister to decide if he wanted me to be a Minister, and that's what I hope will happen, but obviously that depends on the electorate deciding if they want us to be in power, whether they will put their faith in us."

John Woodcock MP
"The MP for Barrow-in-Furness, that is my focus, to ask people to re-elect me, and I very much hope they will stick with me at the next Election. I have got to convince them that I am doing a good job for them, and standing up for them both in Parliament and at home."

This was a hard question for many of the MPs to answer, because as politicians, their future is not in their hands. Normally that will be for the electorate to decide, but also on this occasion, the Boundary Commission will have a major influence. I have talked about this boundary change issue elsewhere in Commons People, but perhaps it is worth repeating. The hard of thinking might think it is a good idea to have less MPs, but in my humble opinion, it most certainly is not. It will damage our democracy and reduce the amount of time an MP will have for each of his/her constituents. I think what Paul Blomfield has to say on this issue is really interesting. But the really sad thing is, I wouldn't mind betting that the majority of the great British Public have no idea that these boundary changes will happen. Neither will they realise or care how it will impact on their MPs ability to represent them effectively.

One of the most thought provoking contributions to this chapter comes from Kevin Brennan, though I suspect it will not be met with much sympathy from the public.

Undoubtedly the most amusing contribution not surprisingly comes from Stephen Pound. What can I say? I just love that man, and it's great that so many of his colleagues do too.

Once again there are a couple of candidates for the last word. In five years time, Sadiq Khan wants to be making sure that there is hope rather than despair. Jason McCartney wants to continue to be a good hard-working local MP, as does Jonathan Reynolds. But you know, the image of Stephen Pound's allotment works for me...

Ivan Lewis

We are imperfect. We cannot expect perfect government.
William Howard Taft

CHAPTER NINE

Boundary Changes

You will have noticed the references to boundary changes within this book, I had not intended to feature a chapter on this subject, but the more I thought about it, the more I thought it was important to give the subject an airing, as I truly believe the reduction in the amount of MPs is a blow to democracy, and does us all a great disservice.

Dave Anderson MP

"It's deliberate, we said why don't you keep the same number of MPs but just divvy the numbers up better. They said no, we need to get rid of fifty MPs to save costs. The government want to cut the MPs but at the same time put 147 new Lords in."

Andrew Bridgen MP

"Under the boundary changes my seat won't exist anymore. We are being cut in half, so there won't be a N.W. Leics. seat, I shall be the last MP for there."

What will you do then?

"Well until the next General Election, I am elected as the Member for N.W. Leics., and my job is to represent the people of N.W. Leics. to the best of my ability, I intend to do that until the next General Election or I am told otherwise. So I don't know, the Boundary Review won't become law for another eighteen months to two years. A week is a long time in politics. But I won't be drawn on saying whether I am going to stand for one end of the constituency or the other, because it's completely wrong, you are writing off 50% of your electorate right away, and I don't think it's right at this stage to get involved in any of that. We will just have to wait and see what happens. But I voted for boundary changes, so I support the idea that people should have roughly the same number of the electorate, because I think that is democratically fair, but when your constituency becomes the victim of a boundary change you don't particularly like, you become very defensive about your constituency, it's where I live, it's where my business is, it's very dear to me. But it's a bit like voting for something you believe in, like the spending reductions, everyone's in favour unless they affect them, aren't they? That really doesn't stand up does it? You can't say that. So I can't really vote for changes and equalising the size of constituencies, and a reduction in the number of MPs to reduce the cost of Parliament, well if that then affects me adversely, I can't say that I have a problem with it can I?"

I think a reduction in the amount of MPs really is a blow to democracy in as much as it being more difficult for me as a constituent to see my MP if he has a larger number of constituents. There shouldn't be less MPs there should be more.

"I think the number of MPs has varied over the years from five hundred and fifty to six hundred and fifty. We have as many MPs as we have ever had, it's not that many years ago that we only had six hundred. You are going to have around 100,000 people per MP excluding children which is a reasonable amount of people. Currently my electorate is about 71,800, and if you add the children in probably about 85,000/90,000. So it's potentially a 10% increase in your workload. At a time when we are looking to make efficiency savings, that's not unreasonable for any enterprise or endeavour to have to deliver a 10% efficiency saving, and that's all that is being asked. And with the current standing of MPs in this country, I don't think that anyone will have any sympathy for MPs and their staff having to work 10% harder, will they?"

Philip Davies MP

If my memory serves me right your constituency is in danger with the boundary changes isn't it?

Yes it's being abolished. I don't know what I will do yet, there may not be anywhere to stand, I need to see what the final decision of the boundary commission is. I really have three realistic choices, one is to stand down, the second is, two of my best wards go into the Keighley constituency, but that already has a Conservative MP called Kris Hopkins, so I could by rights challenge him for the nomination for the new constituency, but obviously two thirds of the new constituency would be his, so it would be unlikely I would beat him. Me and him are like chalk and cheese in our opinions, he has never voted against the Government, where as I regularly do, so I could do that. Or the third option is a third of my constituency goes into Bradford West so I could stand against George Galloway. For a parliamentary democracy to work, everyone has got to feel that at least one person is speaking up for them.

But the less MPs there are, the more people they will have to deal with, the more people they have to deal with, the less time they will have to deal with them, we need our MPs to have the time to deal with us.

"I totally agree, I voted against reducing the number of MPs in Parliament, I don't agree with it all. I think whatever problems the public have with MPs they are not going to be solved by making MPs more remote from them. So I was totally against that. But it's happening now, and we are going to have fifty less MPs, and it looks as though I'm going to be one of them. I don't know what I'll be doing. If I was here, I would still be on the back benches, holding the Government to account, or whoever happens to be in Government."

Oliver Heald MP

I wonder if there are people out there who may have voted for a Conservative MP, and due to boundary changes may end up with a Labour MP?

"That could easily happen. It's not happened recently, but there would have been times where that has happened. In the Stevenage constituency which has often been Labour, and parts of the area around it have often been moved in and out."

Sadiq Khan MP

The hard of thinking may say, oh great fifty less MPs. It's not good it's a blow for democracy as far as I can see.

"Let me tell you why I am so angry about that. If you speak to people like Tony Blair or Neil Kinnock, even Conservative MPs or Liberals, David Steele, they will if they are honest, say to you, when they were first elected in 1979 or 1983 or 1974, they didn't work as hard as the current MPs, they didn't do surgeries, go out and meet constituents, do e-news, make visits, they admit that we work really hard. If you compare this country to others, France, Italy, Germany they have different tiers of Government, so you have your local councillor, you have your regional rep, you have your federal stuff, your city stuff, and your MPs are up here. They have far more tiers of devolved politicians than we do which means the work is divied out. You as a citizen feel empowered. In this country a lot of it is Whitehall controlled. So of course we have councillors but they have very little power, very few cities have mayors with executive powers. No regional government, Scotland and Wales have devolved powers, but no more regional government, so just the councillors and the MPs. Each MP has to service around 72,000 voters. In Tooting, there are 100,000 people, although of course some of them are children, about 72.500 voters, so it's not physically possible to service all of those people, however diligent and hard working you are. I have regular surgeries which are always packed out, I get emails all the time, I have a budget with which I am allowed to employ staff with, but none of my staff are paid well. So all of the budget is used up trying to pay staff, and they work all sorts of hours trying to service my constituents. It's not surprising that citizens get cynical when their MP can't deliver or respond quickly enough.

"Tomorrow is a really important vote on the Health and Social Care Bill that the Government is trying to get through by the back door, in my words trying to privatise the NHS. But there is also a backbench MP Tory Nadine Dorries trying to get through an amendment about abortion. So I have been inundated with emails from people in my constituency who are unhappy with her amendment which is fair enough, but I just don't have enough time today to respond to all of them. So at the moment there are 650 MPs which the Government is trying to reduce to 600, and before the manifesto, what the Tories wanted to do was reduce the number of MPs by 10% which is 65 – o.k.? which goes to 585. The Liberal

Democrats wanted to reduce the MPs down to 500. If you did a straw poll of your mates they would say reduce it to fifty or to ten. So why have they settled on 600 then? The answer is the number of reductions that does most damage to Labour is bringing it down to 600, so for partisan reasons they have chosen this number. What it will lead to it is what's your seat called? Barnsley Central. It's got an identity you know where it is. But they are going to have a crude mathematical formula to decide what a seat is with no necessary local connection. Literally you will get seats that go across rivers, across geographical boundaries, and fewer MPs. I'm not saying I am work shy, but there will be less Members of Parliament with more people to look after, and also no sense of identity at a time when cohesion is so important. So the Government may think they can earn brownie points with the public, but at the same time they have all these new unelected peers in the House of Lords. Where's the sense in that?"

Nicky Morgan MP

This thing about MP's being reduced from 650 to 600, a lot of people may think that is a good thing, but those of us who take an interest in politics know that's it's not. We are keen to create a greater understanding with the general public about MPs. What do you think can be done to do that?

"It is interesting because things like e-petitions have taken off, and I think if people felt that their voice had more of an influence it would make a difference. It's very interesting the whole what is an MP there for? and the fact is you wear lots of different hats, you are there as a local champion, a champion for your constituency in Westminster. Obviously you are elected under a party banner, on a manifesto, although it's been a bit tougher this time, and you are there to help the Prime Minister and the Government implement that, so it's juggling all of that. It's explaining to people. I get people saying to me who are perfectly well educated, do you spend much time in London? And I think yes of course I do because that where the House sits, but why would people know if they are not that aware of what MPs do?"

Derek Twigg MP

Will your constituency be affected by the boundary changes?

"It will be yes. In not too big a way, but two wards will be taken out of Widnes, and put into another constituency which is bizarre, although we gain a couple of wards in Runcorn, we lose what are two historical ones in Widnes."

Dave Anderson makes an interesting point when he talks about the Government getting rid of fifty MPs to save money, and yet they want to increase the Lords by one hundred and forty seven, a little disengenous don't you think.

No doubt Andrew Bridgen is right when he doubts there will be any sympathy for MPs, but there ought to be concern. Personally, I don't believe that this has anything to do with efficiency.

And Philip Davies is absolutely right when he say "I think whatever problems the public have with MPs, they are not going to be solved by making MPs more remote from them."

But isn't it interesting two Conservative MPs with opposite opinions, but both make a reasonable case.

Anyway, I am breaking my own rule, and getting far too political. So the last words on the subject go to Philip Davies and Nicky Morgan, both Conservatives by the way. Philip Davies "For a parliamentary democracy to work, everyone has got to feel that at least one person is speaking up for them." Nicky Morgan "If people felt their voice had more of an influence, it would make a difference."

Jacob Rees-Mogg

*No man is good enough to govern another man without
that other's consent.*
Abraham Lincoln

CHAPTER TEN

Work Experience of MPs

*Do you think the work experience and background of MPs is
representative of the general public?*

*Some of the criticisms often aimed at our MPs are that they are
out of touch, have never done a proper job, and do not live in the real
world, so I thought it may be interesting to ask them what they
thought.*

Ben Bradshaw MP

"Well it's not as representative as I would like it to be. There is a
surfeit of lawyers, journalists and increasingly, career politicians,
who have been involved in Politics as students, who have worked
for the major parties, in the research department at central office,
then they get selected, and get a seat and they haven't really done
anything else. I think that's a pity. I think the bigger challenge is how
you change that, and how you ensure that you get a better cross
section of candidates. We have had some success with that in the
Labour Party, with women and particularly ethnic minorities, but I
think it's a constant battle to ensure that political representatives are
truly representative of the constituencies that send them here. The
advantage of our system of course, is whatever your background,
you always go back every weekend to your constituency, and you
are meeting a variety of your constituents which does give you a
good feel for what their concerns are, and what their life is like."

Kevin Brennan MP

"Well they are not an exact representation of the public, that's obvious.

You just have to look at the statistics for where they are educated, what their careers have been and so on. But I do think being elected from a constituency, and having that constituency link, and regular contact with the public means that they are not as odd as people in the House of Lords are for example *(laughter)* some of them are very brilliant people, but are utterly out of touch with what's happening down on the ground because they don't have contact. I was listening to one on the radio yesterday, and he was asked how do you know what people think about House of Lords reform, he said, well people tell me these things on the golf course, and you think what planet is he on, if he thinks that is how you find out about public opinion. So they are not representative, but I think to a certain extent you have to keep your feet on the ground as an MP because you are dealing with the general public all the time in your constituency."

Andy Burnham MP

"Probably not, I suppose people may look at me and say I've not had a career in law or medicine, I have come through the political route, but my worry would be less about that and more about the backgrounds of MPs. Are they from all parts of the country, from all class backgrounds. I don't think it's generally the way for people in their fifties any more. I think there are a lot of demands as to how hard MPs will work, it's becoming a younger person's game. Personally, I don't see myself being an MP all my life, I'll do a proper shift but then at some point, I think it's healthy to say that someone else should have a go at this. So I don't see this as all I will ever do. My take on it is I might do this earlier on, and then later on do something different, I think that way I will be able to do more and give more. So there is a trade off. If you do it earlier in your career you get the energy, if you do it later in your career you bring the experience. I feel I can do more by doing it this way around. But I also don't think this should be the kind of job where people just dig in and stay forever, we need more turnover in the House of Commons."

Do you think the background of MPs is representative of the general public?

Ann Coffey MP

"It's very difficult when you have 650 MPs to get a representative of every diversity that the British Community is these days. I think there has probably been an over representation of certain professions, there always has been, that has always been a criticism of Parliament. But I think it's good that we are getting younger people, we are obviously getting more representation from ethnic minority communities, and more women, that's very important. Not enough, but more. But I do think that we need to do more to make Parliament more representative, also in terms of occupation."

Rosie Cooper MP

"Sadly I think there are too many career politicians, I've always wanted to be in politics, but while I was a councillor in Liverpool, I always held down a full time job outside it. Not only did I do my full time job, I was on the Board of the Deaf Centre, I did stuff for the Blind School, I was involved in the Roy Castle Foundation. I really got involved in the commercial and social sides of the city. My city mattered to me. So when I see so many young people who have had no business career, who have just been researchers, I worry that when they become Ministers, the decisions they make are distant from the real world. When I worked for Littlewoods I was Corporate Communications Officer for the whole Group, lawyers would stop you doing stuff, not make things happen."

Gloria De Piero MP

"No I don't. I meet amazing mums in the local mums group, and I think my god, you would tell them a thing or two, and they say no we couldn't do it, but by the end of the conversation they were like 'well actually... '. I am trying to work out how it got to this stage where we speak in techno jargon, and everyone speaks on the tele and sounds like an expert, rather than they have a real passion. It doesn't sound like anyone wants to change the world anymore. I'm not saying I want to return to those big ideological battles, because some people got very very hurt in some of those, but there is something about the language going funny somewhere along the line, and somehow we have ended up sounding like managers, experts, civil servants, think tankers, and that isn't good for politics, I think it switches people off."

Stephen Dorrell MP

"The answer to that as a matter of fact is no. MPs have a relatively untypical range of backgrounds. I think perhaps there is another question of whether it matters. Today's generation of MPs is drawn from a narrow band of experience, and I think it is true and it does matter that there are fewer and fewer people, who arrive in the Palace of Westminster having had experience of real life outside the political world. That's something that I think impoverishes the political process, because the more that it is made up of people who were already involved in politics as I was at University, and then as political researchers, they are talking about life outside, which they have never lived."

Michael Dugher MP

"I think it is more representative than it is given credit for. So a lot of people point to people like me, for instance Andrew Neil did that programme about 'Posh and Posher', and actually there was a lot of good stuff in that, he did show just how many members of the Government are privately educated, or how many went to one school, so he did highlight something. But in order to try and balance it he said Labour are no better because their new intake is full of ex-Special Advisors. Well actually I would have thought that there were as many ex Union Officials to be honest. The people I knock around with are people who have been councillors, lawyers, or teachers, who have done all kinds of different jobs, and actually even if you look at some of our Oxbridge lot there are some who were working class kids. If you take Gloria for instance, she grew up in a council house, in a workless household in Bradford, and has

Do you think the background of MPs is representative of the general public?

done very well, ended up being on the tele, but she came from a pretty humble background. My own background, in the end, my mum went back to education and did O.U. and became a teacher, but actually as a kid, I grew up in a pit village in South Yorkshire, with a pretty working class background, and a lot of the Labour MPs I knock around with are from pretty run of the mill, normal, modest backgrounds. I think we could do better. We made great strides in terms of Labour getting more women involved, more people from ethnic minorities, but I still think we need to improve that. We need more working class kids coming into Parliament, so I'm not complacent, there is a lot more that can be done, but sometimes it's slightly over stated how non representative we are."

Natascha Engel MP
"Definitely not. People really make an issue of this that Parliament isn't representative of the general public, and I understand because we are representatives, but I had the same thing when I was at the TUC as an organiser, there was a big thing that we should be more like the people we were recruiting. And I understand that, I think if you had nobody from any ethnic minorities, no women, nobody with disabilities, everyone from a certain class I think the House would be a poorer place. But that doesn't mean we have to have exactly the same percentage as in the general public, because I think that is the reverse, and it's quite patronising. When I was an organiser I was always a bit uncomfortable if I was recruiting someone in a wheelchair, does that mean I should have been in a wheelchair, well no, not really. It doesn't mean that I represent anybody less well. The reasons why I do or don't represent people well isn't because I am not like them, it's because I am either good or not very good at representing them. For example, I am not from Derbyshire, I am originally from Berlin in Germany, so quite far away from people's everyday experience locally, I think if I had the choice I would wish I was from Derbyshire and I would probably make a better MP if I were from the place that I represent, but the

other side of it is that I work so much harder at making sure that I understand where people are coming from, and what their experiences are. I feel really privileged to have had the experiences that I have in Derbyshire, it's been amazing, the most eye-opening learning experience I have ever had in my life. You don't usually get that sort of thing when you get to my age *(laughter)* it's absolutely incredible. So really to get back to your question about representativeness, there are two sides to it, but the answer is definitely no, absolutely not."

Andrew George MP

"The more egotistical side of the public yeah *(laughter)*. There is a good cross section. There seems to be a higher percentage of public school, wealthier people, and you tend to find they become a mutually self-selecting group. I realise I am not the first ever to identify that. So yes we are not wholly representative, but there is a moderate cross section of professionals, and to a certain extent, society as a whole."

Zac Goldsmith MP

"I think we need to open the process of selection up, ideally through Open Primaries. That may or may not bring about a more varied Parliament, but regardless, it would ensure that voters are represented by people of their choosing. I don't support any form of quota or rigging, and prefer that people can choose the very best candidates to stand in their constituencies."

Liz Kendall MP

"No, not at all, it's not. When you are in the House of Commons, despite the big improvements with more women MPs, which I do have to say Labour drove. When I go into the House of Commons, I don't see a representativeness certainly of my constituency, there aren't nearly enough MPs from minority ethnic backgrounds. It is still very dominated by middle and upper class rather than working class – Parliament should be more representative. It's for all sorts of reasons, partly because we politicians haven't done a good enough job showing that politics is about the issues that people care about. So many people say that they are not interested in politics but they are interested in jobs and things like that, that's our responsibility, and also in our own parties that if it costs so much money to be selected as a candidate, that people don't have that kind of support. There is lots more we can do to change it."

Sadiq Khan MP

"No way. You are lucky I didn't start laughing. If you look at Parliament now in 2012, arguably at the last General Election in 2010 we have become more representative than ever before. There were big changes in '97 when Labour won with a big landslide, and we had lots of women in winnable seats, on all women shortlists. But even in 1997, out of 650 MPs, about 100 were women, one out of six. Now in 2010, you have a handful of ethnic minorities, you have a small number of people who are disabled, you still have less than one in six MPs who are women. You could count on one hand the number of working class MPs, or the number of MPs who have admitted having a mental health problem. I think the more representative lawmakers are, the better legislation they pass. You look at the Executive, the Government, I'm not saying if you are rich you don't understand what it's like to be poor, all I am saying is your ability to empathise is more difficult. The fact that I don't have mental health problems doesn't mean that I don't understand how people with mental health problems feel, because I have empathy, so I am not saying that, it would be far too simplistic. But unless the Government reflects our society, I think they do what we have done for hundreds of years and make laws that suit a minority of people.

"The history of our Parliament is Tony, until the 1920's women didn't have the vote, so why did the lawmakers have to make laws that were fair for women, until 150/200 years ago you had to be a property owner to vote, so the laws that were made benefitted them. In my view, the more you can get working class people and the more you can get women into Parliament (more than half of our population is women) yet only one in six parliamentarians are, the more you can get ethnic minorities into Parliament, the more you can get people who come from diverse backgrounds. I am not a big fan of people who dream of being an MP when they are seven years old, you need to have a life outside of politics, have life experiences, apply for a job, be made redundant, have other skills. I was a lawyer before I became an MP, we have lots of ex teachers here, and lots of ex journalists, and people who have worked in other walks of life like industry. It's very important."

Caroline Lucas MP

"Sadly no, not at all. There have been some improvements in recent years, with more MPs coming in from backgrounds other than the well-worn route from private education to Oxbridge then to political advisers. But with the current Cabinet dominated by millionaires and Eton-educated men, this certainly feels like a particularly male-dominated Government, progress would appear to have gone into reverse."

Nicky Morgan MP

"Probably not, because at the end of the day no normal people want to become Members of Parliament. *(laughter)* Most sensible people would think, not in a million years. I have friends who look at me and say, well I am very pleased you are doing it, but I couldn't possibly. But I do think there is a wide cross section of people here with a different variety of backgrounds. I know people always complain about those who have only done politics, and I do think that is a criticism that is well made, and it would be good if more people did things outside before they became MPs. You do need a sense of perspective to do this job."

Greg Mulholland MP

"Not as much as it could be, more work needs to be done, not only by political parties, but actually by society as a whole and through education, to make politics relevant to people so they want to take an interest and see it as a way they can challenge and change things and improve their local communities and society as a whole. This is why I go into schools, particularly primary schools, as often as possible to try to engage and enthuse our younger citizens."

Jason McCartney MP

"In my view as an insider now, I think that Parliament is much more representative of the country. Yes, some people are posh and went to private school, but in our society, some people are posh and went to private school. We have people who were in the military, and certainly on my side, we have three practising G.P.'s, Dr Daniel Poulter, Dr Phillip Lee, and Dr Sarah Wollaston, so when they are talking about the Health and Social Care Bill, they are talking from knowledge and real life experience. We have Sheryll Murray from Cornwall, whose husband sadly died last year on a deep sea fishing trawler, he was a trawlerman, so she has experienced personal tragedy, but now she speaks in the House of Commons on Fisheries issues with a personal life experience of that. We have people like Andy Percy, who was a school teacher in an inner city comprehensive in Hull. And again, people don't get that, everyone is stereotyped as public schoolboys and it is simply not true. There are a lot of down to earth people, although the media aren't interested in that. All they like is the posh boys and girls, but there is real life in there, and I can tell you we have a mixture, we have Muslim MPs we have MPs from different religious backgrounds, we have gay and lesbian MPs, and I think more than ever it now reflects real life society. In fact not all of the new MPs were young, there is a guy, Gordon Birtwistle, a Lib Dem MP for Burnley, I think he is nearly 70 and he was elected for the first time."

Stephen Pound MP

"Not remotely, absolutely not. It's totally unrepresentative. In 1997, there were two of us who came in here from a manual trade background, Clive Efford who was a cab driver and me. Everyone else were barristers, solicitors, teachers or university lecturers, and the place was crawling with them, absolutely crawling with them. Dennis Skinner did twenty one years down the pit, a lot of the South Yorkshire MPs were from the mines, in London we had a lot of T and G employees from the buses, quite a few who had come through the union. People have made a lot of fuss about gender balance, and about disability balance and I entirely agree with that, but class balance is important too. Maybe the working class doesn't exist anymore, but I think it does, and it deserves representation, which it doesn't have at the moment."

Yasmin Qureshi MP

"No it isn't, because a lot of them whether they come from the Labour Party or the Conservatives come from middle class, privileged backgrounds. Some aren't, but a lot are. That doesn't mean to say that they are any less sympathetic or attuned to the general public. I don't think you necessarily have to be born in difficult circumstances to fully appreciate when others are in bad situations. Sometimes you find that people who have been brought up in difficult circumstances and have done very well tend to be harsher against others, because they say well I've done it, why can't they? Whereas with others born into more comfortable environments, sometimes, I think maybe it's a guilty aspect, but you tend to feel more empathy with others less fortunate. So I don't necessarily think that MPs backgrounds are reflective of a cross section of our communities, but it doesn't mean to say that they can't represent the interests of those communities effectively."

Jacob Rees-Mogg MP

"Yes and no. I think they are representative in the sense that they are mainly available to the electorate, and most MPs are responsive to their electorate. Most MPs do their best to try and understand the different lives that their constituents lead. No, to the are MPs 'Joe Average'?, but the reason that is no, is there is no such thing as 'Joe Average', and I think it's a desperately condescending view to take that there is this middle figure who we are all trying to be. I have never met a constituent, or even a non constituent, who I thought was an average person. Everybody is extraordinary in their own particular way, and it's just a question of finding out what way that is."

Jonathan Reynolds MP

"No, I don't think anyone would say it was, and there are probably a few reasons for that. If you did it statistically on gender, ethnicity, and work background, you would probably get a very different House of Commons. I think that people need to appreciate that the job has massively changed through social media, the internet and people's expectations. Those famous old stories about Churchill going to his constituency once a year… the idea that you are sent off to Westminster and no-one expects to see you for four or five years has now completely gone. I guess backgrounds may well be different, I always think the number of lawyers thing is not a good measure because it's very different if you do criminal law for someone on legal aid to being a high end lawyer working on litigation for a top corporation. The thing about Law is you have to take fairly complex stuff and put it in simpler terms because that is what people pay you for, and for politics you have to understand and involve yourself in some quite high level debates, but then you have to explain the position on doorsteps, so there is a similarity and synergy there. Some people say there are not enough people from working class backgrounds there, now I find that a very difficult measure, as I would definitely say that I had a working class background, I went to a comprehensive school, etc, but I went to a red brick University and I've been to Law School. But the structure of society has changed, one of our former councillors who has just passed away, said to me that he didn't consider teachers to be working class, but these days most people wouldn't think that someone who had been a teacher is a fairly tough school had had a privileged background. So the perception has changed. There needs to be more diversification, but there is more than there was, even our Front Bench now, not everyone has been to Oxbridge, and people like Chuka Umunna went to Manchester with me, so it is getting more diverse. I think it looks more pronounced, because incredibly, and I don't know how it's happened because the Conservatives managed to get a cohort, not just from a single school but actually from a single year group. And also I guess that combined with the tax cut for high rate earners, it makes it look as though everyone is on a different planet.

"I do some mentoring for the Labour Party's future candidate programme, it's a new thing for people who want to develop their skills, they come forward with their CV's and the party picks a tranche of people, hooks them up with advice and that sort of thing. The Parties are definitely doing more these days to develop a more diverse range of people coming through. When I went for selection the Party were more interested that I had a commitment to the local area, and could make an impact, but I don't think what school or university I had been to had any bearing on it."

Charles Walker MP

"Definitely, definitely, absolutely, and I think that's very healthy for democracy in this country. We have people who come from successful backgrounds, the city, we have people who come from legal backgrounds, the stereotypical MP some may say. Of course all backgrounds need to be represented, and some are more than others. One of my dear colleagues, before she became an MP was a receptionist in a doctor's surgery, isn't that wonderful? She was a receptionist in a doctor's surgery who became a Member of Parliament. Now of course I am not diminishing the excellent work carried out by receptionists in doctors' surgeries, but it's a lovely thing to believe in and see happen, she was a local activist, she got involved in politics through campaigning for Cornish fishermen, while holding down her job and the surgery and she is now an MP. We still have a few ex coal miners here. We have people from all walks of life representing their constituents. Of course the middle class has expanded in this country, as John Prescott famously said, you will tend to see more MPs from a middle class background, but we have farmers, machinists, nurturers, we have doctors and nurses, we have all sorts of people here, that's healthy for democracy. Could the pool be wider, perhaps it could, and we need to be mindful how we do that by making sure that the best people get here, but I think people should not believe everything they read in the *Daily Mail*, we have a pretty healthy democracy, and some really good people serving in it."

Phil Wilson MP

"People say that there should be more working class MPs, but I don't actually know what that means, because people would see me as being middle class but my dad was a coalminer, and people move on. For me, I think it is the role of Labour politicians to improve of what's gone before, and if people improve their lot and become more middle class, what that means is the party itself has to change, not the people, because we have done what we said we would do. We have given them the NHS, we have given them comprehensive universal education, we have given them everything that people now take for granted, and it's very easy to lose that as we can see with what's happening with the NHS at the moment. I think what you need from politicians is, whatever their background, commitment, belief and a strength to continue on with it. I want to see more people from all kinds of backgrounds get involved. I think there is only 10% of MPs who haven't been to University, and I am one of them. But I want my son to go to University, so does that mean he shouldn't be an MP? You want better things for working class people, and if they become middle class, I think we have done our job really. Nothing's too good for the working class."

Rosie Winterton MP

"It could improve. I think what the Labour Party did when it was formed by the Trade Union Movement, it ensured that there was a far greater proportion of working class people, although I don't like the term, but there is no doubt that happened. Increasingly there has probably been a tendency for people to work in politics and then become Members of Parliament, and we have to make sure that we are able to ensure that we are properly representative, and I think we do need to work frankly with organisations like the Trade Unions to make sure that people are thinking about becoming an MP as one of their options, and encouraging people to do that."

John Woodcock MP

"No they're not and it's a real issue, and it's easy to say and has proved much harder to sort out. It matters that we are not a representative Chamber. There are too few women, there are too few disabled, there are two few ethnic minorities, there is not a broad spectrum of people from different backgrounds, with different professions. And while it is right that you want individual choice for the person you think is best for the job, if we are a Parliament that for whatever reason excludes particular groups of people, we are at severe risk of making bad decisions that don't reflect their interests. One of the things that has struck me is families for example. MPs moaning about their hours, about sitting late in the House of Commons aren't going to get any sympathy, understandably, but where it matters I think is if you are a young mum or a young dad, there is a real risk that many people with young families, if they see what the working culture is like, they will think they don't see how they could balance that with looking after their children, and so maybe it's not the right move, and we will lose out enormously if that is the case."

Does Ben Bradshaw have a point when he says, "You go back

to meetings with a variety of your constituents which gives you a good feel for what their concerns are", and does Andy Burnham have a point with his view that "if you do it earlier in your career you get the energy, if you do it later in your career, you bring the experience" Is it unreasonable to expect both?

As always Natasha Engel makes some thought provoking observations as does Jason McCartney, and certainly many of us would agree with Liz Kendall when she says "we politicians haven't done a good enough job showing that politics is about the issues that people care about" And does Yasmin Qureshi have a point when she says "sometimes you find that people who have been brought up in difficult circumstances and have done very well tend to be harsher against others, because they say, well I've done it, why can't they?"

Many of us raise concerns about the amount of lawyers in Parliament, but Jonathan Reynolds is right to point out the difference between lawyers and the work they do. Besides if all the lawyers and solicitors were like him, Sadiq Khan and Nicky Morgan, the world would be a far better place. Also interesting is the work that Jonathan Reynolds carries out mentoring future candidates. I never knew such a programme existed.

Perhaps one of the most important comments made on this subject is by John Woodcock when he talks about MPs moaning about long hours when they have young families, though not likely to get any sympathy. But isn't he right when he says it may deter people from entering politics and then we all lose out.

For what it's worth, I do believe we still have much to do in this area. It concerns me that there are far too many parliamentarians who have not worked outside of politics, but you know that is down to us, and the ball is very firmly in our court. We can effect change, that is of course if we can be bothered.

On many of my questions in this book, there has been general agreement amongst the MPs, irrespective of their political leanings, but you will have noticed that this question has produced some vastly different answers.

When I decided to ask this question, I was concerned it may not have encouraged particularly interesting answers, but actually the responses it has produced demonstrate perfectly why I feel there is a need for a book such as this.

I'll leave the last words to:-

Greg Mulholland – "More work needs to be done, not only by political parties, but actually by society as a whole."

Jacob Rees-Mogg "Everybody is extraordinary in their own particular way, and it's just a question of finding out what way that is."

and finally Phil Wilson "nothing's too good for the working class." Amen to that.

John Woodcock

A government that is big enough to give you all you want is big enough to take it all away.
Barry Goldwater

CHAPTER ELEVEN

Relaxing?

Many of us lead stressful lives these days, and contrary to what some may think, that includes MPs. Indeed there is a debate to be had as to whether we take enough interest in the mental health of our policy makers, given they make decisions that affect all of us, one thing is for sure, we flipping well ought to.

Anyway, here is what they had to say about what they do to relax.

Dave Anderson MP

"I've had a few problems lately because I've had a knee operation, but I do like walking. Aye, and to keep fit. I have done since I was a kid. I think you would find a lot of people who would understand, that the nature of the colliery villages were mostly rural if not semi rural for obvious reasons. My dad grew up in a time when they had nothing, and they lived off the fields, things like poaching were part and parcel of everyday life. So me dad loved the country side, and passed that down to me. People get quite shocked, particularly in the conservative part of the House that I'm not anti-shooting, I'm not particularly bothered about fox hunting, but normal hunting, shooting and fishing are fine even though I don't do much of them myself. I'm into caravanning, I bought a caravan in the Dales and spend a lot of time there. When we lived in Willington, I really wanted to live in Weardale but we could never quite afford it, so Willington was as close as we could get, but it meant I could be up there within ten minutes, instead of an hour."

"I also like drinking *(laughter)*. I like music, listening to anybody really, Jimmy Rogers, Hank Williams."

Paul Blomfield MP

"Apart from Sheffield United, one of the great things about Sheffield is its' proximity to the Peak District, I spend a lot of time walking, cycling, going to one of our two great theatres. We are going to see Journey's End at the theatre on Friday, it's about the First World War."

Sir Peter Bottomley MP

"Answer questions in interviews like this… *(laughter)*. I don't really get time off in that sort of sense. I love reading and I love buying books. I like collecting portraits of my wife, I have one over there. Occasionally being insulted by my grandchildren, the usual sort of things."

Ben Bradshaw MP

"Certainly as a Minister you never had much time for hobbies. I don't really have a strong football allegiance although I support Exeter City. I even stopped playing tennis which I used to do quite a lot. We walk, and tend to go for walking holidays, because we like to keep fit, and I cycle. I am a utility cyclist I cycle to and from work, and round my constituency. I do the minimum amount of gardening, just to keep the garden from becoming a jungle. One of the joys of not being a Minister anymore is having time to read novels and biographies again, not just government papers, which is what you spend all your time doing if you are a government minister. I also have occasional visits to the theatre and the opera."

Kevin Brennan MP

"Music is probably my first port of call, if I go home at the end of the week and it's been very stressful.

"Everything from people like David Bowie when I was growing up as a teenager, I can still remember picking the needle up and dropping it on to the vinyl on my copy of Ziggy Stardust with that drum beat, and changing it. That one record changed my world completely when I was a teenager. But I actually also do think it's to do with my origin and Welsh background. We used to live opposite a Church, and whenever there was some sort of event there, wedding, funeral whatever, they would all come back to our house, with a bottle of whisky and a crate of beer, they would all gather round while my mother made a stack of sandwiches and so on, and my father would go round the room, and everyone gathered in the room would give a song or recite a poem or something. And there was always the best of order for whoever it was. So I remember at a very early age I thought it happened in every house *(laughter)*. My oldest sister had a guitar too, so that was always lying around the house, so I picked that up and her boyfriend taught me a little bit when I was younger. Then one day my dad came home with a piano, he used to do things like that *(laughter)*, I don't know where he got it from, I think it had been thrown out of a working men's club or something like that. So I started playing on that.

"Music is definitely my therapy. For me to go home and sit at the piano, or knock out a song on the guitar, all the troubles of the world are forgotten. But I also love sport, and the cinema. I more often go to rugby, but football as well, I suppose for me being Welsh that rocks my boat."

Andrew Bridgen MP

"I used to be into fishing, I don't really have any time for any hobbies any more. I have two boys aged eleven and eight, the eleven year old is very into ponies, so I take him to Pony Club, show jumping and things like that, which is quite entertaining. My youngest is into Cubs and we sometimes go camping, so it's generally doing things with the children. We have been to a football match, to Villa Park, and it was supposed to be quite a good game it was 2-2 at the end, Aston Villa v Fulham, but I didn't get through the whole game without falling asleep *(laughter)*. I am actually hoping to take them to watch Leicester Tigers play, which is quite entertaining at times.

Generally there is often an event to go to on Saturday mornings, and then I do try to spend time with the family at weekend if I can.

"During my first year in Parliament I was so keen to make a good impression on the Electorate I went to everything. I was going to four or five things on a Saturday and a couple on a Sunday, there was hardly any time for a family life. I like cars, so I have a nice sports car that I drive sometimes, but I haven't even driven that for six weeks – it's an Aston Martin DB9, I like four wheel drives too. Sometimes I just go out and drive for ten or fifteen miles and don't go anywhere. I also have Donnington Race track in my constituency, so when that re-opened my Aston Martin was the first car to go around the track. We sometimes go to Donnington Park, and if we do go there I can generally wangle for them to take us a couple of laps round in the pace car. That's a very undulating track as well, most race tracks, most are flat aren't they, but that is very much up and down. I do like skiing too, I like things that really occupy you, and that you have to concentrate on."

Ann Coffey MP

"I enjoy quite a lot of things. Spending time in London makes it easy for me to see some very good films that I can't necessarily see in Manchester, I am a member of the British Film Institute, the other week I saw *Who's Afraid of Virginia Woolf*, so that's very relaxing, a very nice thing to do. And obviously I also have access to a lot of Galleries, I like visiting the TATE. I like reading and have a Kindle, so I can read any time and any place, and when I am travelling. I like knitting, I like walking, I like seeing friends for meals and general activities. I like to go on day visits to places, I enjoy visiting different towns and just spending the day there, looking at the architecture and things like that, so they are all very relaxing things to do.

"I like photography, I recently attended a course to improve my photography skills, I have a Nikon 5000, which is a good, bulky camera. I also always carry with me a little handbag camera because I like just taking shots of things, particular buildings in relation to each other, and there will be things I see when I am going over the Thames. So I have a vast collection of digital photographs from different places that I have been. I think they are great things for remembering, because I don't know about you, but my memory is not that good for recalling events, but if you have pictures they immediately take you back to the day spent at Brighton or the day spent in Oxford. What I need to do now is to go on a couple of courses to learn about a software package called Photoshop, so you can actually do things, change the colours, I think that would be an interesting development. I like sunsets and sunrises too. I have a wonderful picture that I took in Australia, in Fremantle, and it was taken on the beach as the sun was going down in Fremantle, with a seagull just flying across but what I really liked about it was that I knew as the sun was going down, it was rising in Great Britain on the other side of the world, and of course I wasn't there I was in the other place, but that was lovely, there is just something about the colours you get. I just loved the bird, because I just caught the bird in a nice position next to the sun which was setting."

Rosie Cooper MP

"I'm an Elvis fan, so I did a long tour of the deep south. I like films, I read biographies, political ones, although not just political ones, Katherine Hepburn for example. I am one of these people who always have a saying for example Katherine Hepburn in her biography, she came out with a quote which I think is fantastic – 'You can't sail a leaky ship, you either get out and swim or you row like hell'. Dr Phil, I love his attitude to stuff. Oprah, all of that. I don't read fiction, and I read too many newspapers."

Philip Davies MP

"I don't have much spare time, I am a workaholic. That's just me I enjoy working and I fret if I'm not. If work is piling up because I am not doing it, that would be a nightmare to me. I work to relax to some extent. But if I'm not working horse racing is my escapism. I went to the Races on Saturday with my kids, I forget about anything else that's going on. Horse racing is definitely what I do to relax."

Gloria De Piero MP

"Coronation Street, red wine, my partner. I'll put him above Coronation Street obviously, though not sure about the red wine *(laughter)*, friends. I don't do sport. I like being with my friends with lovely wine and lovely food… "

Michael Dugher MP

"I do have young kids so they do take up a lot of time. Music is massive to me, I used to play in lots of bands, and I have a house full of instruments. I am always buying new string instruments. I had a major gig last week in St. Helens – I was the support band for a 60th birthday. So I still play a lot, that is probably the other thing I do. It tends to be more for mates and do's but I still play, piano, guitar, bass, I'm always wandering in with a banjo, mandolin or ukulele. It's an acquired taste.

"The Beatles are definitely my favourite band. I listen to a lot of the old fashioned song writers like Sinatra and Ella Fitzgerald. All that Cole Porter and Sammy Khan. But I listen to a lot of new music too, it depends on my mood. Some days, you know, you get up and just think I have got to listen to a bit of Merle Haggard."

So Michael why don't you sing more?

"Well I'm busy in here… *(laughter)* they've got me voting at 10 o'clock at night, I can't be in Las Vegas… I do more now than I did a couple of years ago, because I have a bit more of a profile now so I get asked to do more locally. It's something I discovered when I was twelve, and I was actually a bit of a slow developer in truth, academically as well, and my mum who wasn't a teacher then, but who became one, always used to say if you find the talent, you then unlock the potential. So it's all that stuff about get the kid interested in sport, and they will go to school everyday, the kid who is interested in drama will get better at their English... I really believe that. I was really lucky in that I found I could play a bit, sing a bit, and it's been great for me."

Natascha Engel MP

"I was asked this in an interview before and I really struggled, I ended up saying well I go to bed early with a cup of tea and listen to Radio 4, but for god's sake don't tell anyone *(laughter)*, and of course they printed it, the pigs... But to be honest, an early night is really good cos I've got three little kids."

Andrew George MP

"Quite a lot. Like most MPs, during parliament sittings I probably work at least an 80 hour week, reckon I do way over that, and there actually isn't a lot of time left. But in the miniscule time that there is left, I play cricket, football, cycle a lot, do gardening, go out with the family, walking and swimming. I am an outdoor, team playing sporty type of person, even though I know I'm an old codger, I can still get around a cricket field or a football pitch even in my dotage.

"I play for the parliamentary football and cricket teams on occasion. Although I play every week at home. I play in a competitive League. I don't support a football team as such. I still prefer to play, rather than watch. I like to pretend to myself that I am still young enough to play. That is the nature of a politician, their self image is totally different to the reality."

John Glen MP

"I think like many politicians you never really switch off, you are always an MP, you are an MP at the weekends in the constituency, and you are an MP during the week. You are aware of how many plates you have spinning, some at a higher intensity than others. I enjoy going out for meals with my family, and spending time with them. I play a bit of squash. But you know with two children of ten and twelve, my step children actually, I maximise my time when I am at home with them, doing homework with them, taking them out, while they are still interested in having me around, I try to be around."

Zac Goldsmith MP

"I spend as much time as possible with my children. There's not a lot of time for anything beyond that."

Oliver Heald MP

"Well the children are in their twenties now, so I suppose the family responsibilities are a bit less. I like walking and I go walking quite a bit, particularly in the Lake District and the Peak District. The children enjoy it too, so quite often we have a project. This year we wanted to go up Scafell Pike, on the Eskdale route which is the long route. We had tried it twice before but not made it because the mist came down, but this time we cracked it, and got to the top. So that is something I am proud of. The last time I went up Scafell Pike on the other route, I met John Mann the Labour MP at the top."

Dan Jarvis MBE MP

"I don't get very much spare time because the life of an MP consumes most of the time that you have, and I try and work pretty hard for Barnsley, and have a young family, so clearly I want to spend as much time with my kids as I can. But I have agreed to run the London Marathon next year to raise money for Cancer Research, so I do try and get out and do a bit of running whenever I possibly can. As a new MP I am still trying to settle into the routine, so in order to relax I do like to go out for a run, I find that quite therapeutic, and it gives me a chance to think and exercise and I always feel better for doing that. I do like to be out in the countryside, I do like to walk, and have two dogs so enjoy taking them for a walk. It's really important to be able to carve out some time to sit with a book, I find that really relaxing too."

Liz Kendall MP

"I'm a running nut, I love running, five times a week I go either running or to the gym. I find it very relaxing, it's time on my own, and when you are running you kind of think about everything and nothing. It's not like I think directly about a thing, it just cogitates in my brain. I have my headphones on and obsess about getting the right play-lists, I need the right music at the right place in the run when I am feeling a bit shattered.

"I love films, me and my partner have something called film club, where we say to anyone new we meet, suggest your best ever film, and we will watch it. So what's your suggestion?"

BAT 21 – Gene Hackman, he's a high ranking Airforce officer in Vietnam, gets shot down, and has to get rescued – brilliant film, my all-time favourite!

Ivan Lewis MP

Well apart from football, I read, and walk, I have only been doing that for the last couple of years. I like walking, hiking really is pushing it a bit, but a bit of hiking, walking. Until recently I did quite a bit of swimming and gym stuff, I need to get back into that. I spend quite a bit of time with my kids, I have teenage children. For the last year I had the Culture brief, and I started to really enjoy the theatre, so I do more of that now than I used to do as well."

Caroline Lucas MP

"I've started running in the mornings, which helps to blow away the cobwebs and get the mind and body working. Also, I love long walks on the South Downs with my family and our dog at weekends, and winding down with a gin and tonic, and re-watching episodes of The West Wing."

Nicky Morgan MP

"I was a keen cinema goer before I had my son. With this job particularly, it's quite hard, and then to get babysitters. My favourite film is actually called *Crimson Tide*, which is a fabulous film about a nuclear submarine, really tense and Denzil Washington is fantastic in it. But the things I probably watch most at the moment are children's films, my son is three and a half, *Toy Story*, *Cars*, so if it's *Disney* I have probably watched it. But I think there is nothing like films like *Gladiator*, films you can really lose yourself in with beautiful music."

Greg Mulholland MP

"Not sure if relax is the right word, but away from work and from the job I try to spend what little I have with my family, my young daughters. Although due to the job I don't get to do so as often as I would like, I do like to watch and still sometimes play sport, particularly rugby league (I am Chair of the Parliamentary Group and captain of the Political Animals, the Parliamentary Rugby League Team) and I enjoy walking and of course I do find the time for a pint or two of wonderful local beer in the many excellent local pubs in and around my constituency."

Jason McCartney MP

"Apart from Huddersfield Town, I like tennis as well and I like walking, with our girls. I like going to the pub with friends and playing pool, and having a pint. I am not a big drinker but it's nice to have a pint. I like good food too, I try not to eat puddings but I like pies, beef pie all the kind of stuff."

Esther McVey MP

Cooking (though that doesn't mean to say I'm any good… but I can do a mean cottage pie!)

Chi Onwurah MP

"I really like reading, I have always read hugely ever since I learnt to read, and right now I am reading the Biography of Steve Jobs. I am an electrical engineer by background, so I spend a lot of time following science, but that's also part of my job really because I am Shadow Minister for Innovation and Science. I enjoy music, particularly jazz music, and walking in the countryside. Our local constituency office – Newcastle Central organise what we call Red Rambles, so every three months we go for a ramble. Last month's was a walk along the coast in Easington. Graham Morris, the MP for there is a big rambler too. Rambling is very popular."

Stephen Pound MP

"Apart from Fulham, well obviously nude snowboarding has always been a passion of mine. I played football, I played cricket a lot in fact I still do play cricket, I have a huge collection of comics, my whole attic is groaning with them, by that I mean DC… the early Superman and Batman stuff from the fifties and sixties, from when Marvel started. I got tons of the stuff. The problem is I have never found anything in life that doesn't have some interest, with the possible exception of morris dancing. In almost everything in life there is something. The way I look at it is, if you are in a strange city, and you are one of these boring people who have got no interest in life, you can just walk around the streets and it won't mean anything to you, but if you have you can see a flag or a poster in a window, always something to interest you."

Yasmin Qureshi MP

"I think for me, whatever little time I have, I like to spend it with my family. My mum is nearly eighty and not very well so I spend as many as hours as I can snatch with her. I have a beautiful little niece who is ten years of age who I love to bits, so I try to spend time with her and my brother, and my husband of course too! I go back to

Bolton every week, my husband stays there. So really for me it's about spending time with my family."

John Redwood MP

"I play cricket for my old Oxford College and the Lords and Commons. I enjoy the theatre, good music and good conversation. I enjoy being a non stipendiary fellow of All Souls College, Oxford, and maintaining a daily commentary on the health of the world economy and UK politics at www.johnredwood.com. I wish June and July were longer months, as so many of the events I most enjoy in Britain, from the test matches through Wimbledon to the outdoor music and theatre take place in the all too short English summer."

Jacob Rees-Mogg MP

"That's a very good question, and I love cricket. I am ashamed to say that I am spending Friday and Saturday of this week at Lords, and I shall do so again when the South Africans are over again later in the Summer. I always go to the Lords Tests if I possibly can for a day or two, which I love doing. I've got a young family who I think force me to relax, and that's a great pleasure. I got married quite late really, I was in my late thirties when we married and had children. I have three at the moment and another about to arrive. That's been very exciting, the children have me wrapped around their little fingers, there is no discipline from me at all.

"I thoroughly enjoy reading too, a whole range of things. I never have enough time to read, but it's a great pleasure. I like history biographies, and this will play entirely to my stereotype, so I don't know if I should admit it, P.G. Wodehouse. I absolutely love Wodehouse! There was a brilliant historical biography of Curzon by David Gilmour. I often find biographies very compelling. And our old friend Palmerston who I mentioned earlier, I read one on him recently which was excellent. Kenneth Rose wrote an excellent biography of George V, which actually had the extraordinary true fact his Doctor finished him off to make sure he died in time for *The Times* rather than the *Evening Standard*. He thought it would be undignified for the King's death to be reported in the *Evening Standard*. And Kenneth Rose's book I suppose was published in the late 1980's, so fifty years after the King had died, and nobody had known this – it was an amazing bit of historical research. One of the pleasures of this, was that the doctor was Lord Dawson of Penn, so there was this rhyme ' Lord Dawson of Penn, has killed many men, so that's why we sing, God Save the King'. And little did people know, it was absolutely true and he had killed the King in the end! *(laughter)*"

Jonathan Reynolds MP

"Well I have a young family so that takes up quite a lot of time. My biggest hobby at the minute, which is relatively new over the last few years, and takes up quite a lot of time is that I have got into growing stuff at home, so horticulture basically. I grow fruit and vegetables. We moved to a house just before the Election, and it had a vegetable garden there, and I said to my wife Claire that I had always wanted to grow a bit at home, cos my dad, and my granddad, classically as a miner, when he wasn't working always wanted to be outside at his allotment, growing strawberries, which brings back lovely childhood memories picking them. And Claire said, there is no way you will ever follow this up and you will end up with an empty vegetable plot. Well I didn't, I got into it, it's lovely because I am away a few days a week, things have grown by the time I get back. Quite amusingly, I entered the Mottram Show, it's a big agricultural show round here last year, and was a winner, which generated a bigger press story, than anything else I had done. So basically gardening, the kids, football, I still support Sunderland, which is pretty good as it's pretty evenly split round here between City and United so you wouldn't want to pick. There's not a lot of spare time at the moment.

"Since I got into gardening, I go to loads of primary schools, and it's quite a big thing with the Royal Horticultural Society and they grow things at the schools, and it's a great conversation to have with kids, learning where food comes from, a lot of them have these Eco councils, and you talk about stuff you see in the supermarket, where is it flown from, you can have some really interesting conversations with them."

Derek Twigg MP

"Apart from Liverpool, I love fell walking, I keep myself fit, I go running and like a bit of gardening, but it's all time isn't it. Fell walking is my real love, getting out there in the mountains. I walk anything from four or five miles to ten to fifteen depending on time. I see some lovely scenery I've got some pretty nice pictures. Langdale and Borrowdale are my favourite places, but I just like to get out in the fresh air and exercise. It's nice to be on the top of a mountain looking down and seeing all that peaceful scenery around you.

"I have always had an interest in Military History since I was a kid, the Battle of Crete is my forte. But I do read generally any books I can get my hands on about the Second World War, and a bit about the First World War, but the Battle of Crete, I think I have every book ever written. General Patton is one of my heroes. I know he had his detractors, but he was a brilliant General, he got the job done, he was absolutely superb. Probably my all time top General would be General Patton."

Charles Walker MP

"I am seriously addicted to fishing, I have an addictive personality I have given up coffee, as you noticed when I was told this morning there was no decaffinated coffee *(I said tongue in cheek)* that was almost a firing offence, I'm not good with caffeine, so I gave up drinking coffee almost three years ago, I had one and a half cups of coffee about a week ago in a fishing hut because I didn't want to be rude but seriously it's just devastatingly bad for me. I gave up drinking and smoking eight years ago, but the one addiction I can't break, I have never been addicted to women although I love my wife, the one addiction I can't break is my addiction to fishing I just love it, absolutely love it! It's a total passion! It takes one to beautiful places and I thoroughly recommend it!

"I will turn my hand to any sort of fishing really. I started off with a float, caught my first mackerel when I was three, I caught three goldfish when I was eight, I caught a perch when I was eight, then I went into a sort of hiatus. Then I took up fly fishing when I was ten. But over the last four or five years, thanks to my friendship with the former MP for Reading West, Martin Salter, who is a fantastic coarse fisherman and a champion of angling, I have actually started doing more coarse fishing. I enjoy barbel fishing, river carp fishing, I don't necessarily enjoy sitting at big lakes, but I do love fishing in rivers. I have enjoyed pike fishing for the last twenty years, so all sorts, I do everything, fly fishing.

"My favourite place has to be Islay, on the west coast of Scotland, beautiful Inner Hebridean island, home of the famous whisky which is of no interest to me now, although it used to be, actually it's the beautiful countryside, the lovely ocean and the amazing lochs that draw me back every year. It's a great way to relax, I probably go for far too long in my constituents' minds."

Phil Wilson MP

"Apart from football, I listen to a lot of jazz, probably for Margaret too much jazz, (Margaret, his partner interjects, probably bordering on an obsession) but I love the music. I love reading, I've always got a book on the go, and I like writing as well. So those are the things that I do when I'm not doing this.

"History books, as you can tell (indicates towards the bookcase). I like American History. The thing about America is, it's the first country to be established, to be based on a principle which was the Constitution. At that time no other countries were based on a principle.

"The way I got into jazz is my dad got our first record player, it was one of those where you could stack six LPs, and the speeds on it were 78, 45, 33 and 16. I think it was 16 or 18, I could never buy anything that could go that slow, and he bought three LPs, it was Harry Secombe, the Black and White Minstrels and Glenn Miller, and I loved the Glenn Miller sound. I really liked to listen to it, and this was in the early seventies, and in 1974, that was the 30th anniversary of Glenn Miller going missing, and there was a lot on about it. There was a biography of his life came out by George T Simon, called strangely enough Glenn Miller and his Orchestra, and I read it, and got to identify some of the people in the band and there were people you have never heard of like Tex Benagu, who played the tenor sax, like Louis Armstrong. And then there was Bobby Hackett who was a great coronet player by the way, whose sound was like Bix Beiderbex, and I was thinking I had never heard of these people, so I started to buy their records. So the kind of jazz I like is whatever I am listening to at the time, so I can listen to Louis Armstrong, Hot Fives and Hot Sevens from the mid 1920's, and I can listen to Trombone Shorty, who was a New Orleans trombone player, who merged New Orleans jazz with Eastern European, kind of Balkans music. Fantastic! If you listen to Louis Armstrong's music from that time, if you don't like it, I tell people if I put it on just listen to him play solos, don't listen to the background music, it's very 1920's and it's like finding a diamond in a lump of cement. It's just fantastic, and the same with people like Sidney Besier. But I think Duke Ellington is one of the greatest composers of any music in the 20th Century."

Rosie Winterton MP
"Well I go sailing, and I like reading and going to the gym, going out with friends."

John Woodcock MP
"I spend time with my daughter, and that is so important for me as a dad, and it's so important for her too, she was born a month after I started working for Gordon Brown, and so the first few months were all a bit of a blur, and it's one of the biggest things, that I want

to be a dad to her, I don't want to see her going to school, and secondary school and think well I've not really been around. And we have number two on the way at the moment actually, formally due in three weeks, another girl, so I'm completely outnumbered *(laughter)*. I brought my car down at the weekend to park it down here because my last train is at eight thirty at night, so if I get a call after eight o'clock then I am stuck until six the next morning, so I have the car here now in case."

I loved Kevin Brennan's description of picking the needle up and dropping it on the vinyl of his Ziggy Stardust LP, as I used to do exactly the same, as I am sure many of you did. Not surprisingly, Kevin is in a Parliamentary cross party rock band called MP4, and they have produced CD's to raise money for charity.

As a photographer myself, I can also relate to Ann Coffey, particularly with her love for sunsets and sunrises. Photographing those is a fantastic way to relieve stress, and is certainly one of my coping strategies.

As for Michael Dugher, I know he is not only a great MP for Barnsley, but he is also an awesome singer and musician. He has played several gigs for our charity and he is a really good bloke, who anyone would be happy to share a drink down the pub with, and if you ever get the chance to see him perform, I recommend you do so.

Liz Kendall and her running is also something many of us can relate to, particularly the bit about obsessing over the playlist, and the right music for when we are feeling shattered.

I have to say I just loved talking to Jacob Rees-Mogg. The man has a genuine warmth, and it would be a great shame if people made superficial judgements because of his accent. There is no place for reverse snobbery in my humble opinion, or any kind of snobbery for that matter.

Derek Twigg is another man who exudes a genuine warmth, and I share his interest in General Patton. Of course, he has a very different background to Jacob, but it perfectly illustrates my point about judging MPs by their sincerity, and not by a political leaning.

Charles Walker, another MP with such an engaging personality. I am biased because he is also a champion for mental health. I probably would not agree with much of his politics, but he is a great bloke all the same, with a great sense of humour, and doesn't his passion for fishing really shine through. As does Phil Wilson's passion for jazz.

What struck me in the answers to this question, was how many of these MPs use walking to relax, something many of us will relate to, but I'll leave the last words to Gloria De Piero, someone else many of us will relate to, "Coronation Street, red wine, my partner. I'll put him above Coronation Street obviously, though not sure about the red wine *(laughter)*, friends. I don't do sport. I like being with my friends with lovely wine and lovely food… "

Kevin Brennan and MP4

Democracy is a government where you can say what you think even if you don't think.
Author Unknown

CHAPTER TWELVE

Sporting Allegiances?

*As an ardent football fan myself, this is one of my favourite chapters,
nearly all of us can relate to sporting allegiance, particularly football,
and it certainly breaks down barriers. I asked them if they had any
sporting allegiances.*

Dave Anderson MP

My Team "My team are Sunderland. My very first game, was the
game where Brian Clough got injured in 1962 on the Boxing Day,
and I've been a jinx ever since *(laughter)*. We got beat one nil. Semi-
final of the Cup in Sheffield in 1973, it was absolutely fantastic. We
drew Arsenal, and Arsenal were a phenomenal team at the time. We
beat Man. City in the sixth round, no fifth round, we beat Luton,
and nobody expected us to beat Arsenal, but we absolutely played
them off the park, we won 2-1. And the fact we then had to go to
Wembley, and play Leeds was in some ways not important, it was
the getting there. The fact that we actually won the Cup Final as
well was even better, but in terms of absolute pure joy it was the
Semi-Final at Sheffield.

On the Stadium Move "It wasn't really bad, moving from Roker
Park to the Stadium of Light, because it wasn't very far for a start.
There was discussion initially about it being outside of Sunderland
where Nissan is, and to be honest with you, it would have made
more sense logically in terms of getting there and back, but it would
have taken the football club out of the town, and it would have made
it more awkward, like having a bite to eat and drink before the

match. There was nowhere around there, so it was a good site where they put it, and it's also been a very, very welcoming stadium. People regret moving for simple reasons of nostalgia, but there was never a big campaign not to do it. I was reading stuff last week about Chelsea, I guess at the time Sunderland moved, football wasn't as commercialised as it is now. You look now and think teams like mine are never ever going to bridge that gap, the financial gap.

Favourite Player "My favourite footballer of all time is probably Charlie Hurley, he was born in Ireland, left there when he was ten months old and moved to Millwall, his dad worked at Dagenham, spoke with a broad London accent, he was Sunderland's player of the century. Until recently he was definitely Ireland's most capped Captain of all time. He was a centre-half, left before we won the Cup in '73.

"Sunderland were the longest serving team in the First Division, from 1890 to 1958, nobody touched us, right? When we were finally relegated, it took us six years to get back up and Hurley was the pivot of the team. I was ten when we got promoted, and there was a huge celebration, we come second to Leeds, and Hurley came out on the balcony, and he was big man, and I'm a ten year old kid, he was just amazing. He probably stopped playing in about '70. Me other one would have been Jimmy Montgomery who was the goalkeeper in the same team, he was a bit younger than Hurley and actually got a Cup Winners' Medal with Forest. I see him quite regularly at the games with some of the corporate people, and he's like the Ambassador for the Club.

Current Players "Out of the current players, Sessegnon is class. I like Craig Gardener, one of the midfielders and McLean, who is an old fashioned winger. I'm still not sure about Bendtner though."

Paul Blomfield MP

My Team "I watch Sheffield United but that's not very relaxing! but I have done that since I was nine years old, so I am not going to break the habit now. I have a season ticket. We were the first team to score a goal in the Premier League, and it was against Manchester United. In the first season of the Premier League, Brian Deane scored a great goal in the 4th or 5th minute, and that was the first goal recorded for the Premier League. It's interesting actually because Manchester United got off to a poor start that season, and I think after our game, people were talking about Alex Ferguson being sacked.

Favourite Players "When I was a kid I used to stand behind the goal at the Bramall Lane end, and pull myself up onto the concrete platform, by the wrought iron railings that were there, just behind Alan Hutchinson, the goalkeeper, and I think he probably was one of my favourite players. So it was a real buzz for me when only about three years ago I met him for the first time. He comes to Bramall Lane quite regularly. And I guess the other player I have a lot of time for, was Len Badger, who I have also seen at the Lane a couple of times since.

"Everybody says Tony Currie, and I think it's those first early childhood memories that stay with you, but at that time we also had Mick Jones and Alan Birchenall. He went to Chelsea for £100,000. That was heartbreaking for me as a young football fan, we were pulling the side together, with Mick Jones and Alan Birchenell up front, Mick Jones was the first £100,00 player in the country going to Leeds, I thought why are we selling them… we've got this fantastic team, and look what's happened."

Andrew Bridgen MP

My Sport "Well I went to a comprehensive school and we didn't play much rugby, but I was the captain of the rugby team and we played a few games, and to me, rugby teaches you a lot as a young man. You do get hurt a lot, rugby hurts, you see the signs in the back of people's cars 'give blood, play rugby', and it take a lot of self discipline when you get hurt in a tackle not to retaliate. Rugby Union we are talking about, not necessarily Rugby League, you charge forward with the ball, you get tackled and then your teammates come in to support you, it's the finest team game in the world. It hurts a lot, I have broken lots and lots of bones playing rugby. When I was in business, we used to sponsor a team, and I have been to Twickenham many times. I had the pleasure of last Autumn being a guest of the R.F.U. at an England game and we lost. The referee was French, and I sent a message at half-time to the England team saying 'Remember Agincourt, Remember Waterloo, Remember Trafalgar, because I am pretty sure that the French Referee does!' *(laughter)* He was pretty biased."

Andy Burnham MP

My Team "I am a football man at heart, that's what motivates me and interests me. I've been an Evertonian all my life, and Everton Football Club is more important to me that most things in my life."

Ann Coffey MP

My Sports "I like swimming, and swim every day. I do not do football, please do not ask me about football *(laughter)*. I rode horses when I was younger, and still do occasionally now, but as you get older horses are quite difficult animals, you get a bit nervous about falling off, but I went riding recently, and did in fact fall off."

Philip Davies MP

My Sports "I love all sport, I was brought up loving sport. I am one of those people who read the paper backwards. My football team is Doncaster Rovers, which is probably why I wouldn't advertise it *(laughter)* because I think relegation beckons this season for Doncaster Rovers. But anyway they are my team, and I also support Doncaster Rugby League team. I was born and brought up in Doncaster, so I support my local teams. My biggest passion in life though is horse racing. I used to be a bookmaker, it was a family business, so I was brought up to be a Conservative, and I was also brought up to be interested in horse racing. Those two things were non-negotiable in my household."

Stephen Dorrell MP

No Sport "No I have no sporting allegiances. (laughter). One of my favourite stories is, my father was a genuinely fine sportsman, and I was always a disappointment to him in this regard. But I always say it's one of the last times I saw him laugh, before he died of a terrible wasting disease, a couple of months after I became Culture Secretary, and then Minister of Sport. So I told him I had been made Minister of Sport and he laughed at that, and said that it proved John Major had a sense of humour *(laughter)*."

Michael Dugher MP

My Team "I went to University in Nottingham, and I moved in with a load of Forest fans, so I started going along to reserve matches cos they were free, and I was skint. And then I started to go more, and you get sucked in, so basically I have been a Forest fan for about twenty years. I was also as a kid, a big admirer of Brian Clough, and I mentioned my granddad before (my mother's dad) he had a huge affection for Brian Clough and would talk about him all the time, and he sort of followed Forest when Brian Clough was Manager cos he liked him so much. So I grew up with an affection for Brian Clough and then I moved to Nottingham.

Supporting Nottingham Forest "I have supported them through probably the worst time in their history, I've brought them no luck, and I don't think anyone could describe me as a glory hunter! I have seen more relegations. You know when you are away at Milton Keynes in the snow in the third division. I love football. It's been a long time, it feels a bit like supporting Scotland, a litany of misery and disaster. I think in the 94/95 season when we finished third in the Premier League, and qualified for the UEFA Cup. I mean these days you finish third in the Premiership and you are in the Champions League with a £100 million quid or whatever. In those days, it was the UEFA Cup we finished third behind Blackburn and Manchester United.

Favourite Players "Stan Collymore was fantastic, Brian Roy was playing well for us that season, that was a really good side, Steve Stone, Stuart Pearce was a great hero of mine. And I also think the side that Bassett managed in 98 when we won what was Division One and is now the Championship, and we not only won promotion to the Premier League, but we won the League as well, we were a great side then too. And I remember what I think was the last game of the season against Reading, and we were already up, and the fans invaded the pitch (I didn't join them) and carried the players on their shoulders. It's kind of funny isn't it, I don't have any political heroes but I have lots of football heroes, odd isn't it.

"Politicians are no different to other people, there was a great Ben Elton line, where he said 'football was something invented for blokes to talk about in between pints'. You know whether you drive a lorry or you are an MP – football is a major passion for me and I like talking about it."

Natascha Engel MP

My Team "I used to have a season ticket to Q.P.R., I lived in West London for years. I used to go to all home games when we were bottom of the 2nd Division, I am the opposite of a fair weather fan because I don't go any more. *(laughter)* I don't get to see them now they are in the Premier League.

Favourite player and will your boys support Q.P.R. "Their dad is an Arsenal fan! *(laughter)* so they are going to be Arsenal fans, and they kind of laugh at me, and they go like 'superhoops' ha, ha, ha! and Q.P. ha, ha, ha, ha! *(laughter)*. And they actually laugh at me. I used to like Shittu until I had kids and then I couldn't anymore *(laughter)*. There weren't really glamour players when I was watching, although obviously we had Peter Crouch.

Other Sports "I love all sports. I am very competitive, I cycled from when I was 18 and used to cycle in London, but was knocked off my bike, and haven't been back on my bike, and have put on a stone in weight – almost instantly *(laughter)*. I swim a lot now."

Zac Goldsmith MP

My Sport "I love cricket, of almost any sort. I never have time to watch test matches, although I still rate that as one of the greatest luxuries. The England team is obviously a favourite, but if you love cricket, you have an affinity with all the great teams."

Dan Jarvis MBE MP

My Sport "Cricket is a big part of society in Yorkshire. Yorkshire Cricket Club are not having a particularly successful time at the moment, but they are a great institution, and I am really keen to be involved with Cricket, with Football with Sport. It provides a really great opportunity for young people in particular to have an outlet for their energies. It's a really important part of the fabric of our society."

Liz Kendall MP

My Team "I grew up in Watford, and I went to school in the same road as Watford Football Club, the Hornets, when Luther Blissett, and Elton John were there.

My Sport "But I would say that my big obsession is athletics, and I am dying for the Olympics to happen! The person I would most love to meet is Usain Bolt, I am fascinated by people who train so hard for those few split seconds, how focused they have to be, it's phenomenal."

Sadiq Khan MP

My Team "My team are Liverpool. Listen, when I was little you either supported Liverpool, or Man. United or Spurs, some people supported Arsenal. The reasons were Arsenal were also in the F.A. Cup Final virtually every year, Spurs played quality football, you had Ricky Villa, Ossie Ardiles, Steve Archibald, Glen Hoddle. People supported Man. United because of the old glory days, and Liverpool, well they played some quality football and won stuff. They played some gorgeous football, you know Alan Hansen at the back, Ray Clemence in goal, and I supported them from a really young age. And you know this, when you support a football team, it's in your heart, you can't change it. When I do assemblies now in my patch and ask the kids who they support, most of them now say Chelsea for obvious reasons, but once you start supporting a team you can't change it. You are a proper football fan so you'll know this, when the results come in and you have lost it messes up the whole weekend.

Favourite Players "I've got a Stevie G signed shirt in my dining room, so obviously he is right up there in the present time. But before that Kenny Dalglish and Ian Rush were amazing, some of the moves Dalglish did were just amazing. So Dalglish would be my favourite all time player in relation to his flicks and his goals, his assists… He was a player/manager who won things, and then became a manager. And if you run with a team with John Barnes, Peter Beardsley, John Aldridge…

Yeah I remember Dalglish scoring at the Bridge… You must remember the Shed…

"Yeah I do… my brother is a Chelsea fan, and he remembers being scared and running away from the Shed.

Club or Country "I'm not one of these guys who knocks the foreign investment into football, I think the Premiership is very exciting. But the disappointing thing is if you speak to proper fans, and probably a lot of managers too, they would rather their team, won the Premier League, than England to win the World Cup I don't think that is the same in other countries.

But you would rather see Liverpool win the Champions League than England to win the World Cup wouldn't you?

206

No I don't think so, we have won it five times after all… we own it *(laughing)* unlike you guys, have you ever won it?"

Of course Chelsea went on to win it, as a fan I have to say that!

Watching Liverpool "I didn't see Liverpool at all last year, because the thing is, it's a long drive back, or a long train ride back… if you have lost and you are coming back at 1.30 a.m… I've got two girls who are eleven and ten now, and I have got to be fair, the job I do is time consuming, and as it is I don't see my wife and children enough. I can't justify if I am honest going up to watch a game. This year, the Labour Party Conference is in Liverpool, and on the Saturday we are playing Wolves at Anfield, so I might get up to that Saturday game, cos it kills two birds as I have to go up on the Saturday anyway, but other than that it is just difficult to justify. With being a front bencher too the diary is just so busy. Where I am lucky though is there are quite a few London teams in the Premier League, I will go and watch Liverpool when I can. The problem is though I am always sitting with the home fans, so when Liverpool score, I want to jump up so it can be difficult as I can't celebrate, so it's not as much fun. MPs are always invited to corporate hospitality, it's not the same though, it's a bit sterile.

Playing "I haven't played for the parliamentary football team for a while, but I like to and I play when I can. I play in midfield, I don't have the engine I used to have, so I can't run up and down like I used to, and I'm quite bossy so I play right midfield. Stevie G is the man! In the olden days it would have been Terry McDermott. I am a long suffering Liverpool fan, so I remember the glory team of Kenny Dalglish, Ian Rush, a midfield of… who do you support? **Chelsea.** Oh god! I mean we are a proper team, used to playing some quality football."

Ivan Lewis MP

We know you are a big Manchester City fan, I assume your sons are too…

"They are. They had to be or I would have had them adopted" *(laughter)*.

That's what I say… *(more laughter)*

My Team and Money "People say to me do you have a problem with money and I say not any more. I remember when we went down to the old second division, and the tremendous loyalty of the supporters. We almost became the 'joke' club in the country at one time. And just to see the change is obviously phenomenal. Obviously outsiders will talk about the money, there is no way around that, but what's amazing for us really is to watch the quality of the football, because we spent years watching dire football to be honest, in those dark years. City didn't have a lot of money, United were the dominant team, and we were buying average, rubbishy players, pretty second rate, but you stuck with them and just went to watch rubbish football. But now winning is important, but we are watching world class football every week, you are watching amazing football. Obviously the money has made a massive difference, but so has Mancini. It's does take time to gel people together. I think he has done it quite quickly, compared to other people. Now I don't want to be complacent, we may not win anything this season, everyone is saying we will, but it's not a done deal, there's a long way to go. But that United match was something else. If we can sustain it? It's fun. I used to go with my dad, and that was nice, we went to every home match together, and now me, my dad and my two boys do that together, we have four season tickets, so that is nice as well, to go as a family."

In the interests of balance I will point out for those non football fans that City went on to win the League.

Favourite Games "The famous one against Gillingham, if that had gone differently, history may have been completely different. We are two nil down to Gillingham in the Play Off Final, with about fifteen minutes to go, and we wouldn't have gone up, and then we scored two goals in ten minutes and we won on penalties. And then we were promoted, that was the start of the way back. And we eventually got back to the top league. There were lots of clubs, when I was a kid starting off, and they were such big clubs when they went down you would always think, oh they will come straight back up, but they have not come back up.

Favourite Players "Kinkladze was one, amazing footballer, but he didn't do it over a very long period of time. I don't really remember players like Colin Bell, but he was a hero, Summerbee was just as I was starting. Trevor Francis, not many people know this but when I was a kid 10 or 12, I used to go to the training ground, and wait for the players to get autographs, all that stuff, and the day that Trevor Francis signed, and at that time he was the most expensive signing in the country, I was there. The front page of the Manchester Evening News had a picture of me and Trevor Francis, and I've still got it somewhere, my mum went mad cos I hadn't had a haircut for weeks. So yeah lots.

Favourite Current Player "It's got to be Balotelli!"

Nicky Morgan MP

My Team "I am not really a sporty person to the extent I don't go along every Saturday to cheer a team on. I am a supporter of Leicester Tigers obviously, because they are my local rugby club. My father was a supporter of Arsenal, so I have probably inherited that. **My Sport** "The sport I probably enjoy the most is Athletics, as I do go running, and take a great interest in what our athletes are doing."

Greg Mulholland MP

Playing "I have a keen interest in sport. I play for the Political Animals rugby league team and the Commons & Lords rugby union teams when I can and am also President of my local rugby league club, Leeds Akkies and Vice President of the Leeds Rugby Foundation.

My Teams "In Rugby League I am of course a Leeds Rhinos fan and hope to see them add the Challenge Cup to recent Grand Final and World Club Challenge triumphs, I also support my local rugby union team, Otley. In football, however, due to my Dad being from Stockton-on-Tees I am a lifelong and long suffering Middlesbrough fan!"

Jason McCartney MP

My Team and Favourite Games "Huddersfield Town all the way. In the 1980's we moved to the northern side of Huddersfield, and we could see Leeds Road from our house, so I started dragging my brother there. They weren't very good then and only had crowds of 5000, then things started to turn around when Neil Warnock became manager, and we moved to the new stadium in 1995. I went to Wembley in 1995 when we beat Bristol Rovers in the play off final, I can remember it really clearly, Neil Warnock got us promoted to the Championship. We had Mick Wadsworth who was a coach at Newcastle, Lou Macari, but we have a period of stability now. We did get relegated all the way down to the fourth tier, but came right up, from the play offs in 1994 against Mansfield, and that was great. So I have been going regularly for a long time now, and have a season ticket, can't go to mid week games because I am in parliament, but go to all the weekend games. It's fantastic. They are a really great community club, the chairman is a fan, and fortunately he has got a bit of money, and we had 16,000 last weekend against Preston. We are a one team town, and it's great, we are second at the moment with a 40 match unbeaten run. I went to the play off final at Old Trafford in May which we lost three nil, which was disappointing. Last season the shirt sponsor was the Yorkshire Ramblers. They gave £200,000 to them, and I am so proud to support a club like that. I had a PMQ earlier this year asking the Prime Minister to praise Huddersfield Town, and he did, we have that on a little plaque. A few of the players live in Honley near me. I always think now if our unbeaten run is to end it will be to a really struggling club. It will almost make promotion better this season having missed out over the last two seasons."

Huddersfield Town went on to win the Play-Off Final.

Stephen Pound MP
My Team "I am a season ticket holder at Fulham Football Club.
Favourite Games and Grounds It was August 1958, the first game of the season, I was ten years old, and playing right back for St Augustines, and then in 1959 – Tony Macedo and Johnny Haynes, Fulham beat Stoke 6-0 and I remember walking out of that ground thinking how could life ever be better than this… but thirty years of misery stretched ahead of me and I have never seen us win 6-0 again. Of recent times, the memorable one has got to be the Juventus game with Clint Dempsey's chip, I mean how could Fulham beat Juventus – it was extraordinary. A year ago going to see the away match at Sheffield Wednesday in the Cup, I remember Hillsborough as a lad, but now all the paint was peeling, and of course the Leppings Lane tragedy, it was just so sad to see. So many clubs now, like the lot at the other end of the Fulham Road, grounds are just like shopping arcades, with a ground in the middle of it. My

favourite ground oddly enough is Stockport County, because you know it's got such a lovely frontage there. I mean the beer's diabolical, and the pitch isn't much better but… "

Jonathan Reynolds MP
My Team and Favourite Players "My team is Sunderland. My favourite player was probably Marco Gabbiadini. When I was little it was a dreadful team to support, it wasn't until the Peter Reid era that things improved really. Kevin Phillips was absolutely brilliant! Niall Quinn, obviously because of his role in the Club, I have met Niall Quinn, because David Miliband is now Vice Chair at the Club. He set up a dinner for Sunderland fans, it was the day after we appointed Martin O'Neill and he came. I sat next to him, it was brilliant talking to him about football.

Favourite Game "I got invited to the last game of the season, the Sunderland v Man. United. game, I had never been in a Box before, I was invited by Manchester and Newcastle Airports. So I went because whatever else I always go to certain games, the first and last matches, and Boxing Day with my dad, so they said bring him along as well, which was great. Loads of firemen because they retire earlier than average tend to do stewarding at the Stadium of Light. My dad loved it, his mates were saying to him what you doing up there in the posh seats, and he was saying it's thanks to my son, he's an MP *(laughter)*. It was also probably the most exciting game to have Sky Sports on behind you as well with the score changing at the Eithad."

Derek Twigg MP
My Team "Liverpool FC!
Favourite Games "My first memory would probably be 1972 when my dad took me to see my first game, and we beat Crystal Palace 4-1. I remember being transfixed watching the Kop, with its' amazing sound and aura, never mind the football. But my outstanding memory would be when Liverpool beat St. Etienne in

March 1977 in the quarter finals of the European Cup, the atmosphere that night was like nothing I could ever experience again. It was unbelievable. Your eardrums were splitting it was that loud. Someone said the Inter Milan game in '65 was probably just as good, and the Chelsea match when we went through to the Final was great, but I can't imagine that atmosphere in '77 ever being beaten. It was so packed on the Kop you couldn't even get your hand out of your pocket, and steam was rising because it was such a warm evening and so many people were packed onto the Kop. It was the whole experience and a great game, and of course Istanbul was outstanding too, but my all time greatest memory was definitely the St. Etienne game.

"And obviously in terms of what happened, Hillsborough is something that will never leave me, but that wasn't about a game.

Favourite Players "Probably the greatest footballer I have seen was Kenny Dalglish. My favourite footballer would be Tommy Smith, because he came from a very poor background, he embodied someone who had the total determination to get on, he was from the local community, he was a Liverpool supporter. He was tough, hard as nails, hard working, but also skilful which was never recognised, and really to me he personified the heart of what a footballer should be. 100% tough, but with skill as well, someone who you would want on your side. The obvious ones would be players like Dalglish and Ian Rush, and of course Kevin Keegan, but to me Tommy Smith always had this special place in my heart, because he epitomises everything I liked in a player, heart and courage, determination, but skill as well.

Current Players "As for current players, it's a difficult one to be honest. Suarez obviously has great ability but he's not been there long enough. I probably would say, still Steven Gerrard, although he has been injured a lot more recently. I think Carragher's game is similar to some extent as Tommy Smith, but he is not quite as tough, or as skilful."

Charles Walker MP

My Team "Queens Park Rangers. I am a pretty fair weather fan – I followed them a lot when I was younger, but then you move on, you move away. But I tell you Queens Park Rangers came to my aid because the first seat I fought was Ealing North. I am not a very political person, so I am not looking entirely for the angle, so when they said what's your favourite football team?, I said Queens Park Rangers, and it never occurred to me that they were the local team. So they obviously thought look at this creepy swine. But then I was in a position to talk about the midfield and some of their recent acquisitions. Do you remember when they sold Ferdinand to Newcastle for millions, and Ray Wilkins, who although I have a lot of time for, squandered most of that money on people who never really made a mark. It really impressed them, although it wasn't why I said it. It only occurred to me when I walked out after the interview that they probably thought I was some slimy politician trying to butter them up. My brothers are avid fans.

Favourite Game "I think the most exciting thing was when they beat Manchester United 4-1 at Old Trafford. I was very lucky to meet Michael Meaker, who I thought played brilliantly, but others had more mixed opinions of him. But I was very impressed by his speed on the wing when I saw him at Loftus Road, and he had been to a school in Ealing North which was where I met him."

Phil Wilson MP

My Team "I support Middlesbrough. I'm not really a big sports person, but I'm also a member of Newton Aycliffe Football Supporters Club and the team have just been promoted. So I like football, but I'm not a religious follower of it, but that's my allegiance, Middlesbrough, cos I was born there.

Favourite Players "As for players, I think it would be from when I was a kid, David Mills and John Hickton and players like that, you know, I can remember those back in the day, and also Gary Pallister. So they are the ones I really remember. The other thing about

Middlesbrough is they always concede a goal in the last ten minutes, but I know they haven't got the biggest following like Newcastle and Sunderland have, but I've supported them since day one and I can't change. You can't change sides, unlike Margaret who does *(laughter)*. *(Margaret, his partner interjects – it's the only way to do it if they don't look like they are winning)* We have a friend who lives in Coventry, and Coventry were playing Middlesbrough, and we were down that neck of the woods, so we went to the match, and Margaret said no I don't like them I think I'll follow the other ones *(laughter)*."

John Woodcock MP

My Teams "I am a Barrow AFC supporter, and the team of my birth is Sheffield Wednesday, and both play in blue and white. I am Sheffield born and bred. Well I grew up with Sheffield Wednesday, my golden time sort of started with Ron Atkinson, but then Trevor Francis was the Manager. We assembled an incredible team in the early nineties.

Favourite Players "John Sheridan was an amazing midfield general with passing ability, and Chris Waddle on the wing – sublime. I think he won the sports writers' player of the year in that season, and I have never seen anything like it and I don't think I will again, so that's what stays with me from growing up.

"We have some cracking dedicated players with Barrow in the Conference, and there is real potential for Barrow if we can sort out some of the financial stadium issues that we need to do. Getting Barrow back in the Football League where they belong would be cracking.

Some politicians are accused of pretending to support a football team just to gain popularity with the voters, which Charles Walker alludes to when he talks of his support for Q.P.R. The mistake some politicians make is to say they support a team just because it is in their constituency. If it's not true, people will see through that, and genuine fans understand people's loyalty to their team, and would not appreciate someone switching allegiance to curry favour with the voters.

Certainly Dave Anderson, Paul Blomfield, Andy Burnham, Michael Dugher, Sadiq Khan, Ivan Lewis, Jason McCartney, Stephen Pound, Jonathan Reynolds, Derek Twigg or John Woodcock could never be accused of that. You cannot fool a dedicated supporter like me, and I can tell you, the passion these guys show for their teams really shines through when you talk to them. I truly believe you really relate to someone who shares your passion for something be it football, rugby, cricket, athletics or anything else, and Michael Dugher is a perfect example when he says "football is a major passion for me and I like talking about it".

Natascha Engel talking about her sons laughing at Q.P.R. was really amusing and something I could relate to (no offence to Q.P.R… obviously), but the interview on this subject I enjoyed the most, although it brought back painful memories was the chat with Sadiq Khan, and I will allow myself the last word here "That was real football banter, something so many of us engage in."

Natascha Engel

Majority rule only works if you're also considering individual rights. Because you can't have five wolves and one sheep voting on what to have for supper
Larry Flynt

CHAPTER THIRTEEN

What Causes are Close to Your Heart?

We all have a cause. I was intrigued to find out not only what was important to our MPs, but also what they considered as a cause. Personally I meant charitable, but as you will see, some interpreted the question differently.

Dave Anderson MP

"I am a dyed in the wool Socialist, Trade Unionist, so anything to do with workers rights. Any debate on employment rights, and that sort of stuff. I have also always been into international issues, so I chair a group, Third World Solidarity, I am very involved with the Asian community. I passionately believe in ordinary people, and I don't think they often get a good deal. It's one of the reasons I come here, cos there aren't enough people like me in Parliament, and if you don't do it there are plenty of others who will."

Paul Blomfield MP

"I believe passionately in the social models that we have developed in this country since 1945, where we recognise that we are stronger together than we are apart. That collective solutions are better than individual ones, which is represented well by the NHS, a system recognised and respected throughout the world, which is also very good at delivering positive outcomes. It is also reflected in our education system, in public services, and in providing support for people when they fall on tough times, or get older. It's those values that mean the most to me. I argue for them, and also for the role of the state in protecting people from the excess of the free market, which is a big issue at the moment. We have seen what unregulated systems do in terms of our banks and the financial crisis, we need to ensure that we have a strong accountable, transparent state to intervene when it needs to, and to make sure the market works for itself. That is something I feel very strongly about."

Ben Bradshaw MP

"Well they are not necessarily the ones you might think, I would describe myself as a generalist, I don't have deep or specialist knowledge of any particular area, but there are some areas I am more interested in. I am interested in Foreign Affairs, partly to do with the fact that I was a foreign correspondent and I speak languages. I am interested in church affairs, partly because I am an Anglican, I am interested in what is going on there. I am also interested in human rights, particularly human rights of sexual minorities, we have achieved a lot in this country, but there is still a great deal to do internationally. I am interested in health as a former health minister, and those tend to be the areas where I have got ministerial experience, and have gained some knowledge through my ministerial roles where I tend to focus my time."

Kevin Brennan MP

"Education, I am a Front Bench Spokesperson, and I am pretty passionate about it, as I used to be a teacher, so I get pretty closely involved with that. Obviously I have done a lot of stuff on things like Muscular Dystrophy, and trying to help kids who have got no prospect of living a full life. I take a strong interest in Welsh affairs because that's where I come from. That's probably it education is obviously, my big thing, my speciality."

Andrew Bridgen MP

"The economy and enterprise, the E.U. and the democratic system."

Andy Burnham MP

"Breast cancer has been a big issue, on a more personal basis. Hillsborough, I wear my wristband and I will do until we have finally got some measure of truth and justice for the families. There are causes that matter greatly, and more broadly I am a Labour man through and through, I care a lot about whether it is in good shape, good health and whether it's touching people. Is it ready to face the challenges of this century, and will it still be here in a hundred years time. Those are the sort of things I think and care about."

Ann Coffey MP

"I am very interested in children and families, as you know I was a social worker, before I became an MP, working with children and families and that's an interest I have pursued through my years of being an MP. I chair the All Party Group on Runaway and Missing Children, and Missing Adults, we are obviously very interested in making people more aware of the dangers children face when they run away, local agencies putting in the kind of help that they need before children are harmed, picking up the fact that if a child persistently runs away there is a problem, and they need to find out what it is, because dreadful things can happen to children if they run away.

"I'm also interested in markets, I love shopping and markets, I like the hustle and bustle of markets. It's been very interesting recently with all the news about town centres, and their changing face. People shopping on the internet has had a negative effect, what they may have looked for previously in terms of the bargains a market could offer, they may now look for on line, and that's a challenge for markets too, as they need to change what they sell. I think people do like being in a market, because it feel like their community, it has a connection with the past, you can stroll around, sit and have a coffee, it's a great experience. I don't think that the internet will ever take away from the fact that people like to visit places, smell the coffee and the food and feel things."

Rosie Cooper MP

"Deafness, Cancer – Macmillan and Marie Curie are just unbelievably brilliant. Whenever any stuff comes in from them or Cancer Research I almost always do it. Health related issues generally, they are the big ones, and Alzheimers – a friend's mum died from rapid onset Alzheimers and I watched how horrific that was for the family."

Philip Davies MP

"Criminal Justice is my biggest subject that I spend most of my time on. There are three things really, one is Criminal Justice generally, the second is political correctness, I hate political correctness with a passion. So I am involved with a group called the Campaign Against Political Correctness who I speak up for in Parliament, and also the Nanny State, I hate people being told what they can and can't do, so I tend to get involved in those three things above all else. The only other thing I would add that people tend to associate me more than I get involved with it, is the E.U. because in 2006 I launched the 'Better Off Out Group' encouraging Britain to leave the E.U. so I get a lot of focus on European issue, but I don't tend to spend as much time on that as I do on the others."

Gloria De Piero MP

"Well I am in charge of anti-social behaviour at the moment, that's my job and I really care about making sure that doesn't fall down the agenda. Things that are personal to me. I care very, very deeply about mental health because a close relative was affected, so that has affected my life a lot. So I say to MIND and Rethink, I will be busy, you two are the only ones allowed to ring me and say you have to do this, because that means something to me. With something like that you can actually be here and possibly make a difference, so I feel I owe it to that particular relative to make a difference."

Stephen Dorrell MP

"I am engaged in issues to do with overseas development, issues to do with heritage and how it affects Worcester which is the town where I grew up and still live, and I am also the Governor of an Independent School. I try to be involved in local community life outside of political life, as well as a wide range of other activities."

Natascha Engel MP

"Trade unions and workplace issues are really close to my heart. Youth policy, and welfare really. Welfare is a big one for me as my constituency is an ex mining area so there are a lot of people who are on passive benefits, and lots with mental health problems. We are going into the third generation of people who have been on benefits with no experience themselves, or through their parents or grandparents of work, and you have whole communities who have been forgotten, when you see that, and then come down to Westminster where people are making big statements about work fayre and the other initiatives, when you compare what is said here, with the day to day life in such a community, I really worry about that. There is a massive disconnect. That is what is closest to my heart really."

Andrew George MP

"Too many really. Ankylosing spondylitis is not a cause it's something that I suffer from, a form of Rheumatoid Arthritis, which inflames joints, especially vertebrae, eyes and other organs. If you have it, you need to keep as mobile and supple as you can, because after each bout of inflammation your joints can ossify. It's one of the reasons I do lots of cycling and swimming, I am lucky because many have it more severely and can end up quite crippled, in wheelchairs and so on. There are different degrees of it, I probably have a milder form of it, so I am just lucky."

"Causes that concern me include any matter to do with the consequences of poverty whether it's in this country or the developing world. I am also on the Health Select Committee, so I am interested in Health, and fair access to public services. I Chair the party's Environment and Climate Change Committee. I try to coalitionize stuff with the Tories in DEFRA, because we do not have a Liberal Democrat Minister there. So we try to find common cause and hopefully identify difficulties before they arise. I come from a fishing and farming background, so it's something I feel really passionately about. We need a productive and effective food producing sector in this country."

John Glen MP

"At the end of the day you are driven by what you experience in the surgery, and you experience a lot of different things during your time in the constituency. So I am quite interested in the way that Welfare Reform works and what that means for individual groups. I am interested in Defence, and on the Defence Select Committee, my constituency has lots of defence interests, so I have done quite a lot on that subject. I am interested in Education Policy, and the future of Universities. I am also interested in innovation in the NHS, key new ways of affording innovations for patients to improve outcomes for them. I am very frustrated that sometimes there is a gap between what I see as the common sense approach and the high politics of we can't privatise the NHS. Well I am not talking about privatising it, I am just talking about making things cheaper. The challenge is always to present your arguments and ideas in such a way that is accessible, that changes opinion, and leads to policy changes, and that's a considerable challenge."

Zac Goldsmith MP

"The environment is the defining issue of our day. It is beyond argument that we live dramatically."

Oliver Heald MP

"I am a longstanding supporter of a number of charities. In my early twenties, I spent a period living in a South London Mission, volunteered to work in the social centre and helped to run a Youth Football team based round the Old Kent Road. The Mission focused on support for deprived Inner City people and the Youth team successfully helped some youngsters who had experienced problems with the Law. They gained confidence as the team did well and went on to more settled lives. This gave me a profound belief in the importance of helping others and of the need many people have for some structure. As a lawyer, I often did pro bono work, starting when I was on the Committee of the Free Representation Unit and represented a number of people in tribunal cases. More recently, I spent a week working in a homeless hostel in Sheffield to see the problems of homelessness for myself. This also involved outreach work to those sleeping rough and it was harrowing to see the miserable conditions in which some people find themselves.

"As a young person I collected envelopes for Save the Children and I have been a supporter of the Royston Branch for many years. I believe in wealthier nations trying to deliver benefits such as medicines and clean water to the developing countries. I am a member of the Conservative International Development Group. I support a number of charities in my constituency and have volunteered in a range of charity shops, delivering Meals on Wheels and I helped tidy up Royston. I have helped Conservative Social Action projects such as refurbishing a Community Centre in Bournemouth, and I am a great admirer of mental health charities such as Rethink and Mind and have visited many of their projects. I have also asked many parliamentary questions designed to keep these issues to the fore and I have previously held a Mental Health Summit at Westminster."

Liz Kendall MP

"Well at the moment the whole issue about our ageing population,

I think as a society we are completely unprepared for it. And for myself, being an MP locally, but particularly doing the national job, it's made me think a lot about getting older, what it means, what sort of life people should be able to have when they are older. The fact that we do not see older people as much on the television, in films, in all different walks of life, and yet a third of people are over 65 now."

Sadiq Khan MP

"Well the issue I discussed with the students this morning is very important to me – poverty in the developing world. Public Services are the biggest issue for me, bread and butter stuff, the sort of things that affect my life, my family's life, my neighbour's life, my community's life. Public services are how good is your local Doctor, what are the facilities like at the local hospital, are the tubes and buses affordable for local people, are there jobs? When I left school, a lot of my mates weren't lucky enough to do A Levels or go to University, many of them tried to get jobs and couldn't, didn't have the skills, didn't have apprenticeships, and you know five, ten, fifteen years later they are not doing very well. My worry when I look at this generation now is you have youth unemployment at more than a million. One out of five young people between 16 and 24 is out of work, is not in training, and not in education. If they are out of work now, what's going to happen to them in years to come when they have a family and overheads, so that really worries me."

Nicky Morgan MP

"Mental health is very definitely one, and then obviously representing a university, and being PPS to the Universities Minister – higher education, but also vocational education, skills, and supporting small businesses, manufacturing. We do make things in Britain but we need to talk about it more. Also, women's issues, getting women involved in business, basically empowering women. One of the best things I do is go and speak to young women, girls at school, and say to them you have a choice about what you do with your lives, it's not always easy, but make sure you use that choice."

Greg Mulholland MP

"I am passionate about justice, about seeking to eradicate poverty, about empowering people and giving a voice to those who need one. I am an active member of a number of all party groups on issues I am passionate about – better wheelchair provision for children, older people's issues, abolition of the death penalty, suicide prevention and motor neurone disease. I am delighted to be patron of local charity Kidz in Kampz, who look after orphans on the Burma Thai border. I also am a big supporter of sport and am delighted to support the Leeds Rugby Foundation who transform lives through the power of sport. I am also an advocate for community pubs and am proud to have been named CAMRA's Parliamentary Campaigner of the Year and named amongst their top 40 campaigners, for my work leading the Parliamentary Save the Pub Group."

Esther McVey MP

"Social Mobility; Fulfilment of an individual's potential, hence I work with school children to provide advice on opportunities as well as careers guidance.; Supporting Small and Medium Enterprises, and people setting up in business; Working with victims of crime to ensure that their voice is heard in the Justice system."

Stephen Pound MP

"Causes that are close to my heart are obviously my constituency. Locally, it's housing, issues concerning people who have been excluded, who have been marginalised and who can't even afford to sit at the table, let alone order from the menu. Externally, Ireland is still a huge issue for me, I'm the Shadow Minister, and still doing an incredible amount there. Ultimately the only point of being an MP is to make a difference, and frankly a lot of people don't need

MPs if they have the intelligence, the education, money, they don't tend to need you, but for the people who don't have that, they need someone, and for them the MP is probably the last port of call. It's the hungry, the needy, dispossessed, the angry who really need us, the vulnerable and frankly the shat upon."

Yasmin Qureshi MP

"Whenever you have people who are vulnerable, either because of mental or physical incapacity, or because they are not well off, because of social economic deprivation, or perhaps where there is an issue where a group of people have been systematically discriminated against, those are the sort of issues that really pull the strings of my heart. There are around one million in our country now who have fallen into, not the poverty trap… although poverty is linked, to it, they are not taking any interest in society, people who are disenfranchised, marginalised, so I am concerned about them. I am also always very worried about young men. I am very passionate about young men, not just the 18-24 age group who have such a high suicide rate, but also the younger ones too, from 12/13. I think there are a lot of pressures on them, we rightly recognise about women's rights, but I think we forget how many issues and challenges there are for young men. We talk about sexual abuse of women but we never talk about sexual abuse of young men at all in our society and that really gets to me. I had a meeting with my Chief Super, and said do you keep any statistics, and do you give your police officers any training about dealing with young men who have been sexually abused. Physical abuse is easier to deal with, but sexual abuse is a hidden topic, it's not talked about. Men don't want to talk about it because it's all part of male masculinity, a bit like women used to be like because of issues of morality, purity and shame, they didn't want to come out. What we don't actually realise is how much sexual abuse of young boys is taking place in our country which no-one wants to talk about, and they are not coming forward either. There are going to have to be positive drives, as they did for women to move the agenda forward. In society now a lot of young men don't know what their position is any more, so for me they actually are a big thing. I also support the campaign against Prostate Cancer, I am right behind that."

John Redwood MP

"I have two big causes which I try to advance every day. The first is to preserve and enhance a democracy in the UK. This is proving difficult, with the advance of E.U. and other unelected powers in our land. The second is to help to advance the freedoms and living standards of those I represent."

Jacob Rees-Mogg MP

"I am very interested in our relations with the E.U. and the whole relationship with regard to democracy and decision making in the E.U. as it's constituted. I have great concerns about how that works or doesn't work. I am interested in the constitutional side of things, which is a minority taste, but it's much more important than people think. How decisions are made, often determines what decisions are made. If you don't have the right structures for making decisions, you don't necessarily make the right decisions, so you need to have things in place. I have always been interested in the Constitution. My background is as an investment manager, and I spent a lot of time looking at the economics of various countries, often the emerging markets, and there are lessons you can learn from that and what economic policies work. It's very important."

Jonathan Reynolds MP

"You have your broad areas of policy that you have an interest in, but in terms of specific causes, I am the Vice Chair of the APPG on Autism. My son has autism so it is a natural thing for me to get involved in. You get approached by lots of charities when you are newly elected, and I had a good conversation with them, and was happy to get involved and support some of their work. I am a Cooperative sponsored MP, so all the Cooperative ethos, responsible business, sustainable economics, obviously there is a huge historical thing with it here in East Manchester. So that is something very close to my heart. It depends on if you are talking about areas of interest or causes, transport is very important here, having commuted to Manchester as a trainee solicitor for a fair period of time, I have a lot of sympathy when people email me about their morning journeys.

"I do believe that coming in in this General Election after the crash of 2008, this is a moment of historical transition similar to the Healey Budget in 1978, as we don't really know what's going to happen, but clearly the way we have run our economy is probably going to change quite dramatically, Ed Miliband is asking some really challenging questions about that whole model of economic system, and I think it is a time to look at other countries. I remember as a student studying the German social model, with its' localisation and thought they were going to get taken apart, but if you look at things now it's amazing how much more resiliently they have come through than we have. I think it is a time to look at new ideas, that will be the big question for MPs of my generation, what will our social model and economy look like for the next twenty years, and that is not a criticism of what went on before."

Derek Twigg MP

"There are many really. The biggest cause close to my heart is my own community where I was born and bought up in, so I want to see them and my constituency do better. So that is my number one cause, to fight on behalf of my people. There is a real health problem in my constituency, because of the industrial style of my community and the associated poverty, so health and education are big for me, because we have raised the game on those but we need to raise it further. And defence is always a big concern of mine, because I have a big interest, and you know security is the number one priority of any Government, and defence and our role in the world are key to that."

Charles Walker MP

"Well it's obviously mental health and it's rivers, and fishing, I love fishing, and it's conservation. I am not a conservationist, but I am worried that while all these conservationists, are talking about saving the Amazon Rain Forest and the Niger Delta, we cannot even make sure that our own rivers keep flowing like the Kennet. So I am very sceptical about our ability to save the world when we cannot even save our own waterways, and our chalk streams and yet we are quite happy to let them run dry."

Phil Wilson MP

"There's Butterwick Hospice which does a lot for children, but is also where me auntie went. Politically, it's jobs. Anything that's fulfils aspirations, such as making sure that people do have a job, that they do have access to universities, making sure that they do have access to a universal healthcare system, and that there are buses for them to get to all of these things. The reason that I got into politics, is that I believe in aspiration, and I believe that everybody should have the right to get on, and the reason why I am in the Labour Party to do that is that so many people from my background were only able to fulfil their potential. A lot of people who went to school with me didn't go to University, but I am thinking of one lad in particular whose son is now a doctor, what if his dad had had that chance, if he had had the opportunities that there are today. My dad would say, and he was bought up in a single parent household in the 1930's, because me granddad died in his forties of cancer, so me grandmother had to bring up five kids on her own. If I think back to my dad, I had a better life than he had, but I want my kids to have a better life than I've got, and that aspiration has got to be there for everybody, not just the privileged few."

Rosie Winterton MP

"Let's look at my time as a Minister, and leaving aside the causes that you know I believe in which are equality and fairness and justice. Mental Health was one of the issues that was very close to my heart. My father had mental health problems, and therefore I did have some personal experience of a lot of what families went through, some of the ways in which services operate from quite personal experience, and I found that an area where there was a lot we could do to improve the service.

"Coming back things like my constituency – wheel-clamping is a great issue that I am involved in, and that is very close to my heart. I have been battling for thirteen years to improve the legislation around wheel-clamping. It's a real problem in Doncaster."

Well I don't know about you, but I found these answers really quite enlightening. It was good to hear Dave Anderson say "I passionately believe in ordinary people" – let us hope it is a sentiment shared by all of his fellow parliamentarians.

Oh, and I so relate to Philip Davies, a man of principle and strong beliefs, as I am sure many of you will when he says "I hate political correctness with a passion." It is rather reassuring that there is actually a group that campaigns against it. I never knew such a thing existed, but I would certainly like to join it, and I am sure there are many of us who are totally fed up with the 'Nanny State'.

Natascha Engel is right to express her concern about a massive disconnect, and another example of that is the NHS which John Glen talks about. If we are not careful, the NHS as we know it, the NHS that we cherish and hold dear to our hearts will not exist for much longer, but that is probably a subject for a different book.

Zac Goldsmith is very succinct, and spot on, especially when he says we live dramatically. And isn't Yasmin Qureshi thought provoking when she highlights the worrying problem of high suicide rates in young men, and the rarely talked about issue of sexual abuse of young men.

Given my own experience of mental health problems, and having worked in this area for the past twenty years, whilst I find it reassuring that so many of my interviewees have mentioned mental health, I find it equally frustrating that it is no longer seen as a health priority by this current Government, but again, this is a story for a different book.

It is great that John Redwood's cause is about the preservation and enhancement of our democracy. I just wish more of us saw it as a priority. And I bet Rosie Winterton doesn't struggle for support with her campaign about wheel-clamping!

The last words for this chapter must go to:-

Stephen Pound "Ultimately the only point of being an MP is to make a difference."

And Phil Wilson "Aspiration has got to be there for everybody, not just the privileged few."

Paul Blomfield and his wife

A civil servant is sometimes like a broken cannon – it won't work and you can't fire it.
George S. Patton

CHAPTER FOURTEEN

If You Were Prime Minister

Many of us have said what we would do if we were Prime Minister,
so what would these MPs do?

Paul Blomfield MP

"The key issue we are facing is to invest in growth to create jobs for our young people, to invest in affordable housing so we can provide the homes people need, and also through construction provide jobs and skills for young people, achievable objectives with a different economic strategy.

"I would also look at issues about our ageing population, it's great we can now expect to live much longer lives, but we need to focus of on quality of those longer lives, provide adequate pensions for everyone whether they work in the private or public sector, and proper care when people need it. We need to step up the debate so people recognise the need to dig a bit deeper in our pockets to ensure that is achievable."

Sir Peter Bottomley MP

"The clocks in winter: lives would be saved, the elderly and children would benefit by light before night rather than taken in the morning."

Ben Bradshaw MP

"The one thing I would do if I was Prime Minister, and I could change something it's not a major thing really, but is one of the things that I have long felt passionate about is at this time of year with the clocks going forward, is that I think we should move to lighter evenings all year round, so we can make better use of the daylight hours. It's a way of boosting the economy, improving road safety, and improving the quality of people's lives, by them being able to do more in the evening. It has over whelming cross party support in Government, and I have no idea why the Government don't just do it."

Kevin Brennan MP

"I suppose I would probably reverse a lot of what the Government is doing on education policy at the moment which I think is quite damaging and dangerous in fragmenting the education system. So I think, trying to get a more rounded approach to education, thinking about kids social and emotional needs, their health as well as simply exam results, and getting schools to collaborate rather than compete. A healthy schools system involves everyone working together to try to maximise every child's potential, and I think the way we are going it's not surprising to me that we do have children with all sorts of problems."

Andrew Bridgen MP

"I would change our relationship with the E.U., which controls so much we do in Parliament and the country."

Philip Davies MP

If you were Prime Minister ("oh my god" – laughter) what would be the first thing you would change?

"It would be a toss up between leaving the European Union, and leaving the European Court of Human Rights. It would be one of those two things, because there are so many things we need to do, that we are being stopped doing by those two institutions. So in order to crack on with things, we would need to do that."

Gloria De Piero MP

"I don't want to be Prime Minister but I do want what every other Labour MP wants – for everyone to have a fair crack at being the best that they can be."

Natascha Engel MP

"That's really difficult. There is one thing that keeps coming up. I love the way that this country is so different in the different parts of it, which is not so in other countries, where there is more of a feeling oh I'm in France, or oh I'm in Germany, whereas here you really know that you are in the north, and what part of the north. One thing keeps coming up, and I am not sure how to put this simply. The thing that I am dealing with at the moment, is where I am is semi-rural and there is a really big issue about waste disposal, so whenever there is about to be an incinerator go up, or anything like that, there is no understanding of the consequences of that. It's not even nimbyism, because I don't have a problem with that. If an incinerator has an impact on your house price, and that's your largest asset then be a nimby, I would support that, and if you are worried about your health or the health of your children, obviously I would support that too. But I don't think we as a country are taking seriously enough our energy and waste needs, and as politicians we are not confronting it, that's not something I would change about the country, it's more something I would change about politicians, that we should go out and lead more. Explain to people, yes whilst I support you, we need to think about what the consequences are of this, we are having to import energy which is enormously expensive, and we are landing all the rubbish on someone else's doorstep. There is very little I would really change about the country."

Andrew George MP

"Give local communities more power to regulate the provision of housing, to limit second homes where they impact on the housing choices of others. I'd want more power for Cornwall!"

John Glen MP

"That's a very good question, it probably would be something around the way that we perceive the NHS. It consumes a massive amount of our money, and I believe that it's not really functioning in the best way it could. It's a great institution and does a hell of a lot of good, but I think there is a consensus around not facing up to the inevitable reality of people living longer, drugs and things, and actually scientific discoveries opening up more opportunities to do things, what that means structurally long term for the NHS.

"So that's one thing but I think the other thing is, and this is more difficult because it's not something you can do by pressing a few buttons, but to try and lead in a way that people felt you had real integrity, so that you could improve the dynamics between those who govern and those who are governed. At the moment it's a very big gap of esteem and respect and one would hope you could project it differently, but I am sure that's a rather false hope. I am pretty cynical about how politicians are seen now, what I call the lens of superficial journalism that wants to grab a headline, but doesn't want to vigorously examine an issue, or at least most journalists don't."

Zac Goldsmith MP

"If I had only one shot at it, I would bring in a mechanism to allow people to trigger binding referendums locally and nationally on issues that matter to them. I'm not suggesting we should have Government by referendum, and don't believe it should be easy, but I have been an MP for long enough to know that MPs don't have a monopoly on common sense. I would set the threshold relatively high. Where there is sufficient demand for a change, say 20% of an electorate, it should be possible for them to force their Government or local authority to act. One vote every 5 or so years isn't enough, and this measure would arm voters with the final veto."

Liz Kendall MP

"If I was Prime Minister now I would be getting this deal on how we fund care. If you are a leader, of course there is all the day to day stuff, but you should be thinking about what the big long term decisions are that you need to make for the country. It's not just the vital sort out the care system for older and sick people and their families, but it's about the sustainability of public finances. The primary pressure on our public finances is to look at our ageing population, and to consider not just cost of pensions, but healthcare for older people. If I were Prime Minister, taking the difficult decisions about that, and having a decent system of care for older people would be alongside climate change for me, the biggest challenge in the world."

Sadiq Khan MP

"Wow, I've never thought of that. I would like to know that everybody's potential is fulfilled. I think back to my own experiences, and there may have been somebody at my school who may have found the cure to cancer, there may have been somebody at my school who may have discovered the secret of the Universe but because their potential wasn't fulfilled they weren't able to. If I was in a position where I could do anything I would try and pull a lever so that everyone's potential could be fulfilled. And that means for example when there is a Budget, you can't take money from the poor and give it to the rich, you can't take money away from schools in poor parts of the country, you can't leave people on the scrap heap."

Caroline Lucas MP

"Can I have two things? First, I'd bring in proportional representation – nothing would do more to broaden out British politics from the three main Westminster parties. The current electoral system, first-past-the-post, is an undemocratic, winner-takes-all system which makes it incredibly difficult for smaller parties to break through. The 'safe seats' under this system encourage voter apathy, because people in 'safe' constituencies feel their vote is a wasted one. Our electoral process must better reflect the views of the whole population.

"Second, I'd change the policy of this Government – that of budget cuts and austerity. A Government can't cut its way out of a recession any more than you can dig yourself out of a hole. It's not just a question of "too far too fast", as Labour claims, but the fact that it's precisely in a recession that the Government needs to invest in jobs – and particularly green jobs, since a green economy is far more labour intensive than the fossil fuel economy it replaces. In terms of where to find the money, the Government could start by scrapping Trident, cracking down on tax evasion and avoidance, and introducing significant green quantitative easing directly into the economy."

Greg Mulholland MP

"Being Prime Minister doesn't mean you can click your fingers and solve the world's ills and one of the problems we have is that the media demands that politicians and party's overpromise and oversimplify. Otherwise I would say I would end poverty. So if was Prime Minister (which I won't ever be!), I would seek to lead the country and the world to become more liberal and more just. If I could instantly implement one realistic policy, it would be to find a way solve the social care crisis that politicians have ducked for too long."

Jason McCartney MP

"Well I will never be Prime Minister, so it's not something I have really thought about. I am a very positive person, I think I would outlaw negativity! *(laughter)* get rid of doom and gloom and mithering, and moaning about things. I was chatting to some of the workers in a factory this morning, who had been unemployed for a couple of years previously. There is a lot of good news and positive stories out there.

"One of the schemes that the Government have brought in that I am most enthusiastic about is the National Citizens' Service, a voluntary scheme for sixteen year olds during the Summer which is funded by the Government. 30,000 young people will be doing it this Summer, and it has an element of volunteering, they work on a community project, and go away and do a week of residential. It teaches them teamwork, camaraderie, personal responsibility because they mix with different people. It's about getting young people together to do something proactive, they work on a project, and then they come back to their community from the residential and do that project. I think by doing that with all sixteen year olds in the country, it would become a rite of passage – National Citizens Service, I think it would give those young people a massive boost in their start to adult life, and help shape them for the future."

I have to go off script now because of what you said. Why are you so certain you will never be the Prime Minister?

"Because I think I am very much my own person in the way I am. I have rebelled on tuition fees. Some people sometimes say oh Jason you are an independent spirit why are you in a Party. Well I am in a Party because you can get more things done, I agree with 80% of what my Party does, and I'm very proud to be Conservative and I believe in the Prime Minister. I believe in him as a person to be honest. And you can get more done that way. It's how you deal with the 20% you don't agree with, I think I deal with it in a constructive way, loyalty is important, but it is how you deal with the elements you don't agree with. Do you take your bat and ball home and be a pain in the backside, or can you turn it into a positive, and be constructive. This is where I live, this is the area I love, day in day out my priority is being a good local MP."

Stephen Pound MP

"If I was elected as Prime Minister? I'd demand a recount."

Jacob Rees-Mogg MP

"I would like to see a reduction in the size of the state. I think the state does too much, it spends too much, it interferes too much in people's lives. I would like to see people allowed to get on with their lives with much less intrusion and regulation, and so that is what my aim would be. I think the individual is much more important than the collective, that the collective is a bad maker of decisions, and the old line about the man in Whitehall knowing best is the absolute reverse of what I think. I think the random decisions of millions of individuals make the best decisions for how the country should be run, and they are too constrained by the Law as it is to make those decisions. So personal liberty would be what I would want."

Jonathan Reynolds MP

"That's one of those questions where there are so many things that you want to change. I'll give you an answer now, and then I'll lay awake at night thinking about it *(laughter)*. I think it would be something between a change in the benefits system that got more people into work, but changed the punitive language that whole debate is carried out in. With some of the people, it's not that benefits are too generous, because they are not. Through being a Co-op MP I do a lot of stuff on manufacturing as well, which is really important to an area like this. It would probably come back to setting up a more continental system, a kind of capitalism that is more favourable to an area like this, with a focus on longer term goals, not just short term profit. This is to be a much more Northern business agenda, prioritising skills and apprenticeships, longer term stuff, that realised that was a commodity to keep in the country as well as profit. I've never liked the phrase north south divide, because I don't think it sums it up, if you live in Wilmslow for instance, you probably have the best quality of life in the country *(laughter)*, certainly more than inner city London, it would be something that changed the central gravity into a different economic model that worked better for all of us."

Phil Wilson MP

"I would want to sort out the banks, people like the guy who said he was going to resign because he wasn't going to get his multi-million pound pay out. What I would want to see happen is for people to take control of their lives, because what you've got with the banks and these big companies where the CEO's are awarding themselves an awful lot of money, is the shareholders and pension funds, that's mine and yours, we have got to take control of what is ours. We need to ensure that even though we need to play down the deficit, we also need to use the money that is available for the benefit of all people and not just the few. I would do that in the first week, in the second week I would move on to something else." *(laughter)*

Rosie Winterton MP

"Well apart from the obvious, I would want to change what I think is developing at the moment under this Government which is an approach to the economy, which is having a severe effect on areas like mine in Doncaster for the people who live there. And when I think in terms of what we were going to get in terms of investment in education, Building Schools for the Future, that has just been pulled. So that's quite big picture, but I do think that is important, that you need a different approach."

John Woodcock MP

"We need to put the Welfare system on a sounder footing because we have not done nearly enough to support people who are genuinely in need, and to give people who can work the proper support that they need to get back into jobs. It's awful what is happening out there at the moment, and all of the structural changes that are being implemented are masking a return to a time when people are just being left in a bad way. You run a mental health charity, you see the effects that worklessness has on people's well being. We have to be prepared to do what is necessary to change that."

Once again, thought provoking don't you think? particularly Caroline Lucas and her comments on our voting system encouraging voter apathy. Personally I think apathy is the biggest threat to our democracy.

Last word goes to Zac Goldsmith "MPs don't have a monopoly on common sense." Is there anyone in the country who would not agree with that?

Philip Davies

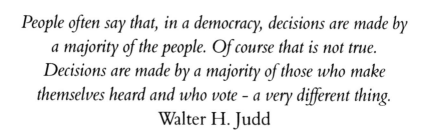

People often say that, in a democracy, decisions are made by a majority of the people. Of course that is not true. Decisions are made by a majority of those who make themselves heard and who vote - a very different thing.
Walter H. Judd

CHAPTER FIFTEEN

What Keeps You Awake at Night?

I suspect we all, at some time in our lives, have something that keeps us awake at night, MPs are the same.

Paul Blomfield MP
"Thinking of all the things I have to do the following day."

Ben Bradshaw MP
"Nothing keeps me awake at night. I have never had a problem sleeping. I get more sleep now than I have ever had. One of things that I have got back is my dream world, I'm dreaming a lot more now than when I was a Minister, which I think is because I am getting a decent night's sleep, rather than waking up, or being woken by an alarm, after four or five hours."

Kevin Brennan MP
"I sleep pretty well actually, if you take it in a literal sense, I go to sleep quite quickly. Work can keep me awake sometimes, if I'm worried about something, or if I haven't done something. I don't have the same sort of dreams I used to have when I was a teacher which were sometimes quite vivid. I never had any problems with discipline in my classroom, but I used to have these dreams about unruly kids."

Andrew Bridgen MP

"Worrying how we are going to stop our country going bust."

Philip Davies MP

"Work. In the last Parliament I can put my hand on my heart and say I never left the office before two in the morning – never ever. The thing that keeps me awake at night, in all honesty, is the thought of have we replied to such and such a constituent or not. I genuinely do wake up at night, and think there was somebody who contacted me last week, and did we get back to him or not."

Gloria De Piero MP

"Working for 7 years on breakfast tv! I still wake up at 4am and it takes me ages to get back to sleep. It drives me crazy."

Natascha Engel MP

"The children." *(laughter)* "Apart from them, nothing." *(laughter)*

Andrew George MP

"Very little I sleep well, mainly because I am perpetually knackered! Like many MPs, I spend most of my time feeling tired, and yearning for the moment my head hits the pillow, so I sleep pretty well. On rare occasions I do wake up, and it's often something really stupid, that you need to let churn over in your mind, and when you get up in the morning, you think, oh no, I had a blinding flash of inspiration to answer that last night and now I can't remember it!" *(laughter)*.

John Glen MP

"I think two things, one is individual constituents' issues, last night I couldn't sleep, I reached for my Blackberry, and emailed my secretary to say what happened with so and so, that I had forgotten to check, so those sort of things. Sometimes people come back into my mind where I have written a letter, and I want to make sure things are resolved. The other thing is as a Member of Parliament you are aware that you are privileged to be put here, and I am always saying to my staff, am I making a difference, could I do more, and you look at colleagues and think why have they done that, should I be doing that, so there is a constant tension between am I being effective, and trying to define what success look like, is it being a Minister, or a Shadow Minister, or being on a Select Committee, you do the role. As a backbencher you have more freedom to define what you spend your time doing, and you can do limitless things. More and more it's about making wise choices in the way you want to define yourself, and using the influence that you have as an individual, and how to combine with others effectively to make a difference, to change things."

Liz Kendall MP

"I focus a lot on work, so usually worrying that I am not being a good enough friend, or daughter, or sister. The people that you love most, should be at the top of your list, and too often they may not be. I tend to wake up worrying that I have forgotten somebody's birthday, and that kind of-thing."

Sadiq Khan MP

"I do have problems sleeping, you are right. It's a good question, it could be the littlest thing or the biggest thing, how my kids are doing at school, did I put the rubbish out, or big things like have I got my speech right I am doing tomorrow, or how can I try and influence Government policy, or should I oppose what the Government is doing in a certain area, or should I try and compromise, have I got enough time in my diary tomorrow to see a constituent. Little and big things, I am not a great sleeper, which I need to work on. There are lots of people in my walk of life – MPs who can switch off, de-stress, I just can't switch off. And I don't necessarily think that is a bad thing actually. I have tried not having caffeine after six, but it's the work I do. When I was a lawyer I was the same. There are some jobs you do where you just can't switch off. There are some jobs where you can just leave the office, switch off and leave work behind, but and I am not saying I am more conscientious than the next person, you just can't help taking your work home with you in your head."

Caroline Lucas MP
"Too many things, and too often. Climate change and the burgeoning environmental crisis. Growing inequality. The social impact of this Government's obsession with austerity."

Nicky Morgan MP
"All the e-mails and correspondence I've yet to deal with and how to juggle life so I see my family, deal with the workload and stay in touch with life outside the Westminster bubble."

Greg Mulholland MP
"I am lucky, I am a good sleeper and it is rare that I lose sleep over things and as an MP, whilst it is important to care about things and I do, you also have to be able to deal with huge amounts of pressure, personal attacks and also cope with hearing about very difficult and sad situations that constituents find themselves in, which can be heartbreaking. However in the end, like any father, it is the worry that I might not be able to support my family rather than work but for now I am just focused on doing a good job and doing what I can to assist the people who need my help, as their MP."

Jason McCartney MP
"Worrying whether Huddersfield Town are going to get promoted or not! *(laughter)*. No do you know what my biggest worry is? I shouldn't really say this, but I had a really important work thing on that I should be doing on the weekend of the Play Off Final, and it's like, do I commit myself to the work thing, or will Huddersfield be in the Play Off Final. I have actually excused myself from the work thing now, so that I can be available to go to the Final now. It

is a big community thing as well, it's very important for the area. And coming back to the positivity sporting success can give an area a real boost, like the Olympics, it can give people the feel good factor. That's why I am looking forward to the summer I think the Olympics and the Diamond Jubilee will be really really good."

"You know generally stuff doesn't keep me awake because I go to bed with a clear conscience, because I know, I do not say anything in private, or behind anybody's back that I do not say in public. I genuinely am what I am. I don't meet someone say something, and then say something different once they have left. It doesn't keep me awake, as I am not having to remember what I have said to whom. I'm not pretending to be what I am not."

Stephen Pound MP
"I'd like to say Angelina Jolie but actually it is my conscience; which I cannot quieten."

Jacob Rees-Mogg MP

Apart from your young children, what keeps you awake at night?

"I have always been a very good sleeper fortunately. You know I was asked this wearing my other hat as an investment manager at a conference, and I said if you have an investment manager who doesn't sleep you should fire him, because you want an investment manager who takes calm decisions, whatever the circumstances are, not somebody who feels under so much pressure, that he makes a bad decision because he is too tired to think things through. So I am very lucky, I have always slept well."

Jonathan Reynolds MP
"Certainly the family *(laughter)* There are genuinely cases where,

people come into your surgery, and their stories really get to you, and I don't mean the human misery stuff, because you see a lot of that and you have to become resilient to it. People will come and see you at the end of a process, if they have had things resolved before, they probably wouldn't get as far as seeing you. You don't object to them coming to see you, far from it, if a system has completely failed someone, you are the person who can change that. It doesn't always mean that you can change it instantly, because there is this huge bureaucratic process that you have to feed everything into and hope it comes out right. There are cases that really stick in my mind, a woman whose partner had cheated on her and moved out, not paid the mortgage when she thought he had, she was then rendered homeless, he had moved in with his girlfriend. She ended up with absolutely nothing, homeless with the kids in poverty. And it's things like that that really make you want to shake up the system. Anyone who says they don't want to be a Minister, I can understand if they don't want the lifestyle, which looks pretty awful, but I can't understand why they wouldn't want to make a dent in this, facing up to the civil servants. In cases like that though, I feel it was down to me to have made it better. What she really needed was a massively generous intervention for about three months, after which she probably wouldn't have cost the State anything ever again. But we don't have that.

"I love meeting people and hearing about their lives, you need a passion to want to know, and I really want to be able to make that better. It's that sort of thing when you are lying in bed, that you think what would a system look like that would have supported and helped that woman."

Rosie Winterton MP

"What keeps me awake at night is usually when Parliament is sitting is what are the big issues, that have either happened that day, or are going to happen the next day, in terms of Parliamentary voting."

John Woodcock MP

What keeps you awake at night? I know what is going to, the new baby (laughter)

"Yeah, the little bundle of joy who is just about to arrive *(laughter)*. No nothing does at the minute, and I am training to walk the Keswick to Barrow, which everyone else in my constituency seems to have done, no matter how unfit they look when you see them. It's 42 miles and you have to do it in one go, so I am training to do that, and when you are training, when you are physically exercising, you just find you are out like a light in the evenings."

The deep concern that Philip Davies, John Glen, Sadiq Khan and Jonathan Reynolds have for their constituents shines through.

And as always, a great answer from Stephen Pound, but I think Jason McCartney sums this chapter up perfectly when he says "I go to bed with a clear conscience."

Rosie Cooper

To rule is easy, to govern difficult.
Johann W. von Goethe

CHAPTER SIXTEEN

What Would You Like to be Remembered for?

I guess we all hope people will have positive memories of us, and MPs are no different.

Paul Blomfield MP

"I have no great expectation that I will be remembered. What is most important is to be a good constituency MP, to spend a lot of time working on local issues and connecting them to Parliament. When we had the debt management enquiry, I had a round table of local debt management officers, to give them, through me a direct voice, and their concerns were reflected in Select Committee report. I have also, when we were looking at apprenticeships, bought the Select Committee to Sheffield which was the first time they had met outside Westminster in this Parliament."

Ben Bradshaw MP

"The thing I would most like to be remembered by the people of Exeter for is being a good constituency MP, someone who has worked hard, gone the extra mile on their behalf. They won't have always agreed with what I have said, done or voted for, you are never going to please all of the people all of the time, but I would like to be able to feel at the end of my career, that I could walk up and down the streets of Exeter and look people in the eye, and that they would continue to look me in the eye too. That's the thing I would hope most to be remembered for."

Kevin Brennan MP

"In a general sense, as someone who genuinely tried to change things for the better. What you will be remembered for in politics is obviously another question, because that is a totally random thing sometimes, because if you mention a few names of former politicians, what would Michael Foot be remembered for? For being a brilliant orator, for being a brilliant parliamentarian, and for being a progressive figure who tried to change things for the better. What will he actually be remembered for? Wearing a duffle coat and falling over. And I actually have some sympathy for that Tory MP, Sir Peter Vickers, who didn't actually buy the duck house. I wouldn't have agreed with him on much politically, but he probably slogged his guts out for thirty years working hard on behalf of his constituents, but the only thing he will be remembered for is the duck house. So actually, funnily enough, sometimes in politics it's the picture you paint that counts, and you will probably end up being remembered for one thing, and the one thing that you are remembered for, won't necessarily be what you want to be remembered for."

Andrew Bridgen MP

"For being an active participator in the debating chamber, and a hardworking and effective campaigner on behalf of my constituents."

Andy Burnham MP

"These are hard questions aren't they? *(laughter)* I want to be remembered as someone who did right by the NHS, who stood up for kids from a similar background to mine, i.e. who weren't born in the golden circles of this country. I want to be remembered as someone who had some integrity and principles. People might not always agree with me, but they would always say that I had been true to the things I believe in throughout my career. I want to be remembered as someone with integrity, not necessarily for big reports and things like that. That people would look back and say he did his best, he did some good things."

Ann Coffey MP

"I think one of the great things about actually being an MP is the very special place you have in your constituency which is very unique to you, and if I was going to be remembered for anything I would like to be remembered as having represented the community well. I think that would be a very good thing to be remembered for."

Rosie Cooper MP

"I suppose as the best MP West Lancashire has ever had. I didn't come here to be, I came here to do, so at the end of it I need to see a tangible result. We've got the College, we are going to have a town centre which could so easily have been paused, and not have happened for a few years. And all of it would have fallen away had Everton gone to Kirby. A Government spokesperson, I don't know who, said Rosie played a ferocious game and she won, and I did. I staked everything, because if it had have gone through, Skem and Ormskirk would have been finished."

Philip Davies MP

"That's quite easy. As someone who stood up and said what they thought irrespective of how popular it was, or whatever the party thought, someone who stood up and advocated unpopular causes, and unfashionable causes, and said the things that nobody else would say."

Stephen Dorrell MP

"I think more generally if through the health and care system we are able to deliver more joined up care, that is more focussed on the service user, and less on a set of institutions that owe their roots to history, I will have made an important difference."

Michael Dugher MP

"Jeez. Thirty or forty years ahead, sat in my rocking chair, with the three remaining hairs on my head turning silver. You know like everyone else I would like to sit there and think that I had been a good father to my kids, been a good husband, that I had been as good a person as I could be, recognizing that everyone has their faults and failings. I think professionally I would like, at whatever point I am no longer the Member of Parliament for Barnsley, I would like people in Barnsley to think that I worked hard for them, that I did my best for them, and that I made a difference."

Natascha Engel MP

"It's really difficult to say anything without sounding completely pompous. The one thing that I have been really excited about with this job doing the Backbench Business Committee and dealing with all the E Petitions, only having existed for 18 months, and it's a committee not just me, but I think we as a Committee have brought in something that is already connecting people with Parliament in a much more worthy way, and I hope that is what I will be remembered for. That is the thing I care most about, making it all relevant to everyday lives."

Andrew George MP

"As someone who sought out the silent voices; who spoke up for those who found it difficult to speak up for themselves, and who stood up to bullies."

John Glen MP

"My major hope is to be known as a superb constituency MP, that I delivered. I can see a new school, a new Sixth Form, investment has been maintained in Porton Down and the jobs there, that I made sure that my constituents received best possible outcomes from Government. That I was always accessible and available, and that I represented them faithfully and determinedly over a long period of time, that very few people said that I wasn't a good MP. That's what you want because at the end of the day, doing your job well in our world is not about public recognition, it's having the satisfaction that your efforts were recognised. Not rewarded, but recognised, by the people who know you most in your constituency. Not to have a big place in history but the sense that you can retire with some satisfaction for the period that you were given, that you did a good job."

Zac Goldsmith MP

"I hope I will have used my time in Parliament as fully and wisely as is possible. It is a great privilege, and also a great opportunity."

Dan Jarvis MBE MP

"I would like to be remembered as someone who always did their best for the people of Barnsley Central, that would make me very happy."

Liz Kendall MP

"Getting a proper deal on how we fund care for older people in the future, which has agreement across the parties, so that people know when they are older, if they need care, that there will be a decently funded care system, and that is very, very difficult."

Sadiq Khan MP

"Politicians often talk about the 'L' word Legacy. To be honest I am really quite pleased with the legacy I have left so far. Working class boy in Parliament, first MP of Muslim faith to be in Parliament, attend Cabinet, all that sort of stuff. There are tangible things too, I can point to a school in my patch that wouldn't be there but for me, I can point to buildings that wouldn't have got the investment but for what I did, so I have already achieved things that I am happy to be remembered for. For me personally, I have two healthy great kids. Maybe they will find the cure to cancer, or the secret to the Universe."

Caroline Lucas MP

"For staying true to my principles, standing up for my constituents and making a positive difference."

Nicky Morgan MP

"I would really like to have been seen to be one of the people getting the big mental health debate, and getting mental health talked about more here. And as the Government I guess we did come in to tackle the deficits which have made life very difficult for everyone in the country, so I think if we are able to look back and say we made tough choices, it was very hard, but we did ultimately get our economy back on track, I think that would have been a legacy that I would like to be a part of."

Greg Mulholland MP

"Being a good MP, and being a good father. For achieving success in some important campaigns, that change things for the better. I will judge myself on how successful I have been in doing that."

Jason McCartney MP

"Well in just opening the factory this morning, I now have a plaque, so people will be able to look at the rusty plaque, and say who was that Jason McCartney MP then? There was a previous MP here called Richard Wainwright, and people remember him as a good constituency MP, I would like to be remembered as someone who brought everybody together no matter what their political background is. Someone who provided incentives and encouragement for young people, good businesses, someone who brings pride to our area, which we have already. For my positivity and for real good community spirit, and that can be at all different levels."

Esther McVey MP

"Helping people, being straightforward, honest and optimistic.

Always finding a solution to a problem. As my granddad always said, don't moan… find a solution."

Stephen Pound MP

"What an incredibly good question. What I want to be remembered for is making a few people's lives better in my constituency, and being part of a government that rebuilt every school in my constituency, and actually valued people, who didn't have the ability to make the case for theirselves, but who needed help from other people. I want to be remembered as someone who was clean politically, who wasn't corrupt, who wasn't venal, but someone who did a fairly decent job, who did everything the best he could. I just want to be remembered as the person who gave 100%. I don't want to be remembered as a playboy or as an amateur. What a great question though."

Yasmin Qureshi MP

"I would like to be remembered as a decent, honest, hard-working person."

John Redwood MP

"I would like to be remembered for the big campaigns I have helped to orchestrate – the campaign to return the wealth and ownership of state owned enterprises to the workforces and customers in the wider community in the 1980s, and the campaign to save the pound in the 1990s."

Jacob Rees Mogg MP

"Well in thirty years time, I will only be seventy-two, so I hope I will still be here, still being returned by the long suffering electorate of North East Somerset!" *(laughter)*

Jonathan Reynolds MP

"Definitely for my constituency work, and you know when you see politicians pass away, people like Lord Ashley, you immediately think about him being a renowned campaigner. I think it probably grows over your career, but what would be fundamental, and it's very hard, because you never know what is going to happen or if there will be another contentious world event like the Iraq War, is that I want to keep living in the centre of my constituency, which is important because people can bump into you in the supermarket as well as by coming to your office. If there is ever a national issue where I feel things are not in the interest of our local area here that I would be seen to stand up for the best interests of the constituency, because that's the legacy. When you're quite young, as well I have no idea what the legacy of the job will bring, my kids will go to school here and it will be remembered in the memory of this area, and I want that memory to be a good one.

"I am also the Secretary of the Armed Forces Parliamentary Group, we have a lot of people serving in the Forces from round here, and that sort of connection you really do take very seriously, with things like Libya. It's things like that that really bring home that the decisions you make can have such an impact on your community. At the end of forty or fifty years you don't want people to say I agree with everything that guy did and said, but you do want them to say he was a decent guy, he worked hard and he was pretty genuine."

Derek Twigg MP
"Being a good hard working MP who achieved the best he could for his community."

I don't know about you, but I find it re-assuring that they want to be remembered as good constituency MPs, and what Kevin Brennan has to say is very interesting, he is right, sadly you may not be remembered for what you may have liked to have been remembered for.

I wish more MPs shared Andy Burnham's sentiment about doing right by the NHS, as we may no longer have one by the next generation of MPs. John Glen also makes a worthy comment in his wish to be remembered for always being accessible and available, shame Government Ministers don't follow his example.

Oh and God Bless Liz Kendall with her objective if we are fortunate enough to reach old age, having contributed to the system all our working lives, surely we are entitled to expect to be cared for. And when you listen to everything Caroline Lucas says, don't you wish there were more Green Party members in Parliament, I suspect Esther McVey's granddad was right when he said "Don't moan, find a solution" a great motto that we would all do well to live by.

The last word undoubtedly has to go to Philip Davies, and it is certainly worth repeating, "That's quite easy. As someone who stood up and said what they thought irrespective of how popular it was, or whatever the party thought, someone who stood up and advocated unpopular causes, and unfashionable causes, and said the things that nobody else would say."

*Politicians have all the answers when in Opposition
and all the excuses when in power.*
Tony Russell

Sadiq Khan

Applause, mingled with boos and hisses,
is about all that the average voter is able or
willing to contribute to public life.
Elder Davis

CHAPTER SEVENTEEN

In Conversation with

During the course of these interviews, there were times when I was fortunate enough to have a little more time with some of the MPs, and the interviews progressed from a Question and Answer session to an often very interesting more in depth conversation.

Paul Blomfield MP

On Dealing With His Brain Tumour

"There are lots of lessons from what I have just been through, firstly, even if you have what you think is a minor symptom, check it out with the GP, particularly if you are a bloke because we have a habit of trying to put out of our minds things that can be more serious. I had a minor sight interruption, which lasted for about thirty minutes and I thought, oh well that's fine, one of those things. Then I thought I ought to check it out with the GP, who thought it was something minor but wanted to confirm the diagnosis, so sent me to the hospital and they said, actually you have a major brain tumour. You have had it for about fifteen years, but we need to operate immediately, because it's pressing against your optic nerve, and if we don't it might permanently damage your sight. So the NHS worked for me, prompt diagnosis, swift action, great care, eleven weeks later I am fine."

You said before we started recording it all seemed to happen quite quickly, obviously it was devastating news, but you didn't get much time to think.

"It was worse for my wife, because at the point I was diagnosed, I sent her a text message saying I thought she ought to pop in to the hospital, and from that point on I was having tests and being prepared for the operation, she was sitting at home having to think about it while I was on the operating table. I was out to the world, so when a predicted six hour operation became a twelve hour operation, she was at home having to worry about it, it was much worse for her."

On why the operation took twice as long
"It was more complicated. The hospital were great, after eight hours they rang my wife to say we know you were waiting to hear, but it's taking a bit longer so we are just ringing to reassure you. I had a great neuro-surgical team and nursing staff. After the operation I was up on my feet again pretty quickly, reassured that the tumour was benign, that there were no side effects from its' removal, and six days later I was out of hospital, with a four by four section of my skull removed and replaced with titanium screws."

Looking at you now, you wouldn't think that you had just been through all that, you look really well!

"I feel really well, the NHS delivered for me, as it does day in day out for thousands and thousands of people."

On whether the NHS would have delivered under 'Lansley's brave new world
"That's why we need to defend it, and why I am so proud of what Labour did. Over the 13 years we were in power, we almost doubled the investment made, and that made an enormous difference, more doctors, nurses, equipment, and treatments. It meant that the equipment was there to deliver effective diagnosis, more knowledge

about the work being done, and more tools to do it."

Has it changed your outlook on life?

"I have become more aware that you never know what is round the corner, maybe you reflect a little more, and spend more time with those that matter to you, which you don't always do as a politician. Apart from that it has just re-energised me."

Andrew Bridgen MP

On The Press

"I think if you look at the popular press, it's open season to attack MPs for everything. There isn't a great deal of compassion out there. Journalists aren't really interested in the truth, all they are interested in is selling newspapers. Good news is never a story anyway, so they actually want bad news about somebody or something, their job is to create a story that people want to read, whether it's true or not. We all know what we are getting into, no-one makes you be an MP. At the end of the day there are hundreds of people who would want this job, so while there is that sort of competition, you are going to have to accept that politics is a rough trade. The press don't take any prisoners, they will print anything that is bad about MPs, and people generally are willing to believe it. Although politicians are regarded fairly badly, if you spoke to people in the MPs own constituency they would say all politicians are pretty awful, liars, cheats, rogues, but ours isn't that bad. I know it's setting the bar pretty low but that is how it is."

On The Public Getting Involved

"When people are really passionate about an issue, they say to me what are you going to do about it? I try to say to them what are we going to do about it? If they don't have true conviction about their arguments, they don't want to do anything, they just want me to, maybe that's an issue I can deal with, but I would rather they got involved as well. Politics isn't just for MPs to get involved in, it's for everyone to get involved. I met this guy who said I'm not interested in politics so I don't want to talk to you, I said to him are you interested in the Armed Forces, and he said oh yes I love the Armed Forces, I said are you interested in the Economy, he said yes, it's in a shocking state, so I said are you interested in the NHS, and he said yes we rely on the NHS, but you are not interested in politics are you?!" *(laughter)*

People should understand that everything in life is affected by politics.

"Tony, you have been to Parliament quite a few times, and doesn't it give you an appreciation of what it's like here, people have to come here to experience it, to really understand it. You can't just tell them what it's really like here, and what the people are like. You have pretty good access to politicians. I have good friends on the Labour side, I go and have a drink with them and they are really decent people, obviously politically completely wrong and lazy thinkers *(laughter)* but not intrinsically bad. Most MPs are here for the right reasons, and genuinely want to do the very best they can for their constituents, and the country as they see it. If someone starts out with that stand-point, you might not agree with them, but you can't slag them off politically, because it's what they truly believe. Oppositional politics sometimes turns into a bit of a slanging match, but the way you get the best legislation, is by someone else pointing out what's wrong with it, you shouldn't get offended because there might be something wrong with it. At the end of the day we have a system of politics that has been reproduced around the world, so it can't be that bad can it? Democracy isn't the answer to everything but it's better than everything else we have tried."

> There are MPs whose opinions I am violently opposed to, but I still respect them for the courage of their convictions. I can't cope with MPs who just 'toe the line' irrespective of what their view might be.

"Because the Government is a coalition, we effectively had to renege on a lot of promises made on the doorstep that we would have delivered on, specifically on Europe which I struggle with, which is why I have voted against them five times I think it is on Europe, and that I have also abstained, when I couldn't vote for what was going on. **So I guess that's not a good career move then?** Possibly not, but it might be because I think Euro scepticism is growing far more popular in the country, so it might prove that the things I have voted against like bail outs for other countries, or the £400 million increase in the European budget which I didn't support because when I worked it out it was the equivalent of £750,000 out of my constituency, £15,000 a week when we are having to cut funding to voluntary groups in Coalville, the most deprived town in Leicestershire. I think we can spend that £15,000 a lot better than the European Union who haven't had their accounts signed off for fifteen years because there are too many black holes. I couldn't vote for that when we told the people we weren't going to give Europe any extra money, I couldn't walk down Coalville High Street and look people in the eye and think I voted for that, so I didn't. I voted for an amendment to the Freedom Bill last week too, because there was a clause that was going to make it illegal to insult somebody – well what's an insult, what one person would think is, another wouldn't. It would have been like a lawyer's charter. I thought a Freedom Bill was supposed to be about Freedom. Imagine going to a meeting, and someone says something that is liked, so someone else says they have insulted them, they could then be arrested, and thrown in prison, well it's just not on is it. It's just not British, so I wasn't too chuffed with that."

You are an entrepreneur, used to running a business, what advice would you give those that work in the charitable sector in these difficult times, particularly new charities, how do we survive in the current climate?

"The less you can rely on funding from Government the better, because that funding is always going to be at risk. I will defend all of my voluntary sector locally. When I became an MP it was pretty obvious what was going to happen, there would be severe spending reductions. A third of all Government funding is through local or unitary authorities. The first thing we did was go to all the voluntary groups, in Coalville especially, the most deprived town in the county, which is generally very affluent, which is the worst place to be, in a deprived area surrounded by wealth, lots of my local groups are part funded by district and county councils, people like the C.A.B. and Turning Point. We met these people and found out where their funding streams were, and lobbied from the very beginning, to make sure that they kept their funding, because they are the easiest things for the councils to cut. When you look at what they leverage in, The Big Society, Home Start, you have seventy four volunteers doing it for nothing, for the cost of two co-ordinators, if you had to deliver those services from the County Council it would cost an absolute arm and a leg. So do not even think about cutting my voluntary groups when they are delivering with such meagre resources all these services. Go and switch the lights off in County Hall if you need to save money. So I think we have been fairly successful, some of them had to have a reduced funding stream, but at least they still have funding guaranteed for a number of years. It's no good being on tenterhooks every year, you need to be able to build for the future and know that you have the money for three to five years."

(Don't we know it.)

"We have East Midlands Airport in my constituency and they operate the Leicestershire, Nottinghamshire, Rutland Air Ambulance which is completely run by voluntary contributions, they have to raise £30-40,000 a week to keep that helicopter in the air. I had a brilliant visit there when they were just taking delivery of a brand new helicopter. They took me and another couple of MPs from the Airport to Derby Royal Infirmary to show us how they work, I said to them at the end, would you take any Government funding, they said no, we wouldn't want any because if we took Government money we would have to have Government inspections, and we wouldn't need £30,000 a week then, we would need £60,000! They said they normally have three or four months money in the bank raised by their fund-raisers and donations, and even in these tough times were ok. Doesn't that say a lot that is good about the voluntary sector and how they work, and a lot that is bad about Government funding that they wouldn't take it even if it was offered. I think that speaks absolute volumes. That's a sad indictment isn't it?"

My hero is Winston Churchill, what part of military history interests you?

"I was always very keen on the Duke of Wellington, the General who never lost a battle in the whole of his military career, and who faced

Napoleon in his last battle, who had also never lost. That was the clash of titans, and changed the face of European history. You know, Income Tax was brought in as a temporary measure to pay for the Napoleonic Wars, you would have thought it would have been paid for by now *(laughter)*. I am always very suspicious of any politicians who say they are bringing anything in on a temporary basis.

"I have been in the Armed Forces, and I wanted to be a leader of men, no offence to ladies, and I have always been fascinated by how you persuade people to stand there when there is a chance they are going to get killed, would they follow you? I can remember my Sergeant in the Royal Marines said to me, 'Mr Bridgen, your men will always follow you because they are very well trained, they will follow you for one of two reasons, either they trust you with their lives and they will follow you into the mouth of hell, or they think you are a complete idiot and they are following you to see what you are going to do next' *(laughter)*, 'and you will never know which reason.' I have always had an interest in the Napoleonic Wars, wars changed after that, the artillery was more powerful, and that changed the tactics, but Waterloo was one of the last powder cavalry battles. I have been to Waterloo to the Battlefield quite a few times. So, the Napoleonic Wars and especially the Duke of Wellington. He had a staff of about thirty four civilians who ran the Ministry of Defence, and ran the whole of the defence of Great Britain with that, we now have 22,000 just in military procurement, so I think there are probably about 70,000 civil servants in the M.O.D., I think we may be a bit top heavy on that one."

On climate change and oppositional politics
"I am not sure that climate change and global warming have been given a fair hearing on either side, it seems to be an accepted norm. Anyone who doesn't totally agree with what the accepted norm is is shouted down. As a scientist, it's a bit like oppositional politics, if you can't defend your argument without accusing someone of being loony, or just saying why don't you believe us because everyone else

does. For me that's not right, people are entitled to have a different opinion, and if you can't defend your arguments maybe there is something wrong with them. Change is always driven by unreasonable people, because reasonable people tend to accept the status quo, things are as they are, but unreasonable people rail against the way things are, as they don't think they are right."

Ann Coffey MP

You have had exciting times with the big landslide in '97, and you have had some really high profile jobs, as PPS to Tony Blair and Alistair Darling, what was that like?

"The use of the word interesting is perhaps an understatement, but when you are in those sorts of positions, and you are very close, watching how the Executive of a Government makes it decisions, it gives you a realisation of the limits of what politicians can actually do, because those two people I know, were always limited in what they could do, by what was possible and what wasn't. And this very interesting phrase 'Events dear chap' also came to mind. In a sense politics is often a reaction to events. The event could be happening on the other side of the world, it could be in the U.K., it could be a natural disaster, it could be a terrorist attack, it could be a slump in the Stock Exchange, or the collapse of the financial markets. People as their elected representative expect you to be able to control these events, but they are outside of your control. It's interesting to watch Governments and very important Ministers like Tony Blair and Alistair Darling faced with events, then try and put the show back on the road which was what the electorate would expect."

On Ministers
"It's important that Ministers have strong views because civil

servants have strong views too. If the Minister doesn't have strong views, then the Civil Service's views tend to prevail."

On changing politics
"I think bits of legislation have changed the way that politics operates, for example the Freedom of Information Act which the Labour Government passed has given much more power to people to ask for information that wasn't available to them previously. The signing up to the European Convention of Rights has given the Courts much more power to decide on individual cases, that has altered where politicians sit in the exercise of power. You have lobby groups, courts, press, public opinion and you have politicians who are all part of the process of democracy. There is a transparency about the democratic process that wasn't there twenty years ago before those very significant acts were on the statute book."

On being in Opposition rather than in power
"I have never been a Minister, so actually the job of a back bencher, in terms of how you do your business isn't a lot different when you are in Government as opposed to being in Opposition. You are a lot freer when you are in Government to pursue your own interests. I think it must be harder for people who were Ministers and used to making decisions, but I have never been in that position. It's been an easier transition for me."

Philip Davies MP

It's interesting that you said you were always a Conservative. Peter Hitchens described you as a genuine Conservative. What is a genuine Conservative?

"Well Peter Hitchens was very kind. I think basically he was saying that I have retained my traditional Conservative views"

(I can't tell the difference between David Cameron and Tony Blair)

"Well quite." *(laughter)* "I think that's how David Cameron likes it. I think he would take that as a compliment."

A lot of MPs in the past have either been lawyers or political researchers, but you came from a supermarket? We have met former lawyers, a hospital porter, a bus driver… but you are the first from a supermarket.

"I'm not quite the first, my boss at ASDA, Archie Norman, was the MP for Tunbridge Wells, and Archie was my referee to get onto the approved list of candidates. Funny enough, there are two other MPs now who both worked for ASDA with me, Mark Menzies who actually took my job at ASDA, and in 2010, was elected as the MP for Fylde, and David Rutley who is the MP for Macclesfield, used to work at ASDA as well, so we are having an ASDA takeover *(laughter)*. This is Wal-Mart's plan to conquer the world. I said in my maiden speech, we had 14/15 million customers coming through the doors, it's a great background for politics in terms of dealing with a cross section of the public. You are right there are lots of people here who were lawyers, researchers, advisors or whatever. I think the problem really is for lots of people politics is their career, whereas as far as I am concerned I gave up my career to go into politics, so I think with that comes a slightly different perspective. In my career, I worked for ASDA, I wanted to get promoted, and the same happens if you see politics as a career you will do what it takes to get promoted, whereas I don't see it as a career, I don't want to get promoted. If I was offered a promotion I would turn it down. It's a completely different way of looking at it."

You might not feel the same if it was a different leader though…?

"No, to be perfectly honest when I said that in my maiden speech, David Cameron wasn't the leader then. I have absolutely nothing against him at all. Whoever was leader, whoever was Prime Minister, I would never accept a promotion."

People say that we live in a democracy, but I wonder sometimes when Members of Parliament, more often than not will vote the way their whips tell them to, it may not be what their constituents want. I question just how much of a democracy we actually have, and wonder if it would be better if there were more independent MPs?

"We do live in a democracy, it's a parliamentary democracy, so our system is that people vote for someone to represent their interests in Parliament, then it's up to that person to do what he or she thinks is right. At the following election people can decide whether they want that person to continue, or whether they want someone else to do the job for them. I'm a fan of our system of democracy. I might be one of the more rebellious MPs but I am a fan of the whipping system, I have no problem with that. The whips tell you what they think you should do, and it's up to you whether you take it on board. It's my right to ignore what they say.

"The thing is, and this is where the dilemma comes in for MPs, in terms of do you vote for things that your constituents want, the honest answer is no I don't, I vote for what I think is the right thing, and it's for people to consider whether they are happy for me to continue representing them. Capital Punishment is an emotive issue, if you're against it, and you had an opinion poll in your constituency which showed that most people were for it, I can't ever imagine you voting for something like that when you are so wholly against it. You have to follow your conscience, and what you believe in your heart is the right thing to do. I go home every weekend to my constituents, and I've got to look them in the eye, and say whether you agree with me or not, I did what I genuinely thought was right. I think as long as you can say that, then you are alright. They will respect you.

"I was elected as a Conservative, when I was first elected in 2005, I don't believe anyone woke up before the election and said I can't stand Michael Howard, and I can't stand the Conservative Party, but I'm going to vote for that Philip Davies, he seems like a nice chap. They voted for me because I happened to have the word Conservative after my name on the ballot paper. That was the only reason I got elected in 2005, it was nothing to do with me. So that is how I have marketed myself, what I have said I am. It's perfectly right that people feel when I get to Parliament I will broadly follow the Conservative line. I approach these things with my default position being to vote with the Conservative Party. If there is an issue where I don't really care one way or another, I will vote the way the Conservative whips ask me to, or if it's an issue that I don't really know much about, I will also vote the way the Conservative whips ask me to, but if I feel strongly they are doing the wrong thing, that's when I will rebel. I think people who voted for me are entitled to think that I will generally follow the Conservative line in Parliament."

You are obviously making a difference, because your majority went up a lot in the last election.

"Yes, it was a surprise, it went from 422 to nearly 10,000. That was a shock, I didn't expect it. I thought it would go up because of the rising tide of the Conservative Party, as opposed to the previous election, and there's no doubt that quite a bit of it was down to that. The night before we had a discussion about how we thought it would go, my guess was that I would win by 6000, I certainly didn't expect to win by 10,000. It was a high point for me."

Dan Jarvis MBE MP

Having been in Barnsley for a number of years myself now, you have done a fantastic job being accepted so quickly, given that you are not from here.

"Thanks a lot. I hope people know that I am utterly committed to our town, and I will continue to work incredibly hard to do my best for the people of Barnsley. I have got big bold ambitious plans, I think Barnsley is a great place to live, but there are a number of big issues in the town, generational things that are not going to be solved today, tomorrow or next week, so this is something I want to do for the rest of my working life. I set pretty high standards for myself and I want to do the best job that I can for Barnsley, a lot of people have put a lot of faith in me, not only selecting me as the Labour candidate, but also by voting for me in the by-election. I am totally determined to re pay the faith they have placed in me."

On his role on the Select Committee for Business, Innovation and Skills
"I was always very keen from the outset not to be known as the person who had gone to Westminster to talk about the Army and Defence. So I quite deliberately did my Maiden Speech on the Budget and I quite deliberately requested to go on a Select Committee that wasn't Defence or Security related. I quickly came to the conclusion that the Select Committee that had the most direct relevance and impact on Barnsley was business, because it's all about the economy. The biggest issue for people in Barnsley is jobs, so the Business, Innovation and Skills Committee was the one that I thought was the most relevant to my role as MP for Barnsley. Fortunately there was a vacancy at that time, and I got that slot, it's been extremely useful in educating me about some of the issues that matter most in Barnsley. I was also asked to chair Labour's Back Bench Business, Innovation and Skills Committee, so I do that too which complements my work with the Select Committee."

Going back to your Army days I was fascinated by this thing in Kosovo with the American NATO Commander who wanted a confrontation with the Russians, can you tell us a bit about that please?

"It was June 1999 and at the time I was serving as a Platoon Commander in 1 Para, the whole battalion were sat in a very large cornfield in Northern Macedonia waiting to move up into Kosovo and we got word, to everyone's amazement, that elements of the Russian Army had made a move towards the airfield at Pristina. This took everyone by surprise, and the then NATO Commander who was a guy called General Wesley Clarke (quite a controversial, difficult character), who was later to launch a candidacy for Presidency of the United States. He basically ordered General Mike Jackson, the Commander of NATO Forces in Kosovo to launch an operation to prevent the Russians from getting to the airfield. The order was that if it were required, we should use force, potentially lethal force to prevent the Russians getting to the airfield. So as I understand it, I was sat in the cornfield oblivious to the conversation that was going on, but Mike Jackson basically told Wesley Clarke that he wasn't prepared to do that. There was a bit of a stand off and Mike Jackson was talking to the Chief of Defence Staff and ultimately to the Prime Minister, back in this country, and in the end we didn't launch that operation to prevent the Russians taking the airfield. The Russians came down and took the airfield, but then UK and NATO Forces went north into Kosovo and met with the Russian Forces, and Mike Jackson led the discussions, and had a pretty aimiable and constructive conversation with them, and they agreed precisely what was going to happen and how it would work. The NATO forces then went on into Pristina, to try to restore some sort of peace and order in the town. It was a highly charged moment."

That could have started World War Three.

"Well that's what Mike Jackson said. But originally we were given a set of orders that were straight out of the Cold War, you will use potentially lethal force to stop the Russians taking the airfield. It was a bizarre, surreal moment. I subsequently then went on to be General Mike Jackson's ADC, when 1 Para when back to the UK having served their tour of duty in Kosovo, I then remained in theatre, and took over the job of personal staff officer to Mike Jackson and stayed with him for a number more months, which was fascinating."

On Being In Opposition
"It is frustrating to be in Opposition, but I still believe we can influence and get things done. Just to give you one example. I am

doing a lot of work around Libraries. So I am putting together a plan for what a Library should look like in the 21st century, and I think because I am trying to do it in a reasonable, sensible straight-forward kind of way, that will give me the opportunity to shape the debate. Politics is like that, Governments come and go, individuals come and go, you enter Parliament at a particular time and I have done that when we are in Opposition. I think you have just got to get on with it really, and do the job to the best of your ability depending on the opportunities that come your way."

On his new role as Shadow Arts and Culture Minister
"If you can't enjoy the Shadow Arts and Culture Role you can't enjoy life. I mean there are some fantastic opportunities and some amazing things going on, with brilliant people. It is wonderful! I am utterly seized by the value of it, partly for young people, but for everyone else too. It's great, I have seen some brilliant things, some great exhibitions, some brilliant shows, quite high end stuff, the opera and the ballet, through to the more commercially available stuff, it's really great fun. But I really, much more than when I first met you am better placed to understand the benefit that people get from access to the arts. I hope you are proud of me, I am doing a lot, and now I am saying what you were saying to me when we first met a year ago.

"I think because of my own personal background, I got it perhaps more than other people did, but because I have had such privileged access in many respects to arts, culture, museums I completely see the value that they add to our lives."

It's funny because you were quoted in one of the broadsheets, I can't remember the exact quote, but it was about military life not equipping you for this role.

"I didn't say that, people have said that about me." *(laughter)* "I think the headline was 'An Unlikely Culture Minister'. It's quite an interesting debate, as you know I think being in the Army equips you fantastically well for politics. I was the first to say that I hadn't spent the last fifteen years in and out of the ballet, because I hadn't and if you haven't done these things it's best to be up front and straight about them. But that's not to say I wasn't interested in going to the ballet or museums or to be looking at the visual arts, but my life then didn't neatly lend itself towards doing that."

Sadiq Khan MP

Looking through your biography there are a lot of firsts and many awards that you have won.
On being a member of the Privy Council – tell us about that and what it means

"Basically when you see written before an MP, the words The Right Honourable, it means that he or she is a member of the Privy Council, when it is just Honourable, they are not. If you go back a few hundred years, the king or queen would have advisors, and this would be members of the Privy Council, so they were the entrusted servants of the Royal Family so to speak, of the king or queen. In more recent times, the role has changed because obviously there is more democracy now, and of course a Prime Minister. Privy Councillors have less influence than they used to have hundreds of years ago, but even now there are meetings for the Privy Councillors with the queen on some issues."

On how proud you were to be the first Asian – the first Muslim to attend Cabinet
"Yes I have been blessed, when I was appointed to that position and the Privy Council by Gordon Brown in 2009 it was an amazing

experience, when I had just been elected only four years previously. Obviously I am very proud, but I don't see myself in that way. We all have multiple identities. Of course I am Asian, and I am a Muslim, but I am also a Londoner, I am a father, I am a husband, I am British. You can't define yourself by just one part of your identity. So of course I am really proud. I have just come from Oxford where I have been giving a talk to deprived students about leadership, one of the things I said to them is that you should always aspire to do more, if you are from a humble background, like me, whose dad was a bus driver, and you can go on to be a Privy Councillor and in the Cabinet then that's not bad."

On being the first western Minister to visit the Holy Cities of Mecca and Medina
"That's because the rules of Islam are quite strict, they are the two holiest cities of the Muslim faith, and you can only visit Mecca or Medina if you are a Muslim, so non Muslims are not allowed. You must have seen pictures of the Kabba, the black cube where we go round that to worship. So obviously because there had not been a Muslim Minister from the west previously I was the first to go there. Globalisation has made the world a smaller place, east meets west. Christianity against Muslim is a lot of nonsense. Obviously I am a Muslim, but I am also British. I think it is the beginning of a trend, touch wood, and I think you will see more and more, as Muslims continue to do well in this country, in Europe and America too – more and more Ministers who are both Western but Muslim going on pilgrimage, and that's a good thing."

On the whip's office, and do they bully people to do what they are told
"You can charm people as well. One's persuasive tactics can vary. The whips serve a very, very important purpose. When I was first elected, it wasn't unusual for me to vote against my own Government, so I am not just a patsy, I have been outspoken when I need to be. I have always maintained that it is very important in a

parliamentary democracy for there to be some sort of discipline, and the reason why the whips are important is this. If you are a hard working, busy MP, you can't know what is going on every single day in Parliament, there are different bills virtually every day this week, so how would I know how to vote in a certain way if I have not been following the detail. The whips will look at all the legislation going through, and at our party's policy, look at what the Government is proposing, and then advise colleagues to vote in a certain way. On a serious note, it's a quite important management tool. Even in business you have people whose job it is to administer, and to advise, the same as in politics, but where I think you have got to be careful is on certain issues of conscience where the whips stay out of it. But generally speaking they have a very important role to play, and it was good training ground for me to spend time there, and learn how this place works."

On being chair of the Fabian Society and what they do
"The Fabian Society is the world's oldest think tank. A think tank are people who come up with ideas, and then they hope that policy makers take them up. For example years ago, the Fabian Society came up with the idea of having a welfare state that provided those who were basically socially disadvantaged, and who had fallen through the cracks with some minimum provision. Often the Fabian Society like other think tanks come up with ideas that may not be taken up by politicians, sometimes they will. The Fabian Society is left of centre. There are also right of centre think tanks. It is a membership organisation. The people who founded The Fabian Society also founded the London School of Economics, and lots of the thinking about the welfare state. Some of the thinking Gordon Brown did about alleviating poverty was driven by Fabian Society documents, work life balance and all the rest of it. It is still very important in helping to make policy decisions for political parties."

Jacob Rees-Mogg MP

On The E.U.

"One of the reasons we find being in the E.U. so uncomfortable, is that we have a common law system, where the laws are consented to, by the people who are governed by them, and it's always been lawful to do anything that isn't specifically prohibited. In the Napoleonic system it's rather the other way around, unless it's allowed, it's not allowed. So for generations we have accepted the Laws, and obeyed them because that has been the right thing to do. On the Continent, for generations, they have avoided the Law, because everything was covered by the Law, so intrusive that they couldn't do anything else. What we find very uncomfortable is that we are now applying our system to a Napoleonic system, and there are far too many laws many of which don't work, and the two systems don't work together. It's creating a serious clash of cultures between us and the Continentals. I call it Napoleonic although it goes back much further than that. There is a wonderful book written by John Fortescue, on political Government and he defines it very neatly, he says the difference is the King of England is the king under the law, and the King of France is the law, and it's those differences that have had a continuing long term effect."

I hope I am not doing you an injustice, but I read somewhere that you were described as 'David Cameron's worst nightmare'?

"I was, by *The Times* of all newspapers, and it goes back to what you were saying about not sleeping at night, so I would hate to be his worst nightmare, because it's important that the Prime Minister gets a good night's sleep! It would be difficult for him to govern the country otherwise." *(laughter)* "What it comes from, and this was unfortunate, is that I was selected, as was another MP, similar in some ways to me, just at the time that the Party was leading a big push to have different, more diverse candidates. So there was a big policy to do this, and then who gets selected, yours truly. It was just that the timing was not necessarily ideal for the Party."

On using the longest word in the Chamber and why
"I have no idea, it just came into my head.

Please can you pronounce it for us?

certainly it's Floccinaucinihilipilification. I wanted to be rude about the European judges because they have behaved very, very disgracefully, and what's interesting is we were debating what in my view, was a real scandal. The European judges had decided to increase their own pay. It's fundamentally against the basic principle of justice you should never be a judge in your own case. We had an hour and a half debate, lots of serious minded speeches were made, and the only thing that got it any publicity was the word Floccinaucinihilipilification. So it was jolly lucky that I used the word. It wasn't deliberate, I wish I was clever enough to have thought through a strategy to highlight the issue, but it did have the effect I wanted."

I have interviewed some MPs who may be considered rebels, but I can't see why you are?

"I am not really a rebel, and you know I enjoy reading a great deal, have probably read too much Trollope, that an MP ought to be relatively independent minded, representing his constituents, and not somebody who is just there to toe a party line. As it happens, I very often support the party line, overwhelmingly I think what the

Party is trying to do is right, but if I disagree, I have been given this platform by 69,000 electors and therefore I use it."

On voting against the whip
"Mainly on Constitutional issues, so on the fixed term for Parliament that was set, I consistently voted against the Party line as I thought it was a dreadful piece of legislation, dealing with the immediate problems of coalition, not dealing with our Constitution in a serious way."

Two MPs that I have interviewed, are more typically and traditionally Conservative, can you help me understand the Conservative Party a little?

"I think that is interesting. I think that the Tory Party has always had a variety of characters in it, and is there a typical Tory MP? I don't know? I think it changes as well, ten years ago the typical Tory MP would have been the Chairman of the 1922 Committee, Charles Walker is the Deputy Chair, so he is a suitable character, somebody who is upright, proper, full of integrity, completely loyal. But I think MPs recently have become much more willing to vote against the Party line. Twenty years ago, if you were looking at the typical Tory MP, he would never have voted against the Party Whip in his whole career in Parliament, and I think you would be hard put to find anyone in that category now."

Did you say 'I gradually realised that whatever I happened to be speaking about, the number of voters in my favour, dropped as soon as I opened my mouth?'

"Yes I did, I said this when I was canvassing in Central Fife, which was a Scottish constituency, the more I spoke, the more English they realised I was, and the less likely they were to vote for me *(laughter)*. So it was better if I shut up. They were very nice to me actually in Central Fife, they knew the Tories had no chance of winning. I would knock on doors and say, 'Hello I am Jacob Rees-Mogg, the Conservative Party candidate,' and they would say, 'Are you a Tory?' and they would laugh. *(laughter)* ' Tories don't normally stand here do they?' So anyway, I enjoyed Central Fife and they couldn't have been kinder. However much they were not going to vote Conservative, they were broadly welcoming that I was taking the trouble to go round, and they were good people who, just like everywhere else, wanted the best for themselves and their families."

This accent thing is really funny, my wife was in a taxi earlier today with a Cockney driver, who said he found it hard when he picked up people from the House of Lords, as he was embarrassed by the way he spoke, and concerned that he came across as being common, so he said he found himself trying to speak differently when he was in that situation.

"It's the George Bernard Shaw line isn't it, about as soon as an Englishman opens his mouth, another one makes a judgment on him. I think it fundamentally doesn't matter actually, I think what George Bernard Shaw said, is both true and not true. We all form snap judgments on people depending on what they look like and sound like and so on. If then what they say is interesting, then the accent doesn't matter at all. If what they say is completely banal, however grand the accent, you are not going to want to listen to them." *(laughter)*

We have read about you canvassing with your nanny – was that true?

"I never canvassed in central Fife in a Bentley or Rolls Royce or anything like that, that was all invention. Nanny is true, and someone I am very proud of. Veronica has worked for my family for 46 years, she looked after me as a child, and was with the family before I was born, she is now looking after my children, who are absolutely devoted to her, and she is terrific, she is part of the family. In Central Fife, my mother and father came, one sister came, my brother came and brought all his children with him, so the family helped, and Nanny is part of the family. I am not going to pretend that she doesn't exist, because she does. If you are in politics you need a thick skin, whatever you do, people will say something about it. You just sometimes have to be a little more careful what you say."

Sir Bob Russell MP

On the last election and suddenly belonging to the party holding the balance of power

"Actually I had mixed emotions. It is on the record that my prediction was by the weekend David Cameron would be Prime Minister and I was right, but that we would have a second general election between May and October next year, and I was wrong. Days later talks were in full flow and we had a coalition. I think the record shows that I am not the most enthusiastic supporter of the coalition, I voted against tuition fees, as I had said only a few months before that I would. I voted against VAT going up to 20% because as a tax it impacts proportionately more on low income families. And I have actually proposed that we should target a VAT reduction on tourism. I voted against the civil service pensions being changed, if people have signed up for something you shouldn't retrospectively change it, as a point of principle. But the record will show that I have supported the coalition more than some of the right wing Tory head-bangers."

On the Party Whip
"I used to be an Assistant Whip, but in those days it was more business management it is far more serious now. The Lib Dem Whips are part of the Government, and we have to make sure there are enough people in the right lobby. I got into terrible trouble, not because I voted in the wrong way, but I didn't tell them I was not going to be here for a three line whip, I'm buggered if I can remember what it was for now. I told them I wasn't going to be here, but I didn't fill in the form and get it sanctioned. The records will show that I have the best voting record of any MP over the fourteen years I have been here."

On making darts a recognised sport
"John Whittingdale, the Chair of the Culture Select Committee, and MP for Maulden, has in his area darts' leading activist, who has completed a thesis on the history of darts, so he knows all about it. John previously had an adjournment debate on the issue. I was in my first or second year of being an MP, and there was an event in my constituency attended by Bobby George one of the country's more flamboyant darts players, who lives in my area too, and he started talking about getting darts registered as a sport so I told him I would go for it. I then discovered there are two darts organisations in this country and the buggers don't talk to each other. I then got involved with the Professional Darts Corporation, the ones with the money.

"Bobby George's people are like the F.A. for everyone, while the others are like the Premier League and they got all the money. For two years running I went down to their big event at Purfleet, and was on Sky Sports, and constantly raised the issue on the floor of the House, and Dick Caborn to his credit ran with it. The serious issue is, it really is a sport, almost like indoor archery. Darts is the only sport I know where you start by throwing closest to the bullseye, cricket and football are all on the toss of a coin. And yes it is a pub game, but it's more than that it can be played by people of all ages, so it's an all inclusive sport, and I do think one day it will become an Olympic sport. Darts is the fastest growing sport in the People's Republic of China. So if we don't get it as an Olympic sport soon the buggers will beat us at that too. I also got Dick Caborn to come to Colchester for cycle speedway, at a track opened by Trevor Brooking when he was Chair of Sport England."

> The last thing, and one of the things I love you for the most, is one of your constituents complained about the cost of the Royal Wedding, and you told them they needed to get a life. Now this is what a politician should do.

"There is another one too, this bloke contacts me on a whole range of issues, as he is entitled to do, he is a serial complainer, it gets a bit boring when they write to you on so many things, so now we wait until the end of the month, and give a collective response. My caseworker drafts most of my letters, but I have them on the machine and I titivate them, put a 'Russell' flavour to them. She had had written a really polite letter, and I said no, I'm not having that, and I wrote him a blockbuster which I do from time to time. Well he should have kept quiet. I got a lot of publicity out of that including Matthew Parris who started off his article *'Bob Russell is my Hero'*. I try to be myself, my wife and I have always lived in the same house for forty three years, opposite what used the be the Highways Depot, we have no graces in that sense, we are ordinary people. My wife is an Essex girl, fourth generation, so I think that is why people accept me because I don't live in a big house in the posh end of town.

"At the weekend, the *Guardian* phoned round various Lib Dem MPs expecting them to be outraged at the sentencing for the rioters. Well I am to the right of the Tories on this one so they didn't use it. I wrote them a letter and said I assume my comments were not what you were looking for. A few days later this Rector guy in Ealing, wrote in about my 'vile' and 'disgraceful' comments. The *Colchester Gazette* published this same story on the Bank Holiday, this resulted in a whole page of letters, the *Gazette* website praising me to the hilt. This is read by someone who told me that this Rector in Ealing is, or was a Labour Councillor. Funnily enough, he hadn't mentioned that. So I wrote to him, Dear Comrade Vicar… and he emailed me back saying he could have been more explicit perhaps, but that he wasn't making a political point. I have emailed him again this morning, and told him that I thought his political affiliation was an important aspect and that he had hid behind his clerical position, and that our Lord had never hid, anyway, I think I am going to let this one run a bit more."

Paul Blomfield, another really good guy, had previously joined me on one of my charity walks. Not long after, I heard he had been quite seriously unwell, so I was both relieved and happy when I met him in *The Palace of Westminster* many months later. Obviously I needed to talk to him about the trauma he had been through and how the NHS, something I am passionate about, had performed for him.

Andrew Bridgen is the sort of guy I could talk to for hours, and what started as an interview, just developed naturally into a conversation. To me, he is a conviction politician, and as far as I am concerned, they are worth their weight in gold.

I have known Ann Coffey for nearly twenty years, she has held some interesting positions within her party, without ever being a Minister. Nevertheless, she has had a positive impact, and she is a genuinely nice lady. Ann also hosted the launch of our charity *Reflections Art in Health*, and shares my love of photography.

Philip Davies is probably in many ways at the opposite end of the political spectrum to me, but I have a great deal of respect for him, like Andrew Bridgen and Jason McCartney, he is a conviction politician, not afraid to upset his own party. He also shares the same background as me in supermarket management.

At the time of writing, Dan Jarvis MBE was the newest addition to the House of Commons. I first met him when Colonel Bob Stewart was kind enough to allow me and my charity walk support team the use of his office, when we dropped in on Westminster. As Dan is my MP, I let out quite a bit of frustration during that first meeting, god knows what he must have thought, but a taxi driver friend of mine who is passionate about his home town of Barnsley tells you all you need to know about Dan when he says "Ere, that Dan Jarvis may not come from here, but he really cares about Barnsley you know. He'll do well here."

Dan, like many of us has been through a rough time. It is not for me to talk about, nor would he want me to, I just want to say, as with Michael Dugher, the people of Barnsley should be proud to have two great and totally committed MPs.

And what an interesting time Sadiq Khan has had with so many firsts. He is another MP that just makes you feel so relaxed. By the way, he also got me addicted to twitter.

I have said elsewhere in this book that Jacob Rees-Mogg is the type of guy both Angie (my wife) and I just wanted to give a big hug to. He is the perfect example of why you should not make judgements based on someone's accent or background for that matter. He is another thoroughly decent guy.

Sir Bob Russell is the first, and one of only three Lib Dems I interviewed. Someone else it is easy to relate to, a down to earth guy, who like he says has no airs and graces.

Finally, to my favourite quotes from this Chapter to end on:-

Andrew Bridgen – "Politics isn't just for MPs to get involved in, it's for everyone to get involved."

Ann Coffey – "It's important that Ministers have strong views because civil servants have strong views too. If the Minister doesn't have strong views, then the Civil Service's views tend to prevail."

Philip Davies – "I don't want to get promoted. If I was offered a promotion I would turn it down."

Stephen Dorrell

"If you don't take an interest, bad things can happen."
Dave Anderson MP – Chapter 19

CHAPTER EIGHTEEN
Off Script

When I began the task of interviewing these MPs, I had a list of questions I wanted to ask, but occasionally the conversation went in a different direction, here are the results.

Dave Anderson MP

On All Party Groups

"All Party Groups are voluntary, if you want to be on one of those, or if you want to start one you have to get twenty like minded parliamentarians from across the House, to say yes we will come together and do this work."

Being in Opposition

"It is frustrating, but if you believe in what you are trying to do, you just have to get through it. It doesn't stop things happening on the ground, which is probably the best part of the job, I have a tremendous amount of success in day to day issues, (not me but it's in my name) helping people with benefits, housing issues, everything. You know they call it an MPs surgery, and it's just like a doctor's surgery, people walk through the door with issues, or they ring with them. I have three full time members of staff who all work longer hours than they are payed for, and I have a number of volunteers. I think our volume of work is reflected in the votes we got. It's not rocket science, but if you deliver for people, because most people even if you can't give them what they want, it's the fact you've tried for them."

Sir Peter Bottomley MP

Working with Margaret Thatcher

"She was very straight forward, and if you were very straight forward, you got on very well, but if you started looking like a doormat, she'd walk on you. She and I first really met in 1975, she was leading the Tory Party, and there was a By-Election in a Labour seat, I was the Tory candidate and they asked if we were going to win, she said yes. She came down to help, drove around town in an open car waving at bus queues, and there was enthusiastic support. When they counted the votes, it had been a success for us, she was asked what's your reaction, and she took out a card that on one side said sick as a parrot, the other side said over the moon. There was a headline saying Maggie was over the moon about Woolwich, and a man called Michael Marshall, who that day had been elected Bishop thought she was excited about that rather than me becoming an MP. The following day my picture appeared in the papers again and this time she had given the photographers a Churchill victory sign, but she had her hand the wrong way around, so it was more of a Harvey Smith *(laughter)* and we got on very well since."

On Mental Health

"I take an interest, the MIND group in my constituency in Worthing is admirable. But it's not just the organised things, if you reckon that one teenager in four is going to be depressed, one teenager in ten is going to be seriously depressed, how do you help people recognise what's normal, what is part of the normal ups and downs of life, and how can you get people to talk about mental health and mental illness problems, in the same way that they could if they were dragging around a broken leg, or if they had a skin cancer? You can talk about skin cancers, you can talk about breast cancers, you can talk about prostrates, you can talk about virtually anything, but you can't talk about, at least not yet, mental illness in the same way."

You are a long serving MP, but you don't seem to be ground down.

"Well you can do what you can do, and you can't do what you can't do. And you can fit it what you can fit it, but you can't fit in any more, although it's a little trite to say so. I think you can probably do more by listening that you can by preaching, so I do a lot of listening."

Ben Bradshaw MP
On voting for your local MP, rather than the party or because of family tradition
"I think some people do, an increasing number of people vote on personal issues, you know the voter tribalism that dominated our politics for many years is weaker than it used to be. A lot of people do still vote on party lines but there are lots of variations within that. But you have to be realistic about this, in a constituency like mine where I've got one hundred and ten, one hundred and twenty thousand people, it's impossible for me to meet them all, so it's not really possible for everyone to glean a personal opinion of me. They might if they meet me but otherwise they are dependent on what other people say and on what they read in the papers, and that can make a difference, positive or negative. But I think if you look at democracies round the world, all the successful ones do base themselves on some sort of party system. If you didn't have some sort of party system you would have anarchy in Parliament, you would never get any decisions made."

On being in Opposition rather than in power
"I don't find it difficult at all, because I have always considered myself to be one of the lucky ones. I am one of those people who came into politics by accident, it wasn't something that I had planned for a long time. Just before the big Labour landslide, I came

into Parliament and then came into Government. But there are many other people on the Labour side, and indeed the Conservative side, who have never had that opportunity. I will always be incredibly grateful to have had those opportunities. To be perfectly honest, I don't agree with bemoaning the fact that I don't have them anymore because that's politics, and that is democracy. You just have to get on and to do other things, although I would rather be in Government. It does have its' compensations though, as I can see more of my friends and family, who I had neglected really in the last few years. I think the thing is that you make the most of the cards that are dealt to you, rather than wonder and complain and wish for other things."

Kevin Brennan MP
On voting against the Party Whip
"The implications of doing that depends on the circumstances. My thinking at the time of the Iraq War vote in 2003, was this will probably mean the end of the possibility of a Ministerial career or it could be. But the second part of my thinking was I just have to put that out of my mind on this issue, because it is an issue of such importance, people are going to go and get killed. You have to be absolutely sure that you are doing the right thing if you are going vote for it, and you certainly shouldn't be doing that thinking about personal career prospects. In practice, in my case it probably slowed down my career path within the Party, simply because when opportunities came, there were people who were seen to be reliable and loyal, and I didn't object to that. But in the long run, it has probably made no difference whatsoever. Ultimately, I think most people who were here at the time and voted, respect the decision that others took, because no-one took the decision glibly.

"I was a Government Whip myself, so I have seen it from both sides of the fence, and people do exaggerate a bit. There isn't the kind of bullying that sometimes people mention, it's more like personnel management in a way. MPs like other people, come in all sorts of shapes and sizes, some of them are prima donnas, some are very friendly collaborative people etc. etc."

On what's more stressful, being a teacher or an MP
"Being a teacher definitely. I have never as an MP, or when I was working in the office for Rhodri felt like I did at the end of term when I was teaching, I couldn't wait. For the first few years when I was teaching every Christmas at the end of term, we would go up the pub, have a couple of pints, and I would fall ill. I assume my immune system had taken a battering, and then I would be ill for a few days. I can tell you that several of my mates who were great teachers, particularly men for some reason, very together people, a lot of fun to be around, hard workers, got to their fifties, and there is a certain length of time, had done it for thirty years probably, and they just couldn't do it anymore. In one case literally, one of my mates was driving into work one day, and just turned round and went home, and never went back again. There is something about it I think."

On teachers not being appreciated
"It is a tough job to do well. Such a lot of demands are placed on people, and I know people talk about all the holidays, but I never ever in this job, or others did that. I don't actually take the recess off in this job, that's another misconception people have *(laughter)*. I take fairly normal holidays like other people, I just have more flexibility because of how the job works. I'll give you an example of that, over Easter I went into the BBC Llandaff studios to do an interview for the *BBC News Channel* on education policy, and one of the journalists said to me' Hi Kevin, so you're on holiday now then'. 'I said yeah that's right this is what I do when I'm on holiday, I come into TV studios and do interviews about education policy for the BBC, you're probably on holiday as well aren't you as you are here too!' *(laughter)* He said 'oh I'm sorry I didn't mean anything by it."

Andy Burnham MP

On being in Opposition rather than in power

"I enjoyed being a Minister, not because of the trappings of it or anything like that, more, because you can really do things, and that's what everyone gets into politics to do, you don't get into politics to be a loud mouth from the sidelines. Well some people do maybe, but I don't get my enjoyment from that, I get it from being able to do things, to change things, so Opposition is frustrating for that reason. And what is frustrating is that things that I worked on when in power and committed to, seeing them get wrecked now is quite frustrating to watch. Opposition isn't great and I'm on a mission to make it as short as possible!" *(laughter)*.

Rosie Cooper MP

On being Lord Mayor of Liverpool

"Well I turned it down in 1987 when my mum died, so when I was offered it in 1992, my dad was still alive, I thought he would love it. This deaf guy who had worked his way up, he was a plasterer, fantastically intelligent, value driven. So I became Lord Mayor, and I decided I was going to have a breeze, I was going to have a really good year, and enjoy it, but it was also going to be funny. And I did that because Liverpool had gone through Militant, and the city was on its' knees a bit, I just wanted to do it really well. At the end of my year in office, the future Lord Mayor had a fax machine, (which was sponsored by BT) the lining of the Lord Mayor's robes had been all ripped, cos Militant hadn't invested in anything like that, so I got the local universities to design and make new robes and they payed for them. We did all these entrepreneurial things, and I went out there and if I didn't have it, I got it. The Chief Exec said to me I was going to be the most sponsored Lord Mayor in the history of the city. It was a brilliant honour being Lord Mayor, I loved it, I had a great laugh. I did my best to put Liverpool on the map, really worked hard. I became Lord Mayor early in May, and I think the first day off I had was towards the end of August. By the end of that year, I had also got the Liverpool Publicity Medal, which is voted on by newspaper men, media people and opinion formers, and I am the only politician ever to have got it. So being Lord Mayor was fantastic although it was a hard year."

On being in Opposition rather than in power
"To me it makes no difference at all. I used to shout at Labour Ministers, so shouting at Tory Ministers is perhaps a bit more fun. It's not made a lot of difference to me in the sense that I will fight for what I believe to be right whoever it is, and they will get the same treatment."

On moving parties
"I am a conviction politician, what I say is what I mean, and what I mean is what I'll do, and that's the end of it, as we got closer and closer to power as Liberal Democrats, in my view principles because more and more fluid, and I just didn't want to be part of it anymore. It was my intention to leave politics altogether, and I signalled that when my term was up, that was it, I wouldn't be standing again. But obviously some people in the Labour Party heard that, and eventually convinced me to join the Labour Party, and the result of that is where we are now."

Gloria De Piero MP
From the heart
"I am just really emotional, things move me, wonderful things move me, and bad things really make me upset and angry. You are moved to tears sometimes. In my surgeries sometimes, when someone hasn't got enough money for the leccy and it's the week before Christmas, you think oh my god, and I am thinking have got all my Christmas presents yet. Things like that really make me cry.

"When you get older, like I am thirty nine now, I don't want children, and you just start to think what the hell is life about. You start to think there must be more to life than this, going to the pub and hanging out with my friends. There must be some reason. Kids are a ready-made, give your life meaning thing, but if that isn't for you, you think I'll have to do something. This is my something – this is my baby. People still think that I will change my mind about having kids, and I'm like I'm thirty nine!!"

On her transition from journalist to MP
"It's really funny when I go on television, and I keep thinking, well I would ask me this… I have to remember that these days my job is to answer the questions *(laughter)*, but I do keep thinking I wonder why they haven't asked me that… or that was a rubbish question, and I have got to get out of that. But when I first went into television, after all my teenage years with the Labour Party, I couldn't put together an objective question. It was just like I had to retrain my brain. But I am really good at asking questions."

Stephen Dorrell MP
On his favourite Ministerial role
"I have done a number of things while I have been here, and I have enjoyed most of them, if not all of them. I think the one that was most fulfilling, I hesitate to use the word enjoy, was when I was Health Secretary because it was such a big job, and one of the most important Departments in the Government."

On working for Margaret Thatcher
"She wasn't an easy person to work for, although I admire what she did as Prime Minister, she would not describe me as a Thatcherite and nor would I. If you look at the history books, whatever the rights and wrongs of individual things that happened, and all Governments make mistakes, between 1979 and 1990, her opponents have recognised, so her supporters should recognise that what happened in those eleven years transformed the economic life of our country."

In the nicest possible way, you have been around a long time (laughter). How do you think things have changed since you came into Parliament, when you were called the 'baby' of the House?

"I have effectively spent most of my life in politics, but I have also always had a life outside. I was a businessman when I first came in, and I remain an active businessman now. I think things have changed in that the political class is more uni-cultural. It tends to be more a class of professional politicians rather than those coming in from medicine or the trade union background or wherever. There are fewer people with real roots outside, having said that, I think there is also a tendency to look back at some old golden age that never really existed. There is one thing that the present generation of politicians has always had in common with their predecessors, and that is that they are pygmies in comparison to those who went before."

Michael Dugher MP

On Committees
"It's changed now, it used to be sorted out by the whips. They would place people on Select Committees with the membership reflecting the House, but now you are elected by your peers to Select Committees."

On All Party Groups
"Those are different, you choose. It can be frustrating as you don't have to time to do all of the ones you would like to, there are so many good causes, but being able to give a bit of time to some really good causes is great. I do it locally too, whether it be the British Legion or things I am Patron of in the constituency. But in Westminster, there are various things I try and help. Heart Disease is obviously a big issue in my constituency, and I am Vice Chair of that All Party Group, but there is a huge list of other A.P.P.G's I am involved in. I am also Chair of the A.P.P.G on brass bands."

What was it like being the PPS to Ed Miliband?

"Well I have enjoyed being on the front bench, and being a Shadow Minister and I will miss that, it's a great opportunity. As I said I have worked for a lot of people over the years, and I think the public are just getting to know Ed Miliband. Someone said we are the third most interesting political party at the moment, inevitably the focus is on the Government, but as the next Election draws closer, the focus will be back on the Labour Party again, and Ed Miliband is a future Prime Minister. I have known him for a quite a long time and having worked with him closely in recent months he's very determined, he's a very nice guy to work for. I am also struck by his very strong convictions, he's not someone who is in it to look good at the Despatch Box, or someone who just wants to flounce around. He has got very strong beliefs on how he wants to change the country, I think for the better, and that sort of determination is quite infectious as well. On a personal level if you are working very closely with him day in day out, he is just one of life's nice guys."

Natascha Engel MP

On Party Whips

"They don't tell you what to do, or how to do the job, they tell you how to vote. And I wouldn't overstate that too much, some people really go overboard about the Whips. My relationship with them has always been that they are people, and they are MPs too, so you sit down, and if you have any issues with them, certainly when we were in Government, there were a lot of issues that I didn't entirely agree on, and so you talk to them. It's important to recognise that it's not just, this is what you do and you can't argue it, the important thing is that you can and you do argue it. You make your case inside the party."

On being an MP and bringing up three small children

"Well it is and it isn't hard. First of all they ground you, so you never disappear where others sometimes go, because you can't, secondly, it does tend to keep you in the real world when you drop them off at school and pick them up it keeps you in a normal place. The other thing is being an MP is a sort of vocational job, but there are lots of women, and men too, who do jobs like being lawyers, work in the city, that sort of thing, and we don't really ask the same of them. I knew what the job was like before I had kids, and I made the choice. I have three boys of 8, 6, and 4."

Andrew George MP
On being marked down as a rebel
"I have not been trying to go out of my way to become one, I am quite a loyal person really."

I described you as a giant amongst political pygmies *(laughter)* particularly when you led the rebellion against the Health Bill.

"That's obviously depends on your perspective. *(laughter)* Yes an awful Bill, it was one of the most upsetting moments of my political career, seeing that go through after all the efforts of so many, including my own."

It must be soul-destroying to be judged on what your colleagues or Party Leader may do, even if you don't agree?

"Yes. But you have to accept the rough with the smooth. On the one hand, when things are going well, you bathe in reflected glory. You can't only want it one way. So, I don't actually have a problem with that. And I don't believe in personality politics. I may find myself disagreeing with something Dave, Ed or sometimes even Nick has said. But I don't attack him as a person. I do find myself occasionally disagreeing with Nick, I acknowledge that he is basically a decent bloke. He may come from a different background, and that may affect his perspective on life, but he is someone who wants to do the right thing. And, considering the pressure he faces, he seems to withstand it very well."

On running a charity
"I did a lot of different charitable work, I worked for Cornwall Rural Community Council which did loads of work in housing, employment schemes, charity fund-raising, offering advice to village halls, community centres and a range of charities, playing fields, a lot of development work. Trying to cover a wide range of subjects, which if you like, fill the gaps in society which statutory agencies cannot fill. What we were trying to do in all those areas, was providing the glue between where the needs were, and where the state was unable to help. That's what it was primarily about. I was working with a large range of organisations, from housing associations to councils and voluntary services. I suppose I would describe it as being a 'charity worker'. You are up at the top of the premier league table of public approval with people like Bob Geldof and Nelson Mandela. And now I'm an MP I am down at the bottom of the conference league below estate agents, Beelzebub and even bankers!" *(laughter)*.

John Glen MP
On what is a conservative
"I think at its' core a conservative believes that individuals are better arbiters of their own destiny than the state, and believes that individuals when motivated in the right way and given the right incentives will create a better quality of life and living for them and their families I think a conservative is someone who believes in looking after themselves, taking responsibility, looking after the most vulnerable, and there is a role for the state but it is smaller, and it

should never lead to dependency. That is where there is a big philosophical difference, and we believe that there is meant to be potential in the less well off parts of society, and the state's role is to try and enable the fulfilment of that potential, whilst still looking after the most vulnerable. But not to believe that it is the state's role to arbitrarily determine a level of income that should be acceptable, and transfer money from the most wealthy to the poorest, you have to find a formula that can help them to improve themselves. That will mean better investment and education in specific targeted programmes of welfare reform, but it fundamentally believes that individuals need to be allowed to fulfil their own potential."

On his interest in mental health
"Well my brother-in-law has experienced severe mental health problems, at close hand I have seen the impact it has had on his family, and my wife and our lives. That has been very distressing, and has given me a real sense of the unpredictability of it, the stigma surrounding it, the challenges of finding an effective prescription of state support that deals with that unpredictability. I have also visited constituents, and had a couple of cases involving suicide of a constituent, seen the impact it had on the family, and the gap between their emotional pain, and the reality of what the mental health services were trying to provide for them. So that has given me a real sense of the complexity of it, and a recognition in a period of intense pressure on resources, there is often a tendency to look for ways of finding 'savings' in mental health. It's incredibly complex because actually you cannot find a complete insurance against people who are determined to commit suicide. You cannot account for the way that the different kinds of drugs interact with people's mental state and find a solution. And the culture around politics and politicians is that the state can always find a solution, and it's a lack of money or will, but actually that is unrealistic. That whole area of policy brings many complexities which need a lot of hard work to get right, to project what best practices are, and to try and find the

right solutions. I don't have the answer, but as an MP eighteen months in, I am keen to be a part of finding a solution."

For what it's worth we need more MPs like you who take such an interest in mental health.

On the public's perception of MPs
"There was a very useful piece written on the conservative home website three or four weeks ago written by a guy from one of the think tanks which was basically a complete job application. It was a very real assessment of what we actually do, it did justice to the life of an MP. One of the things that really gets to us is when people say 'oh so you are on holiday again during recess.' I recently had two weeks while on recess, and I am a J.P. as well, so I sat for three days, and that is discretionary for me, but not a day went by when I didn't call my office, or answer several emails. So it amuses me, when people say it but it is just not true to my experience, but you also don't want to defend yourself."

Zac Goldsmith MP
On the bill he has introduced
"I am committed to trying to make the job of being a backbencher more important, and the single biggest step we can take is to introduce a genuine recall mechanism, so that MPs can be removed by their constituents at any time, if enough people agree. That would, at a stroke, remind all MPs that the only 3-line whip that counts is the one imposed by their constituents. It would encourage far greater independence in Parliament, and would, I think, go some way towards restoring people's faith in the political process."

Oliver Heald MP
Has the type of people becoming MPs changed
"There is a big new generation and they are different. We haven't

really had a big new generation since 1997, and at that time the big new generation were all Labour. The last time we had a substantial new Conservative intake was when I got elected in 1992, so really it's been a long time since we have had a whole new crowd of Conservatives in. I think they are very much 'Cameron thinking' in some ways, they are very interested in the Big Society type agenda, they are more against the E.U., and I think they are slightly more rebellious. But I don't mind, my feeling is it's marvellous to have the 7th cavalry come over the horizon. And they are Conservative, it's just they have a different set of views."

On differing views within the party
"You need some people pushing the margins, taking a very strong position, but also you need some people who can get things done, and that's about looking at the law, seeing how you can change it. I'm the Chairman for the Executive of the Association of Conservative Lawyers, and we've got a long tradition of doing that, of getting things done. Looking at how you change a law and making that change happen, not necessarily by means of a big bang that is going to change everything at once, but moving things forward, I do think that you need both."

On mental health and the 2001 summit
"I became a health spokesperson, as number two to Liam Fox. Liam had been a hospital doctor, and he was very shocked by the way mental health was being tackled in England. This was of course quite a while ago, and he said to me I want you to find out what's going on and see what we can do to help. He felt that much more prominence needed to be given, particularly to carers, and also so that modern drugs were available for people with mental health problems. We held the two summits, the first of them looked at a range of issues, more around the treatments that were available, and the second one concentrated on young people. We were particularly worried about the transition from young people's to adult services,

and how to improve that, because it was very variable across the country, I think we did quite a lot to help move the agenda forward. Certainly pretty soon afterwards NICE agreed that the drugs could be used, and we had some support from the drugs companies, particularly in the area of schizophrenia. We were also pushing that it shouldn't be the poor relation, when a lot of areas round the country were short of money, it's always mental health that is the first to go, because it's more of an unseen condition, and I think there was a time when the stigma of mental health was certainly used against it. Not many people were going to stand up and shout if mental health services were cut, and Liam and I both thought this was wrong"

On time for another mental health debate
"I think it would be a very good idea to get a group of MPs to put in for one. When the Mental Health Bill was being proposed and there were a lot of criticisms of that, there was a lot of discussion going on about mental health, because we didn't want to go down a route that was against the civil liberties of the people with mental health problems that it concerned. So it's probably time to have a fresh debate."

Ivan Lewis MP
On his fairly unique background in the voluntary sector
"I think what makes me more unique is the fact that I didn't go to University. Even though I was elected to here at the age of thirty, I basically had worked for thirteen years in the real world before being elected, so that is quite unusual, also I think representing my home town constituency where I was born and where I have lived all my life is quite unusual. I guess all of those things make my journey to Westminster quite different. I obviously feel a great sense of pride to be representing my home town constituency, it's not like being a politician who builds a career just anywhere, it's about having an emotional attachment to where you represent."

On being in power or not
"Politics is to some extent about luck, in the earlier generation of Labour MPs they never had the chance to serve in Government as we were out of power for so long from 1979 to 1997. Some really special people, never served, they were born at the wrong time in the wrong place, whereas we have had that wonderful opportunity. It's the same with the Tories, in 1997, say you were in your forties, and then you were out of Government for thirteen years, you may have missed the boat to ever serve as a Minister. Now that doesn't mean that being a constituency MP is not a privilege and an honour, because it is, and you should never forget that, because it is your first priority. But serving as a Minister for your country, and feeling that you can make a difference is really, really important."

In the next Election you will be quite a senior figure.

"Is that a nice way of calling me old?"

(Laughter) No not at all, it's just with so many newer MPs, you will be one of the most experienced ones by the time the next election comes round.

"I think our generation has got to get used the fact that there is a younger generation emerging, therefore we are now in that category of being the more senior politicians, with the younger ones coming through. I think what you need is a healthy balance."

Nicky Morgan MP
On Select Committees and how they work
"You used to be allocated them, but this is the first Parliament, where

you stand for election amongst your peers, I think the parties sort it out amongst themselves as to which party is going to have which chairmanship, and the whole House votes for them. But in terms of membership, each party votes for its' required number. So I stood for the Business Select Committee, because my background is in working with businesses, and that's what I was most interested in, and was elected. It is up to people to choose, although it used to be in the gift of the whips which probably made them more powerful then."

On the All Party Mental Health Group

"I am the Vice Chair of the All Party Parliamentary Group on Mental Health, and that's a cross party group looking at mental health issues. I decided that mental health would be one of the issues that I was really going to focus on for family reasons, because you have to be focused on one or two key issues to make anything happen. At the moment we have been looking at the Health and Social Care Bill, I think we now need to broaden it out into other areas, and to also make sure that we are involving a wide cross section of the public. The public can attend meetings, and I take the point that you have made to me before which is there are lots of bigger mental health charities who often tend to get a lot of air time, and we need to be able to listen to everybody's voices."

Jason McCartney MP

On whether being a journalist previously has been an advantage

"Having been a journalist and also having also been a Royal Air Force Officer, I am a big fan of people having done things in the real world, having real life experience. I think people are very cynical about politicians, particularly if they haven't really done anything else in life, apart from work for other politicians. I am very in touch with reality, I live in a three bedroom semi-detached house in Honley, I am in the heart of my community. I drive a normal hatchback car, this is the only job that I do, I am not mega rich or posh or anything like that. This was the first time I had stood for

Parliament. In fact when I went down to Parliament on the Monday for the first time having been elected on the Thursday, I had only ever been twice before, once for a twenty minute meeting, and once when I was younger to watch PMQ's. I didn't even know how to get into some of the different buildings, so it was a massive learning curve, but it made it all the more exciting."

So you epitomise what my book is really about, because I think if we want to take advantage of the democracy we are supposed to have, people need to get involved. I am hoping that this book will show MPs are just normal people doing the best they can for others, and that there is a lot more to being an MP than most people think.

"The good thing now is that there are 250 new MPs of all parties, some because of seat changes, but also because a lot of the existing MPs who were involved in the expenses scandal stood down thank god, so there is a fresh approach. There are more people from Asian backgrounds, there are more Muslims, women, and younger people. I think the youngest MP is now twenty-four, and the oldest is eighty-one. There are still people that have been to Eton, who had a private education, but there are plenty of others like me who had a regular education. I didn't even go to University at eighteen, I joined the Royal Air Force instead, and went to University a little later. There are people who have worked as solicitors, some who have run their own businesses, we even have three or four G.P.s. A good friend of mine, Andy Percy, MP for Goole, who gets in the train at Doncaster, when I travel down to London, was a teacher in a comprehensive school, a regular guy, and now he is a Tory MP, has a great knowledge of his local area, and talks passionately about the issues that affect it. So I hate when people say you are a Tory MP you must be a rich toff, not in touch with reality. I am sorry that is just not true."

Stephen Pound MP

You have had a really wide and varied background, how do you go from the navy to buses to hospital porter?

"It was the uniform." *(ha,ha)* "I'd always liked the structure and order. Like a lot of people, I came from a huge family with nine of us. And it just got ridiculous, I used to share a room with three brothers, and I remember my dad taking me over to the Royal Navy recruiting office in High Holborn. It wasn't till years later I realised he had booked a return, and only booked me a single, and by six o'clock that night I was on HMS Ganges. I don't know if it's a male thing, but men seem to like teams, there was always a group of us who played football, and in the Forces it was really nice to have that, it's also one of the reasons that the Labour Party has worked for me, because it's more of a collegiate group, it's not about individual achievements, it's what we do collectively."

On his experience on TALKSPORT Radio on the Ian Collins show where he crossed swords with Philip Davies MP
"Yes I 'lamped' him! My great memory of that is Sean Dilley, the political correspondent, who is blind, and his guide dog who broke up the fight. Me and Davies were rolling around the studio, and every time we went past the microphone we stopped, and all I could hear was 'woof, woof, woof' 'he's not worth it' 'woof,woof,woof'."

From what I hear you could probably have a full time job on the after dinner circuit so say your fellow MPs.

"Lying bastards…" *(laughter)*

322

On mental health
"One of the things that have changed since I came in, is the recognition of mental health issues with Members of Parliament. It was always stiff upper lip, shoulders back, crack on. And it was if you are tough enough to get here you are tough enough to stay here. I always think what Scott Fitzgerald said *'in the still dark night of the soul when it's forever 3 am,'* and that affects every single one of us. Every single human being on this planet is affected by mental health issues, either directly or indirectly."

I am hoping to make a documentary from the book

"But it will be all about the sensationalist side won't it? The trouble with MPs is we have a few nymphos, a few that suffer from rampant priapism (those with a permanent hard on). Do you know of the satyrs? They were ancient Greek gods who couldn't stop 'knobbin', and Priapus was an ancient Greek god who was cursed by the fact he could never ever get 'it' down. He was what we call a 'chin slapper'."

I still can't see you on an allotment.

"You have to think of this, you've got an upturned bucket, and I've got me daisy roots on, and an open necked shirt, pipe and cap, copy of *Readers Wives* tucked in me back pocket… "

Yasmin Qureshi MP
On being in power or not
"Because I am starting life as an Opposition MP, it can be frustrating, whereas if you are in Government you have more opportunity to

influence your Ministers and effect change. It is still the best job in the world though I really do love it."

On being the first female MP for your constituency, as well as the first Muslim female MP
"Yes I am the first female MP for my part of Bolton. I am really proud about that, and I was chosen from an open shortlist as well."

John Redwood MP
On working with Margaret Thatcher as her Chief Policy Advisor
"Margaret Thatcher was the best boss I ever worked for. She was prepared to listen to my case, argue it through on its merits, and accept the advice if she thought it was well founded and sensible. She always wrestled with what was right for the country, and then worried about how to explain it and sell it to the electors once she had decided what was right. She cares very much about the UK and all who live in these islands. When in office she spent all her waking hours worrying about how to improve things and how to do her job well."

Derek Twigg MP

Have the type of people becoming MPs changed since you were elected?

"I actually think the '97 generation probably changed the landscape, in terms of the current generation coming through they are much more at ease with things like I.T. I think '97 started that process. MPs being much more active in their constituencies, being more accountable, holding more surgeries, with the advent of the internet, emails have completely changed the landscape over the last seven or eight years, people being able to contact you, the amount of correspondence has really increased from when I first started, it's tremendous. People expect more from their Members of Parliament now, as they are more visible and more accountable. So I am not sure if the new generation coming in now have made a huge difference, although I guess I could just be saying that as I came in in '97. I think there was such a big influx of new MPs who came in then, either the biggest or second biggest influx ever, that was what changed the landscape and this is just a natural progression.

"I suppose the current generation have changed it with Twitter. I haven't gone down the road of Twitter or Facebook. I can see the arguments in its favour, but I'm just not convinced about it. There's a lot of talking about yourself isn't there too. It's something I haven't ruled out. In my constituency I am out and about a lot, and I know a lot of people, but I guess it's just a way this generation communicate more, and maybe that's something I've got to look at in the future. I do think that's probably been the biggest change in the last year or two, but not just because this new intake have come in."

On changing position in the Shadow Cabinet reshuffle
"I came off the Front Bench, I was a Health Spokesman, but I asked to come off. I wasn't going to go back on, after losing my post in 2008, I refused another job offer the following year. I was really surprised when Ed Miliband rang me, and because I was so concerned and angry about the Health Bill, I took the job, but had asked to come off in the next reshuffle. I intend to stay on the back benches now with much more freedom to do things."

Charles Walker MP
On mental health
"It's an oft told story, and I have mentioned it in the House of Commons on a couple of occasions, but about a decade ago, I was coming home on the Tube, I think it was the Piccadilly Line at South Ken, when I saw a girl, young woman, in a terrible state of distress, dishevelled, covered in soot, shoelaces non-existent, obviously in a

great state of upset and distress. I obviously wanted to reach out and help, and I tried to, but in the end the only thing that could be done was to call the Police. I was just thinking if that had been my daughter or someone I cared for I hoped there would have been more in place for them, and I wished there was more in place for her. As a caring individual I wanted to take her home to my wife, get her looked after, give her a bath, feed her, give her security and shelter but obviously we don't live in an ideal world. But we really need to care for people like her, it was very, very upsetting."

On being chair of the All Party Mental Health Group
"The All Party Mental Health Group is going from strength to strength, it is very exciting to see so many Members of Parliament taking an interest, not just the members of the group, but also colleagues that I talk to about mental health. Just today I was pitching to the Backbench Business Committee for a debate on mental health, and particularly, the need to be able to access acute care, whilst recognising of course that community based care is very important, there is still a need for acute beds. When I first went to present, I had lots of signatures, but only myself and Nicky Morgan turned up, and they responded by saying they would like to see more Members of Parliament, to which I said well I have just been sitting here for forty minutes, and if we had brought more people they would all want to have a say, and it could just go on and on. So anyway, I went away, and when we returned, we had twenty odd signatures, but there were seven of us, so that put the wind up them slightly. They said they were very pleased to see such support. What is very interesting, as I said to them, was when I was getting the signatures from people to support the debate, some of them I didn't know had an interest in mental health, extended beyond that of a constituency MP, but most of them wanted to have a chat about cases going on in their area, so it is a very interesting subject.

"When you scratch below the surface, there is a huge amount of interest amongst colleagues about mental health and access to services, but I am not sure that they know how to progress that interest. We need to look at how we can help them to do that. For example, one colleague is concerned about people coming to see him, clearly with mental health problems, and what strategy he should adopt to make sure that they get seen by someone who is in a position to help them, because everyone gets caught up in this confidentiality clause. If you were presented with a constituent who had cancer or heart disease, you wouldn't think twice about getting a clinician involved, but people get very nervous about mental health. So I think there are strategies out there to help colleagues cope and support people with mental health problems. I have no compunction if someone comes to me who has a mental health problem, and clearly they do, it's not just gut, I ask how they are feeling. Are they feeling under a lot of pressure? If it's to do with a psychotic episode, they may be feeling persecuted, so I ask them how they are and say it must be having a terrible effect on their own health, and they 'Mr Walker, I feel terrible this is really stressing me out', which in a sense gives me what I need to be able to say, 'well can I get someone to get in touch with you, to help support you?' and they say 'well that would be very nice thank you.' There are ways of doing it so that people feel comfortable and happy. There have certainly been two instances, possibly three, where I have felt sufficiently concerned about the person I am seeing to feel that an intervention is necessary, and a rapid intervention in one particular case where I felt she was in a state of huge distress and there was a danger that the young woman might do something very 'foolish', she might not have thought it was foolish at the time, but I felt there was the potential for her to take that further, and wanted to get someone involved quickly.

"So that's a long winded answer to your question, but I am very excited because one of the concerns that the Backbench Business Committee has is ok you have a debate in Westminster Hall and that will be well attended, but if you have a full three hour debate in The Chamber are you going to get the numbers there. Well I am pretty sure, that we will get a very, very good turn-out. A lot of that work has been motivated by Nicky Morgan, who you know well, James Morris, who is an outstanding Rowley Regis MP, and others. There are lots of great people out there going about their work, Oliver Colville has done some great stuff, as has Gloria De Piero. I think the tinder is very dry, and if we put a match to it whoosh, we are going to spread it quickly. Maybe not the best analogy, but it will spread like wild fire. The interest is definitely there and I am feeling very confident."

Phil Wilson MP

On what it was like to follow a Prime Minister

"I had worked for Tony for a few years, and had known him for twenty seven/twenty eight years. I was on the original selection committee when he became the MP for Sedgefield. I have been involved in politics for about thirty years, in one way or another, have always lived in Sedgefield, in the constituency, and had worked for Tony both down here and up there. When I knew he wasn't going to stand thinking the election would be 2009, I knew that he wouldn't stand again for Parliament, because he was packing in being Prime Minister, I though well I'll have a go at the seat, and because I knew him, it was a bit easier. I think it's a state of mind, I thought, I'm not Tony Blair, don't try and fill his shoes, just plough your own furrow, which is what I did."

On being in power or not

"I had only had two years in power, well two and a half years, obviously you don't know what's going to happen, but five years in Opposition and it does feel like you are banging your head against a brick wall a lot of the time. It is frustrating, because you know you are right on things, and you can see the problems that are arising in the constituency and you can't really do too much to put them right. So we need to use this time to re-energise ourselves and to get ready for Government."

Rosie Winterton MP
On talking more about politics in schools
"I spend a lot of time going to schools, talking about politics and encouraging them to have visits down to Parliament, so that they understand more, about my job, what it's like to be an MP, and I think there should be more about politics in schools. Things like the school councils that have developed are very interesting, because when you can say to people well it's a bit like being elected onto the school council. You represent people, you have to help make changes in the school, and that's quite helpful in making them see the connection. We have done research into why people don't vote, at one time we went back to a young woman who said she would vote, but didn't vote in the end, and when she was asked about it she said well I didn't want to go back to that school cos I went there, and didn't have a very good time, and was nervous about going back, and I didn't know what I would have to do. It's simple things like that, maybe we just don't spend enough time explaining the processes. I think she thought she was going to have to answer all sorts of questions before she could vote. Citizenship is supposed to be part of the curriculum."

So there you have it, a few random questions, some of which could only apply to the individuals, such as those who had worked for Margaret Thatcher, but what really strikes a chord with me, is the genuine warmth that exudes from these people.

Understandably my background is in mental health, so it was always going to be difficult not to talk about it, but the fact is, mental illness has such a devastating impact upon all aspects of our society, and it affects so many people, it would have been negligent not to mention it.

I hope also that you found the stuff about how

committees and all party groups are formed interesting, because it rarely gets mentioned, but much of the work they undertake can have a direct effect on our lives. Perhaps also we can now better understand how the transition from power to opposition impacts on our MPs.

Anyway, coming from the charity sector, but also in the small minority of people with sympathy for our parliamentarians, I loved the words of Andrew George "I suppose I would describe it as being a 'charity worker'. You are up at the top of the premier league table of public approval with people like Bob Geldof and Nelson Mandela. And now I'm an MP I am down at the bottom of the conference league below estate agents, Beelzebub and even bankers! *(laughter)*.

But the final word goes to Yasmin Qureshi. "It is still the best job in the world though, I really do love it."

Tony with Rosie Winterton

"If the public don't take an interest in the work of MPs, they let the lazy, idle and venal MPs off the hook. Every time someone sits on the sofa and says, 'I can't be arsed with this politics stuff', some MP is rubbing his hands with glee... "
Stephen Pound MP – Chapter 19

CHAPTER NINETEEN

A Message to the Public

In many ways this is the most important Chapter, a chance for our elected representatives to explain what they do, and tell you directly why you should take an interest. I don't think that opportunity arises too often, so I hope you will find it interesting. The question was: If you could deliver a message to the public about the role of an MP, and the importance of taking an interest what would you say?

Dave Anderson MP

"If you don't take an interest, bad things can happen. If you think people are watching what you are doing, it makes you think more about what you are doing. If 310 people write and ask you what you are doing about a Bill, of course you can ignore them, but you are crackers if you do. One of the sad things over the last twenty five years is with my party lurching to the right, and the Conservatives going more to the left trying to capture the middle ground, the whole argument is that patch in the middle. And it's always been said in this country by those people who couldn't be bothered to vote, well you are all the same, and that was never really true, but it's been more true in the last quarter of a century than ever before, and I think people have become more disenchanted because of that. I just think, the more that people don't engage, the easier it is for people in here to get away with things that they shouldn't."

Paul Blomfield MP

"Like Winston Churchill would point out, parliamentary democracy might not be the best form of Government but all the others are far worse, and in my lifetime, we take democratic politics for granted. A lot of European countries have not always enjoyed democracy over the last fifty years or so, Spain – Fascist, Portugal – Fascist, Greece – Military Dictatorship, authoritarian regimes, the truth is someone will always govern, choice is better democratically elected. The aspiration to have your society run by people who are accountable runs very deep, it is important we try to counter the media cynicism about politics, and cherish and work hard to build democracy. Politicians are ordinary people, and might not always get it right, they may make mistakes, but it is important to work to maintain the sort of system where you can kick politicians out, elect different people, and where politics will reflect the people who elect us. For all of those reasons, we need to ensure people are involved, and take an interest and know what they are voting for and why."

Kevin Brennan MP

"Don't believe the hype about your MP, or about MPs in general. Yes we have faults, as all human beings do, including vanity and greed, and all the other seven deadly sins, but pretty much in equal measure with other human beings. But for the most part, whichever political party they come from, my view is that the vast majority of MPs are motivated by a desire to change things for the better. Although we kick lumps out of each other on the pitch, off the pitch, I have cordial relations with people from other political parties. They are not my friends in the same way that people are from your own party, but people do work together to try and do good things here, and of course that doesn't get highlighted, that's just a fact of life.

"When I first got into Parliament I served on the Adoption of Children Bill, and a group of us went to see Alan Milburn, who was Secretary of State for Health at the time, and said we want to introduce amendments from the backbenches to this Bill to allow couples to adopt, whether or not they are married, and including gay couples. Alan said, 'look I support you all the way but Tony Blair will never back it with a three line whip, but I will argue for you to have a free vote on this.' So we put our amendments down, we got a free vote on it, and the Tory Party at the time were led by Ian Duncan-Smith, he put a whip to vote against it, and John Bercow who is now the Speaker resigned from the Tory Front Bench, because he wouldn't be whipped into voting against allowing gay couples the right to apply to adopt. I think that was a turning point really in the history of the Tory Party in one sense, because thereafter, a lot of them in their ranks realised we've got to be more socially liberal because Britain has changed."

Andrew Bridgen MP

"Parliamentary democracy is not perfect, but it is better than any of the alternatives. My first role and duty as an MP is to protect and preserve our democracy for future generations from those inside or outside our country who would seek to diminish it. We serve in the Parliament, it is not ours it belongs to the people.

"MPs are human too, if the public keep knocking them then they might end up with the MPs they least want, but who are willing to do the job."

Andy Burnham MP

"If you don't take an interest you are letting other people determine things for you. I worry a lot about the cynicism around politics, which was at its peak around the expenses scandal, and obviously that still clouds it. What troubles me is sometimes you have to break through a wall of cynicism, if you are in a meeting and people haven't met you before, they often have a view which is very hard to try to change. I think it's more difficult for local councillors, it's alright for us at one level, but for people who devote their lives to politics locally it can be really hard going, because they get a lot of the cynicism created by the Westminster scene, but they get none of the excitement and the glamour if you like. That is dangerous at the end of the day. The great fear is if people don't get involved, periodically through our history you can see where cynicism is exploited by extremists, and in parts of the north you can see that. That's what worries me if those on the middle ground do not speak."

Ann Coffey MP

"I think the general public probably know that General Elections matter, that what kind of Government you have matters. But it is still a matter of regret for me that in my constituency over a third of people did not vote at the last General Election, and younger people tend to vote less than older people. I think the message I would give is that it is very important to hold your representatives to account, and you can't do that if you don't vote."

Gloria De Piero MP

"Do you know what? I would turn that on its' head, because if Joe Public aren't interested we are doing something wrong, and this is a really big thing that I have discovered, and I am going to try and do some work on this myself. Normal people, and they are normal, not us, they don't think we are like them. They don't think that they could come in here, and I keep saying that all you need to be an MP is to care about your community, to care about the future of your country – that's it. You don't need to be able to speak in long language, you don't need to be able to go into the Chamber and speak in that weird nonsense speak that nobody understands, you just have to stand up for your community. I think all political parties need to think about how we can get Parliament to look like Britain, because it doesn't at the moment, and that's a problem. Particularly for the Labour Party, because we are the people's party, and we have got to look like the people, and we have got some work to do."

Stephen Dorrell MP

"People often say, 'oh I'm not interested in politics', but then they go on to say they are interested in what goes on in their local communities in terms of land use, or what goes on in their children's education, or the Health Service, or Afghanistan, or overseas aid. All of these things are influenced by politics, and if you want to make a difference one of the ways of doing it is to be engaged in political life."

Michael Dugher MP

"It's their Parliament, I am a Member of the House of Commons but it's their House of Commons. I am only here by virtue of the trust that people in my constituency showed in me at the time of the Election and they can change their minds about me at the next Election if they want. I think things like the e-petions have been really important. When you get nearly 200,000 people saying we are really worried about what is happening to the Health Service, you need to drop this Bill. The fact that now levels of public support can trigger debates in the House is great. We need to bring the House of Commons and the people who elect us as close as possible, and I think the fact that good MPs now are very accessible to their constituents is a good thing. But I don't care what the issue is, if anyone from Barnsley comes down to the House of Commons I will see them, that gets top priority, because they are the boss. If you see this as a job, where the boss is the public, then I think that's not a bad attitude to have."

Natascha Engel MP

"That's very difficult, because I think we have got ourselves into a bit of a situation, and it's not just MPs, it's councillors as well, all elected representatives versus the people that they represent, and there is a bit of a passive aggressive thing going on where we get payed through taxpayers money therefore some people say well I employ you so you do what I say, that sort of attitude. And MPs and other elected representatives have become very defensive, and have made loads of things to make it seem as though they are working very, very hard on people's behalf, so there are lots of EDM's (Early Day Motions) and that sort of thing. It's very time consuming, and you can demonstrate how much you are doing on theyworkforyou.com but I am not sure how effective it is in engaging people and making the process two way rather than one way. I don't think we are having an honest enough conversation with people about the changing role of an MP, it used to be that you would go down to Parliament and make and change laws on behalf of those people who had elected you (and there are still a few MPs like that), and you did go back to the constituency, and do surgeries, but those were much more about what the consequences were of what you had done in Westminster making and changing laws. What you have now is people talk about being a glorified counsellor, or a glorified social worker, which is a bit disrespectful to counsellors and social workers, but you do have a recognition that letters to constituents are like direct mails, when you have surgeries you have face to face contacts, all these things will make it more likely for that person to vote for you at the next election. So we have become incredibly sophisticated in what we call campaigning, and that has actually meant in terms of what we do as MPs it has changed very dramatically, I would say we have de-skilled councillors because we are doing their jobs for them. It's easy stuff, we write to the council and say get that fixed and they do it, and we take the credit. And so unless we have a really honest conversation with people, it's not possible, if I do all of that, I cannot be as good as being in Westminster and holding the Government to account, scrutinising what they do, making and changing laws, if I am doing all the other stuff as well.

"I think it was interesting how few people, especially during the expenses scandal understood that I lived in the constituency, and I lived in London because I went to Westminster every week. People didn't know that, it might not have even been that they didn't know, they just didn't think about it, and I think that level of not understanding what their representatives do on their behalf is not healthy for democracy."

Andrew George MP
"Well, forget the tribalism and Punch and Judy show. Politics can have an effect on every part of your life, your community, environment, your car, your garden, your school, your hospital etc.

If you could deliver a message to the public what would you say?

Everything in your life; the things that you care about, there is a political dimension. It's not just party politics and a shouting match up in Westminster, which has nothing to do with your life, we should be debating ways in which we believe we can make your life better. I hope people aren't put off by the Punch and Judy tribalism of politics. That's what puts me off."

John Glen MP

"We are obviously in a pretty difficult place with regard to the standing of MPs, but I think most MPs are motivated by a desire to help their constituents and to deliver improved outcomes, be an advocate for them in the systems of government. By engaging with an MP, by informing the MP about the experience they have in a measured and balanced way, rather than a party political one, you can actually go a long way to putting your views into their mind. So I would say, by careful and thoughtful engagement, by doing a lot of work to try to help them understand things, to see the ways that policies influence their lives, you can make a big impression on people."

Zac Goldsmith MP

"Politics doesn't belong to MPs. It belongs to everyone, and there are countless ways to become involved. I believe politics has become far too remote, and I am actively backing reforms. But instead of complaining about its remoteness, people should get involved and help shape it."

Liz Kendall MP

"I would say they are the boss. Every Friday morning I visit a different Primary School, and try and talk to them about what it's like being an MP and what we do. They often say who do I work for, do I work for Ed Miliband, someone asked me if I worked for David Cameron *(laughter)*, and I say, no, I work for you and your parents. I also invite them all to come to Parliament, and I say because it's your Parliament, it's not mine. I invite all the schools down, and they are now starting to come and see me here."

Sadiq Khan MP

"What I would say to people, and I met some students from a local secondary school earlier today, is the more active you are, and the more you lobby your MP, the better he or she will be. If you don't make him or her realise the issues that matter to you, he/she won't take them seriously, and a good MP can really improve the quality of life both in your local community, and the country as a whole, but also can do a huge amount of good for people around the world. But if you don't lobby your MP, if you're not an active citizen, you can't then complain if you've got a poor MP."

Caroline Lucas MP

"My experiences as a political activist for the past twenty years have helped me realise exactly what is possible when you have a lot of people coming together, all of whom believe something strongly and feel they can really make a difference. Politics must never be seen as just something done by men in grey suits behind closed doors at Westminster – politics is something you can do whoever you are and wherever you are."

Nicky Morgan MP

"I would say that everyone should really be interested in politics, and when I go to speak to schools, I always remind them that politics affects everything that they do, when they can get married, when they can have their first drink, when they can leave school, so everyone should be interested. And also I suppose, to give Members of Parliament the benefit of the doubt about their motives. There is an assumption that we all don't work very hard, that we are all self interested, and obviously like in any profession there are going to be people who don't behave to the standards we all hope for, but there are lots of people here working very, very hard trying to do the right thing, and the right thing by their constituents, and so just a bit of understanding I guess. But it's also up to MPs to tell people what we do."

Jason McCartney MP

"If I had the opportunity to, it would be great for each of my constituents to spend a day with me in Parliament and a day here in the constituency, because I think a lot of people do not realise what we actually do. I think my mum and dad have been amazed at the variety of issues, as have the people that do work experience with me, usually only for a few days as we are so busy. It's just the variety of things, whether you are helping someone with what could be a very personal issue about housing, benefits, health issues or the child support agency. I also have the Pakistani Kashmiri Association in my constituency so there are lots of visa issues. There are also the big policy issues, about whether or not we should intervene in Syria, Somali piracy, the economy big issues like that, and then all the parliamentary stuff too.

"Also we are in recess at the moment, and I know the BBC are obsessed with this, they think when Parliament is not sitting MPs are on holiday. Well here I am. I have opened a factory this morning, I've just had a wonderful young lad in the office talking to me about graffiti, and how we can get rid of tagging, and get the graffiti artists to do something positive with art on community walls. I meet lots of wonderful young people, and I can support then, come up with ideas, put them in touch with groups, funding streams, all sorts of things like that. Last night after a busy day, I was doing emails till about eleven o'clock, and I rang a couple of constituents between nine and ten o'clock in the evening. I live and breathe it, and I think a lot of others MPs do too."

Esther McVey MP

"I would say, if you have a burning issue, something you want to do or to change, then the first and best person to contact is your local MP."

Stephen Pound MP

"If the public don't take an interest in the work of MPs, they let the lazy, idle and venal MPs off the hook. Every time someone sits on the sofa and says I can't be arsed with this politics stuff, some MP is rubbing his hands with glee, and so what I would say is MPs work for you, and they are paid for by you, so get out there and make them work. If you don't make them work, then don't moan about it."

Yasmin Qureshi MP

"I would say to them that MPs irrespective of what party they belong to, are generally very hard working people, and they do take the interests of their constituents to heart. They will do whatever they can to help their constituents, it's just sometimes you can't always achieve everything for everyone. I think, irrespective of party politics, MPs do work really hard and do try to represent their constituents as well as they can."

John Redwood MP

"An MP's role is a privilege to represent people to Government, and to explain Government to voters. Everyday when I go into Parliament I am impressed by the building, by the ceremonial and by all that it stands for. I am all too conscious of the sacrifices that many made to bring democracy to all voters in the UK – the battles fought by Parliamentarians in the civil war, the Restoration settlement, the Bill of Rights, the widening of the franchise, the suffragette movement and recent battles to widen and uphold the liberties of the public. It is a lot to try to live up to."

Jacob Rees-Mogg MP

"Well there is the obvious point that you get the party in Government that you want by voting for an MP, which affects people in their daily lives in any number of ways. Although people say that politics is now all the same, that's actually one of those criticisms that comes up of politicians over the ages, it's not a new one. And actually the parties are very different in many ways, and so how life is will depend on who you elect. Whether you have your roads repaired or not, may depend on your local politicians, whether a new road is built or not, may depend on your national politicians, the level of your pension may depend on the politicians you elect, all these things that affect people's daily lives. Then on a local level, who you elect will affect you if you need the help of a Member of Parliament. If you are facing a bureaucracy that isn't answering you, if you have got a hard working MP, and this isn't party political at all, if you have an MP who is responsive, that MP by writing to the Child Support Agency or HMRC whoever it is, will get you a response, because if they do not get a response from the bureaucracy, they can ask a question in Parliament to the Minister, and then they can raise it in a debate. They can really embarrass the bureaucracy if a constituent isn't looked after, that depends on the individual and how far the individual is willing to go."

Jonathan Reynolds MP

"First of all, an MP definitely makes an impact, whether it's on local stuff like how dirty your canal is, or bigger stuff like foreign policy questions. Don't just look at the Miliband's the Cameron's and the Osborne's, there are different types and ways to be an MP. MPs like Dennis Skinner, and David Davies on the Conservative side are very different, and while it is true that there is a general type, position and ethos on either side, looking at the Conservative intake this time around there are some interesting people like Andrew Percy, who is a former teacher, and voted against the tuition fee rise, but in favour of the referendum. There are people with more diverse voting records than people probably expect.

"By the next Election I will probably have about 80,000 people in my constituency, nine towns, five of which are in Thameside, if the proposed changes go through for this area, which they probably will. I am always looking for a way to get my message out through twitter, or through my email news letter, or direct mail. But people do need to have a certain reasonableness, if you take 80,000 divided by a five year Parliament, and divide whatever number you get from that by the number of weekends in a year, because obviously I am in Westminster

Monday to Thursday, and then take off Christmas and Bank Holidays. I do a lot of doorstep work which I enjoy, because people tend to come to my surgery with specific problems, but I also need that more general conversation about things like the tax system and the NHS and you get that on the doorstep. If that was all I did though, I still wouldn't get around everybody. So people should look at how their MPs communicate what they are doing, but also what happens if they approach their MP for help. It seems to me that generally MPs are available to the public and that they are doing a pretty good job, I mean just look at Twitter *(laughter)*. Some of my older colleagues say, why would you take the risk of saying something controversial or unpopular and causing yourself a problem, if you see it as a threat rather than an opportunity, then it isn't going to work for you."

Derek Twigg MP

"That's a good question. *(laughter)* What did the rest of them say? *(laughter)* It gives ordinary people a national voice in Parliament, your MP can help you, and is someone to listen to your opinions. Churchill always said democracy is the least worst form of Government *(laughter)* – I think it was something like that, as no system of Government is perfect. It gives local people a national voice. It can help the ordinary person, although often seeing their MP is the last resort. An MP is someone who is there to listen to your concerns, and do something about them if he can.

"We can't always do something about what people want, life just isn't that way, some things are impossible, or are not for an MP to do. A councillor is a local politician, but an MP is a local, come national one."

Charles Walker MP

"Well I would say that we didn't become the fifth or sixth richest country in the world by accident. However big our problems are, and of course it is all relative, it's all big if you live in this country, we still have a great NHS, great public transport, great social services, we have all the things needed to be a great society, and that didn't come about by accident. It came about because of our democratic tradition, and through representative democracy. So it's all very easy to slag it off, but actually we are so lucky with our institutions, and being in Government is very difficult, you don't always get it right, but I liken it to *Radio Five Live*. They have *606* on Saturdays after the matches, and you get people calling in who say 'well I play quite a lot of football for my local pub side, and where Alex Ferguson is getting it wrong… ' you know the most successful manager in the world, and I love it, and everyone is entitled to their view, but if Alex Ferguson can be criticised by the great British public, and be given management tips by someone who may not have kicked a ball for thirty years, then only for their pub side, politicians are going to get slagged off too. It is difficult and I am sure we would all like to do it better, but I am so reassured by the quality of people I work with here. We are very lucky and we have got to make sure that people continue to want to be elected representatives. It's very easy for the *Daily Mail* and the *Express* and newspapers generally to slag off politics in this country, but the reason we have the Freedom of Press in this country is because of our democratic institutions."

Phil Wilson MP

"MPs are much maligned at the moment, probably because of things like the expenses scandal. All three main political parties have a problem because of that, there is an anti-politician mood around. The reason that I think politics is a noble cause is because there are very few people who are prepared to take the responsibility. Everybody wants the right to criticise, but what MPs do is to take on the responsibility of making decisions, sometimes they get them right, sometimes they get them wrong. After every four or five years you could end up not being an MP anymore because of the decisions that you take. You have to believe in something to do this job, you have to be a self motivator as well. It you are going to be working sixty or seventy hours a week and you don't get overtime for it you have got to do it for a reason, so the only thing that's left is belief, that you believe in the cause that you are fighting for."

Rosie Winterton MP

"I would like as many people as possible to want to become Members of Parliament, because that would indicate they were interested in politics. One of the key things about our society is that our democracy is so precious, when you see what is happening around the world where people are fighting to get the vote, and dying in order to get a vote, particularly women, it's very depressing when people say I can't be bothered to vote. People say well everyone is the same, it's absolutely not true, we have very distinctive policies and distinctive differences. We need people to get involved in politics because it does make a difference.

"If you don't participate in the political process, and by that I mean, we are at local election time at the moment, and the number of doors that you knock on where people say oh I'm not going to vote this time. When I see women with children, and you say hang on a minute, people all over the world are fighting to get a vote because so many people and traditionally women in many countries and even this one till not that long ago have been denied a vote, and you are saying that you can't be bothered to. Don't complain if you don't have a say, this is about your children's future too, it's not just about you, it's about shaping their society for the future."

John Woodcock MP

"Who passes laws on behalf of the country is of fundamental importance. There will always be MPs and they will always make important decisions, but I think what is happening at the moment is really damaging. Ultimately it's damaging for the groups of people who are quite understandably being switched off by politics. If they are not engaged, they are not interested in potentially putting themselves forward as a Member of Parliament. More and more people will take up the interests of the people who they think are going to vote for them, and if people are switched off, and not voting, they are less likely to be able to influence the decisions that are being made and which will affect them.

Contrary to what the lazy thinkers might say, it is clear by the answers to this question, that the MPs I have interviewed take the role of representing their constituents very seriously, and certainly do not take it for granted.

They are also offering some very good advice, and we would be wise to take it on board, as Dave Anderson says "If you don't take an interest bad things can happen", and don't we just know it. The current ongoing destruction of the NHS is a perfect example, naughty me, I'm getting political again *(slaps wrist)*.

It is good to see so many of them share Andrew Bridgen's view "We serve in the Parliament, it is not ours, it belongs to the people", and as Ann Coffey advises "It is very important to hold your representatives to account, and you can't do that if you don't vote."

I just love Michael Dugher's philosophy, "If anyone from Barnsley comes down to the House of Commons, I will see them. That gets top priority, because they are the boss." Presumably Michael wants them to make an appointment, and not just turn up because that would be chaos, wouldn't it?

Many of them such as Andrew George and Nicky Morgan point out that politics has an impact on every part of our lives, everything has a political dimension, and I don't know about you, but I find it quite reassuring that Liz Kendall, Sadiq Khan and Nicky Morgan, and I'm sure many others, take the time to go into schools. Hopefully the next generation of voters will take much more of an interest, and be far more active.

Sadiq Khan is right when he says MPs can really improve the quality of life, both in our local community and the country as a whole. Sadiq also has a point when he says if you don't lobby your MP, if you are not an active citizen, you can't then complain if you've got a poor MP. As Stephen Pound points outs, the MP works for you, they are paid for by you, if you don't make them work, then don't moan about it.

Zac Goldsmith is spot on "Politics doesn't belong to MPs, it belongs to everyone. Instead of complaining about its' remoteness people should get involved and help shape it." Jonathan Reynolds sets a great example with his lots of work on the doorstep, a very interesting way of keeping himself informed of what's exercising the minds of his voters. More of his colleagues should take this approach. Normally, for understandable reasons, we only see them on the doorstep when there is an election looming.

Charles Walker in a way that only he could, draws a brilliant analogy, when he compares the criticisms MPs get, with the caller to the football phone in show *606*, criticising Alex Ferguson. And I feel for a passionate Rosie Winterton when she so rightly says "Our democracy is so precious" and how "depressing" it is when people say they can't be bothered to vote, given the sacrifices so many people have made. She is also right to point out "It's about your children's future too, it's about shaping their society for the future."

Obviously I am passionate about getting people to take an interest and get involved, it is one of the main reasons for writing the book. Apart from your health, your family, friends and loved ones, nothing is more important than politics. I will refer back to Dave Anderson "the more that people don't engage, the easier it is for people in Westminster to get away with things they shouldn't."

Anyway, not for the first time, I'll leave the last words to Caroline Lucas "Politics is something you can do, whoever you are, wherever you are".

Yasmin Qureshi

"It's important that Ministers have strong views because civil servants have strong views too. If the Minister doesn't have strong views, then the Civil Service's views tend to prevail."
Ann Coffey MP –Chapter 17

CHAPTER TWENTY

So There You Have It

OK, so firstly I want to thank you so much for reaching the end of my book, I know only too well how precious everyone's time is these days, and I really appreciate you spending some of yours with me.

So there you have it, a fairly randomly selected group of MPs, who as far as I know, are pretty representative of your average parliamentarian. I'm biased of course, so I suspect when it comes to ability they are way above average, but you know what I mean. We should bear in mind they are representatives of us, like us they are mere mortals, and as such have the same human faults and frailties as the rest of us. In the U.K. apparently it is only football referees who are beyond reproach, but that's another story. MPs are human too, and share the same hopes and aspirations as the rest of us.

You will recall I started this book by saying I hoped in my own small way I could help create a better understanding of the people that make the decisions that affect all of our lives, and to encourage everyone to take more of an interest in the work of our MPs, and throughout this book, I have constantly nagged you, sorry about that, but you know it works both ways. Caroline Lucas spoke of the need to find a more effective way of making Parliament more accessible, and Nicky Morgan says "If people felt their voice had more of an influence, it would make a difference." Well I would venture to suggest our Members of Parliament need to do much more themselves to encourage our engagement in the political process. It is not all one sided, yes we need to make more of an effort, but our parliamentarians need to as well. Jonathan Reynolds is a great example as he still makes time to talk to people on the doorstep.

I really hope this book will dispel some of the myths the media are partly responsible for creating. For example, it is after all, complete and utter rubbish to suggest MPs are only working when they are in Westminster. So much of their work takes place within their constituencies representing us and dealing with our problems, and it certainly isn't their fault if we don't make use of the resources they have to offer. Perhaps we should ask ourselves what we would do if we were an MP, would we really be any different from the people featured in this book?

One thing I need to get straight at this point. I am no apologist for MPs, and anyone who follows me on Twitter will know I am perfectly capable of criticising some of them. I have no time for unprincipled, power-crazed, incompetent politicians, who renege on their promises, of which by the way, there are far too many. But for the purpose of this book, I am working on the principle of, if I can't say something positive, I would rather say nothing, that is why you will see no mention of David Cameron, Nick Clegg or Andrew Lansley. So be assured, I take a balanced approach when dealing with politicians, and I have no party political allegiances. To be honest, I practise what I preach. If I am not happy about something, I don't just moan down the pub, I campaign and lobby because in my opinion, it is the only way we can ever change anything.

No doubt you will draw your own conclusions from this book. I really hope you have found it both interesting and informative. I do believe it provides a fascinating insight into the life of an MP. I could say so much more, but this book is not about me, besides, I do not want to bore you, or I may have to come and clean your car.

None of the people I have featured in *'Commons People'* would want any sympathy from us, nor do they expect any appreciation. They are just normal people trying to do a good job. It is just worth bearing in mind what they do, and the decisions they make can affect all of us. So perhaps it would be smart to take more of an interest in their activities, provide them with the right environment/equipment to do the job to the best of their abilities, and perhaps most importantly of all, look after their mental health.

For the sake of all you hold dear, parents, children, brothers, sisters, friends, and loved ones, I urge you to take an interest in our politicians because the decisions they make affect us all.

Zac Goldsmith

Acknowledgements

For your co-operation in providing a remarkable insight, and for making me feel so welcome: Dave Anderson, Paul Blomfield, Sir Peter Bottomley, Ben Bradshaw, Kevin Brennan, Andrew Bridgen, Andy Burnham, Ann Coffey, Rosie Cooper, Philip Davies, Gloria DePiero, Stephen Dorrell, Michael Dugher, Natascha Engel, John Glen, Zac Goldsmith, Oliver Heald, Dan Jarvis MBE, Liz Kendall, Sadiq Khan, Ivan Lewis, Caroline Lucas, Nicky Morgan, Greg Mulholland, Jason McCartney, Esther McVey, Chi Onwurah, Stephen Pound, Yasmin Qureshi, John Redwood, Jacob Rees-Mogg, Jonathan Reynolds, Sir Bob Russell, Derek Twigg, Charles Walker, Phil Wilson, Rosie Winterton, John Woodcock.

For all the transcribing, editing, typing and believing in me: Angie Russell.

For all your encouragement and feedback: Marie Lynn, Judy Wilson, Mark Bradshaw, Julia Hatley, Paul Myers and Karen Oogarah.

For help with the title: Hayley-Ann Youell.

For help with research: Josh Seagrave

For giving me the confidence to write: David Brindle, Lynn Eaton, and Dan Parton.

For being there to repair my mind when needed: Lambton Phillips (my therapist) and all the other mental health professionals who have helped me in the past.

For the faith you have shown in me over the years : John Boyington CBE, Stuart Bell CBE, Mike Farrar CBE, Jim Easton, Sue Silk, Stephen Firn, Issac Batley, Simon Barber, Professor Heather Tierney-Moore, Gary O'Hare, Michael McCourt, Steph Palmerone, Martin Barkley, Kevan Taylor.

For always being there for me: Jim Easton, Mike Farrar CBE, Professor Andre Tylee, and Judy Wilson.

For loving and taking care of me: My wife Angie, without whom I most probably wouldn't be here now.

And to you dear readers, thank you for having an open mind, the patience and good sense in taking the time to read this book!

THANKS!